# THE ADULT ATTACHMENT INTERVIEW: PSYCHOMETRICS, STABILITY AND CHANGE FROM INFANCY, AND DEVELOPMENTAL ORIGINS

## EDITED BY

Cathryn Booth-LaForce
University of Washington

Glenn I. Roisman
University of Minnesota

## WITH COMMENTARY BY

John Ruscio and Marinus H. van IJzendoorn

Patricia J. Bauer
**Series Editor**

MONOGRAPHS OF THE SOCIETY FOR RESEARCH IN CHILD DEVELOPMENT

Serial No. 314, Vol. 79, No. 3, 2014

**WILEY**

*Boston, Massachusetts    Oxford, United Kingdom*

**EDITOR**
PATRICIA J. BAUER
*Emory University*

**MANAGING EDITOR**
ADAM MARTIN
*Society for Research in Child Development*

**EDITORIAL ASSISTANT**
STEPHANIE DEFOUW
*Society for Research in Child Development*

# THE ADULT ATTACHMENT INTERVIEW: PSYCHOMETRICS, STABILITY AND CHANGE FROM INFANCY, AND DEVELOPMENTAL ORIGINS

## CONTENTS

# INVITED COMMENTARIES

# ABSTRACT

Bowlby's Bowlby (1969/1982) attachment theory has inspired decades of empirical work focusing on antecedents and consequences of variation in attachment security across the lifespan. However, significant questions remain about individual differences in attachment in adulthood and their developmental origins, requiring a large sample and a long-term, longitudinal design. We address these issues, reporting analyses based on Adult Attachment Interviews (AAIs; Main, Kaplan, & Cassidy, 1985) collected at age 18 years from the largest longitudinal sample of its kind ($N=857$). Participants had been enrolled in the NICHD Study of Early Child Care and Youth Development from birth through age 15 years, allowing us to capitalize on extensive longitudinal (including early attachment) data collected on this sample. Part 1 (*Psychometrics*) questions the prevailing view of adult attachment security as a unitary construct, providing confirmatory evidence that relatively independent AAI dismissing and preoccupied states of mind—along with variation in inferred maternal and paternal experience—capture the full range of participants' coded AAI discourse. Moreover, taxometric analyses demonstrated that individual differences are more accurately represented dimensionally than categorically. Part 2 (*Stability, Change, and Developmental Origins*) reports evidence of weak but statistically significant stability in attachment from infancy through late adolescence, and lawful sources of continuity and change over time— maternal sensitivity, father absence, paternal depression, and negative life events. A specific focus on individuals who described below-average childhood experiences in the AAI but did so in a coherent manner (i.e., "earned-secures") replicated evidence that they actually received average or better parental care, but also experienced significant family stressors in childhood. Additional analyses suggested theory-consistent developmental

Corresponding author: Cathryn Booth-LaForce, University of Washington, Box 357920, Seattle, WA 98195-7920, email: ibcb@uw.edu

antecedents of the four AAI dimensions (i.e., dismissing, preoccupied, inferred maternal and paternal experiences) identified in psychometric analyses. Together, the results reported herein represent a significant step forward in our understanding of adult attachment and its origins.

# I. INTRODUCTION

*Cathryn Booth-LaForce and Glenn I. Roisman*

The development of the infant's enduring emotional bond to the primary caregiver and the consequences of the nature of this bond have been the subjects of clinical and scientific interest for over a century. In a departure from the extant psychoanalytic and social-learning theories of his day, Bowlby (1969/1982) focused on the biological, evolutionary, and psychological bases of the child's tie to the mother, thereby changing the course of scientific thinking about early social-emotional development. In the ensuing decades, Bowlby's theory of attachment has inspired voluminous empirical work, synthesis, and revision (see Cassidy & Shaver, 2008), becoming one of the most well-established and well-validated theories in developmental science. In addition to focusing on universal attachment processes, Bowlby called attention to individual differences in the quality of attachment—secure or insecure—as well as the sources of these individual differences and their developmental consequences. Specifically, a central tenet of attachment theory (Bowlby, 1969/1982) is that the quality of early caregiving experiences (i.e., parental sensitivity and availability) forms the basis for the child to develop a relatively secure or insecure specific attachment to the caregiver, which generalizes to an internal representation of attachment that guides future relationships and social-emotional development. These ideas received empirical support and elaboration from Ainsworth, Blehar, Waters, and Wall (1978), who inspired a great deal of research in the infancy period and beyond.

Although a life-span perspective was a fundamental aspect of Bowlby's work, much of the initial (and current) research based on his theory has focused on the predictors and sequelae of the early mother–child attachment relationship (see Cassidy & Shaver, 2008). This is perhaps not surprising given the centrality of the infancy and early childhood period in attachment theory, as well as the relatively early development and validation of a laboratory-based

---

Corresponding author: Cathryn Booth-LaForce, University of Washington, Box 357920, Seattle, WA 98195-7920, email: ibcb@uw.edu

method for assessing individual differences in infants' attachment security—the Strange Situation procedure (Ainsworth, Blehar, Waters, & Wall, 1978). That said, a growing number of researchers have focused on attachment in middle childhood, adolescence, and adulthood, made possible by the development of assessment measures and procedures pertaining to these older age periods.

## ASSESSMENT OF INDIVIDUAL DIFFERENCES IN ATTACHMENT

In infancy, the classic, gold-standard assessment of individual differences in attachment is the Strange Situation (Ainsworth et al., 1978), a laboratory procedure designed to activate infants' attachment behavioral system via a series of increasingly stressful separations from and reunions with their primary caregivers. In brief, infants are classified as *secure* in the Strange Situation when their separation distress is effectively relieved upon their caregiver's return. Infants are classified as insecure if they either ignore their primary caregiver upon reunion (i.e., *anxious-avoidant*) or simultaneously seek, yet resist, their caregiver upon reunion (i.e., *anxious-resistant*). Finally, infants who exhibit a momentary, yet striking breakdown of one of these organized strategies are classified as *disorganized* (Main & Solomon, 1990). Two somewhat less-commonly used but well-validated childhood assessments of individual differences in attachment security, featured in our analyses and described in more detail in Chapter 4 of this volume, are the Attachment Q-Sort (Waters & Deane, 1985) and the modified Strange Situation procedure (Cassidy, Marvin, and the MacArthur Working Group on Attachment, 1992).

In adulthood, the most widely used and well-validated assessment in developmental research for studying attachment in adults is the Adult Attachment Interview (AAI; Main & Goldwyn, 1984–1998). The AAI is an hour-long interview in which participants are asked a set of questions regarding their childhood experiences, including memories relevant to loss, separation, rejection, and trauma. The development of the AAI (George, Kaplan, & Main, 1984–1996; Main, Goldwyn, & Hesse, 2003–2008; Main, Kaplan, & Cassidy, 1985) was based on an effort to understand how adults organize their discourse when reflecting upon their early childhood experiences (Hesse, 2008). Through careful analysis, informed eventually by the insights of the linguistic philosopher Paul Grice (Grice, 1975) about the nature of collaborative discourse, Main et al. were able to discover which aspects of parents' narratives about their childhood experiences predicted whether their own children would be classified as secure or insecure in the Strange Situation procedure (Van IJzendoorn, 1995).

The primary AAI scoring method developed by Main and Goldwyn (1984–1998) consists of a set of ratings on each transcript that inform

2

assignment of individuals to one of three mutually exclusive primary attachment categories (*secure-autonomous, dismissing, preoccupied*) that reflect the coherence of the discourse produced in the interview. The majority of adults, described as *secure-autonomous*, freely and flexibly evaluate their childhood experiences, whether described as supportive or more challenging in nature. The next largest group of individuals, described as *dismissing*, defensively distance themselves from the emotional content of the interview by normalizing harsh early memories, for example, or by idealizing their caregivers. The smallest group consists of *preoccupied* adults, who are unable to discuss their childhood experiences without becoming overwhelmed (see Hesse, 1999, for more details). In addition to these three categories, coders also classify individuals as *unresolved* if their discourse becomes psychologically confused while talking about loss or abuse experiences.

An additional scoring method that yields dimensional ratings rather than categories is the AAI Q-sort (Kobak, 1993), derived from the original Main and Goldwyn (1984–1998) system. The Q-set consists of 100 items that raters sort into nine "piles" from most to least characteristics of the individual, based on the AAI transcript. In most published work based on the AAI Q-sort, the Q-sort for each individual is then correlated with prototypical Q-sorts for security/insecurity and deactivation/hyperactivation. Prototypically secure (in contrast to insecure) descriptors include "responds in a clear, well-organized fashion," and "is credible and easy to believe." Prototypically deactivating/dismissing (in contrast to hyperactivating/preoccupied) descriptors include "subject persistently does not remember" and "provides only minimal responses." (See Table 2.3, this volume, for the complete list of items.)

## CONTEXT OF THE PRESENT STUDY

The scientific yield of research exploring developmental questions using the AAI categories has been substantial (for comprehensive reviews, see Bakermans-Kranenburg & Van IJzendoorn, 2009; Hesse, 1999; Hesse, 2008). Of particular note is that the development and validation of the AAI provided researchers with the ability to study attachment longitudinally from infancy through adulthood and to address some of the most significant questions about stability and change in attachment security over time. Such studies are important for testing central aspects of attachment theory while also shedding light on developmental risks and protective factors more generally. However, the task of conducting a long-term longitudinal study of this sort remains daunting. Of the few studies that have followed young children into adulthood (see Chapters 4 and 5, this volume; Roisman & Haydon, 2011, for a review), most have enrolled relatively small numbers of participants, thereby limiting power, especially in relation to the less common attachment state-of-mind categories. Moreover, smaller samples have hindered our ability to address important psychometric questions about the AAI.

The present study, in contrast, provided an unprecedented opportunity to address questions of significance about adult attachment because it included 857 participants for whom we had a comprehensive set of assessments from infancy through late adolescence. This large sample size, as well as the other longitudinal data available on this sample, allowed us to address questions of significance for attachment theory, measurement, and research.

More specifically, all of the chapters in this Monograph used data from an NIH-funded study that followed participants from the NICHD (National Institute of Child Health and Human Development) Study of Early Child Care and Youth Development (hereafter referred to as the SECCYD) at age 18 years. The SECCYD was a long-term longitudinal study that followed 1,364 study children and their families at 10 sites across the United States, from birth through age 15 years.[1] The primary purpose of the SECCYD, using an ecological model, was to predict children's developmental outcomes (language, cognitive, social-emotional, health) from characteristics of relevant contexts (child care, home, school, neighborhood) and individual characteristics of the child and family. Although the initial focus was on the child-care context, the study was designed to include comprehensive information that could be used to address significant questions about children's development over time. Importantly, classic assessments of mother-child attachment security were included—the Strange Situation procedure (Ainsworth et al., 1978) at 15 months, the Attachment Q-Sort (Waters & Deane, 1985) at 24 months, and the Modified Strange Situation procedure (Cassidy et al., 1992) at 36 months. (See NICHD Early Child Care Research Network [ECCRN], 2005 for more information about the SECCYD).

Following completion of the SECCYD at age 15, NICHD awarded a separate follow-up grant to a subset of the primary SECCYD investigators (C. Booth-LaForce, Principal Investigator; G. Roisman, M. Cox, M. Owen, M. Burchinal, R. Parke, Co-Investigators). This study (Stability and Change in Attachment and Social Functioning, Infancy to Adolescence), which was based at the University of Washington, followed the entire national cohort at age 18. The primary purpose was to investigate pathways to the nature and quality of social functioning and attachment from infancy to late adolescence, and to answer key questions regarding sources of continuity and change in social functioning over time, the predictive significance of early versus later attachment quality, and the continuing role of contextual factors. Though labor-intensive to collect, transcribe, and code, we made the commitment to administer the AAI to all available participants and to collect other data via web-based questionnaires.

4

In the next section we outline the issues and questions addressed in the chapters of this Monograph, placing them in the context of attachment theory and research. In the final section, we present the details of the data collection and coding methods we used, as well as descriptive and reliability information specific to the AAI.


## ISSUES AND QUESTIONS

### AAI Psychometrics

A number of fundamental measurement issues have arisen in the extant AAI literature that we are now able to address more readily with our large sample size. As noted in the preceding text, one issue we tackle (Chapter 2) is the latent structure of the AAI, to address the question of how to conceptualize what the AAI actually measures. In the classic Main and Goldwyn AAI method, raters use a number of different rating scales to infer adults' current state of mind about earlier attachment experiences with their primary caregivers. Coders then assign these adults to mutually exclusive primary attachment categories (*secure-autonomous, dismissing, preoccupied*) that reflect the assumption that attachment security in adulthood is a unitary construct. However, more recent factor analytic work (Bernier, Larose, Boivin, & Soucy, 2004; Haydon, Roisman, & Burt, 2012; Larose, Bernier, & Soucy, 2005; Roisman, Fraley, & Belsky, 2007) has suggested that adult attachment can be represented more accurately in relation to two weakly correlated components—dismissing and preoccupied states of mind. In Chapter 2, we advance this work by addressing the factor structure of the AAI state-of-mind scales as well as the factor structure of Kobak's (1993) Q-sort. Moreover, in Chapter 3 we focus on a related measurement issue—whether individual differences in attachment security are best represented categorically or continuously (see Fraley & Spieker, 2003a; Roisman et al., 2007).

These measurement issues are of interest in their own right. However, from a broader perspective, what is at stake here is our ability to advance attachment theory and research by representing the variation in AAI responses in the most psychometrically sound and valid ways (see Fortuna, Roisman, Haydon, Groh, & Holland, 2011; Haydon, Roisman, Marks, & Fraley, 2011; Haydon et al., 2012). For example, an individual's attachment classification might be an effective descriptive "shorthand," the meaning of which is arguably clearer than would be a combination of scores on a variety of dimensions. However, if dimensional scores prove to be psychometrically superior to categories, the increased analytic power accruing from retaining the variance in the relevant dimensions (particularly in modest $N$ studies; Fraley & Spieker, 2003a) is likely to yield more accurate (and perhaps different) results—thereby enhancing our understanding of attachment processes (see Chapter 7 for an example).

An empirically informed understanding of the factor structure of the AAI is likewise important because it also has implications for hypothesis development and theory testing. For example, researchers have consistently found that individuals who produce secure discourse are less likely than adults who produce secure discourse to provide sensitive care to their children (Van IJzendoorn, 1995). However, evidence reported by Whipple, Bernier, and Mageau (2011) demonstrated that insensitive caregiving was actually specifically associated with dismissing states of mind whereas maternal intrusiveness (vs. autonomy supportive parenting) was uniquely associated with preoccupied states of mind. Importantly, this pattern of results would have been obscured by assuming that individuals vary on secure versus insecure states of mind and that preoccupied and dismissing states of mind are mutually incompatible (an assumption implicit in coding systems that force insecure adults into the dismissing or preoccupied group but not both for analyses; See Chapter 2 for elaboration of these points).

### Stability, Change, and Developmental Origins

Bowlby's (1969/1982) theory assumes that individual differences in attachment security are relatively stable over time, but that changes in attachment security (e.g., secure to insecure) should be related in "lawful" ways to changes in the caregiving environment. Specifically, according to attachment theory, individuals develop internalized representations of their early attachment-relevant experiences with primary caregivers, which are reinforced under conditions of relative stability in parent-child relationship quality over time. Thus, it might be expected that individual differences in infant attachment would be associated with individual differences in adult attachment as measured by the AAI, but that positive or negative changes in parental availability and sensitivity would serve as lawful agents of change in attachment security.

Of the few, relatively small sample studies addressing longitudinal patterns of attachment, some have reported statistically significant stability in security from infancy to adulthood and others have not (for a meta-analysis, see Fraley, 2002). Some have also begun to identify aspects of the caregiving environment that promote stability or lead to change in attachment security (e.g., Beijersbergen, Juffer, Bakermans-Kranenburg & Van IJzendoorn, 2012; Van Ryzin, Carlson, & Sroufe, 2011; Weinfield, Whaley, & Egeland, 2004), but there is considerable variability across studies in the predictors that have been investigated and findings from studies including the same predictors have not always converged. Consequently, the SECCYD provided an excellent opportunity to address the stability question in Chapter 4, both for attachment categories and dimensions, and to focus on sources of lawful, within-person change in attachment security from early childhood to late adolescence in Chapter 5. The issues we address in these two chapters are of critical importance for supporting (or not) a central tenet of attachment theory, as well as advancing empirical work deriving from the theory.

Chapter 6 addresses stability and change in attachment security from a different perspective, by focusing on the AAI "earned-secure" classification. Those receiving this classification coherently describe their childhood experiences and are therefore classified as secure, but the inferred nature of their experiences with parents is negative, thereby leading to the assumption that these individuals were likely insecure in infancy but overcame their early adverse experiences and became secure in adulthood. But did these adults actually experience a negative caregiving environment leading to early insecurity, or is their discourse about their childhood experiences colored by other factors such as current internalizing symptoms (Pearson, Cohn, Cowan, & Cowan, 1994; Roisman, Fortuna, & Holland, 2006; Roisman, Padrón, Sroufe, & Egeland, 2002)? Very few studies have had the data to address this question directly, but frequent assessments of the SECCYD cohort from early childhood through mid-adolescence of both mother–child and father–child interactive quality, as well as other relevant aspects of the family environment, provide this valuable opportunity. Beyond demonstrating the validity or lack thereof of the earned-secure classification, the results of our analyses are important in the context of the general question of sources of lawful discontinuity in attachment security over time.

In Chapter 7, we turn to the question of the developmental origins of both dismissing and preoccupied classifications, as well as state-of-mind and inferred experience dimensions. In so doing, we focus on whether distinctive elements of experience during childhood and adolescence predict dismissing versus preoccupied states of mind, and whether core antecedents supported by attachment theory (e.g., parental sensitivity) remain predictive controlling for alternative antecedents (e.g., general cognitive ability). This approach addresses theoretical expectations while also adding to the sparse literature on developmental origins of adult attachment and providing a methodological blueprint for future work.

Finally, in a Supplement to this Monograph, we address another possible source of individual variation in attachment security—genetic polymorphisms. Specifically, all dopaminergic, serotonergic, and oxytonergic molecular genetic polymorphisms featured in the infant attachment literature (Roisman, Booth-LaForce, Belsky, Burt, & Groh, 2013), as well as gene by environment interactions, were examined as potential predictors of the AAI state-of-mind dimensions.

## METHOD

### Participants

Participants were 857 adolescents with a targeted age of 17.5 years (actual mean age was closer to 18 years [17.8 years with a range of 17.2–19.1]; for that reason we refer to 18 years as the assessment age throughout the Monograph). All participants had been enrolled from birth through age 15 years in the SECCYD ($N = 1,364$ at 1 month of age). Of the 997 participants in the SECCYD at age 15, 86% (857) participated in the present study and completed the AAI. We compared demographic characteristics of the AAI sample ($n = 857$) with those of the original SECCYD sample for whom we did not have AAI data ($n = 507$). The AAI sample was significantly more likely to be female (AAI: $M = 51\%$; no AAI: $M = 44\%$), $\chi^2$ (1, $N = 1,364$) = 6.06, $p = .014$, and to be White non-Hispanic (AAI: $M = 78.2\%$; no AAI: $M = 73.4\%$), $\chi^2$ (1, $N = 1,364$) = 4.08, $p = .043$. Their mothers had significantly more years of education (AAI: $M = 14.6$, $SD = 2.4$; no AAI: $M = 13.7$, $SD = 2.5$), $t(1,361) = 6.35$, $p < .001$, as did their fathers (AAI: $M = 14.7$, $SD = 2.6$; no AAI: $M = 14.0$, $SD = 2.6$), $t(1,278) = 4.64$, $p < .001$. The AAI sample also had a higher family income-to-needs ratio (AAI: $M = 4.1$, $SD = 3.1$; no AAI: $M = 3.1$, $SD = 2.8$), $t(1,354) = 5.82$, $p < .001$. (Family income was reported by mothers at each major data collection point from infancy [1 month] through mid-adolescence [15 years] and converted to an income-to-needs ratio by dividing total family income by the U.S. Census-based poverty-level income for that family size. For this analysis, mean income-to-needs from 1 month through age 15 years was computed).

## MEASURES AND PROCEDURE

### Adult Attachment Interview

Personnel located at the 10 original SECCYD data-collection sites administered the AAI, an hour-long interview in which participants are asked a set of questions regarding their childhood experiences, including memories relevant to loss, separation, rejection, and trauma. The interviewers were trained to administer the AAI by the second editor of this volume, who certified them after they successfully completed at least three practice interviews that were audiotaped and extensively critiqued. (Interviewers were subsequently monitored by the second editor for drift at regular intervals). At birth, the participants and their families lived within a relatively small area around the 10 sites but by age 18 they were more widely dispersed. Thus, the majority of the AAIs (79%; $n = 679$) were conducted in person, but 21% ($n = 178$) had to be completed by phone due to travel distances. Note that phone administration of the AAI has been used effectively in other longitudinal investigations, including the Minnesota Longitudinal Study of Risk and Adaptation (Sroufe, Egeland, Carlson, & Collins, 2005) and in follow-ups of cohorts studied by Dr. Everett Waters and his colleague Dr. Judith Crowell at SUNY Stony Brook (Treboux, Crowell, & Waters, 2004). Interviews were digitally audio-recorded, transmitted electronically, and then transcribed verbatim by teams at the University of Illinois at Urbana-Champaign (UIUC) and the University of North Carolina-Chapel Hill. AAI transcripts were coded at UIUC by six trained and certified coders, under the direction of the second editor (who served as one of the AAI Q-sort coders for a small set of reliability cases). The coders all received training at the 2-week Minnesota AAI Training Institute by Dr. June Sroufe, after which they passed a set of reliability tests over 18 months administered by Dr. Mary Main at UC Berkeley.

### Other Measures

Participants and their parents also completed web-based questionnaires that provided information about the participants' social-emotional functioning and relationships, and the parents' characteristics, such as depressive symptomatology (See Chapters 5 and 6 for a description of relevant measures and Fraley, Roisman, Holland, Booth-LaForce, & Owen, 2013).

### AAI Scoring—Main and Goldwyn Method

Two sets of 9-point rating scales were used by the coders to inductively assign individuals to attachment categories [See Table 1.1 for a complete list of the ratings]. The first set, known as the *inferred-experience* scales, reflects AAI coders' impressions of participants' experiences with caregivers during childhood, including assessments of maternal and paternal love, rejection, neglect, pressure to achieve, and role reversal. Note that several investigators have made use of a sub-set of these scales to distinguish between secure individuals with putatively negative early relationship experiences with at least one parent (i.e., earned-secures) and secure adults with largely positive experiences with their caregivers (i.e., continuous-secures; see Pearson et al., 1994, and Chapter 6, this volume).

The second set of ratings reflects the coherence of participants' discourse regarding their childhood attachment experiences (i.e., their *state of mind*), for example, the tendency to idealize and/or normalize childhood experiences with caregivers (*mother idealization* and *father idealization*), the inability to recall events from childhood (*lack of memory*), the extent to which one or both caregivers are derogated (*derogation*), the expression of unreasonable fears that their child (or hypothetical child) may die (*fear of*

## TABLE 1.1

DESCRIPTIVE AND RELIABILITY DATA FOR ADULT ATTACHMENT INTERVIEWS, MAIN AND
GOLDWYN SCORING

| AAI Subscale | Descriptive Data | | | | |
| --- | --- | --- | --- | --- | --- |
| | Mean | *SD* | Min | Max | ICC |
| AAI Life Experience Scales | | | | | |
| Maternal loving | 4.4 | 1.1 | 1 | 9 | 0.87 |
| Paternal loving | 3.7 | 1.5 | 1 | 9 | 0.87 |
| Maternal rejecting | 2.0 | 1.1 | 1 | 8 | 0.86 |
| Paternal rejecting | 2.3 | 1.3 | 1 | 7 | 0.75 |
| Maternal neglecting | 1.6 | 1.1 | 1 | 7 | 0.83 |
| Paternal neglecting | 2.4 | 1.5 | 1 | 8 | 0.88 |
| Maternal role reversal | 1.8 | 1.1 | 1 | 7 | 0.86 |
| Paternal role reversal | 1.5 | 0.8 | 1 | 6 | 0.75 |
| Maternal pressure to achieve | 1.4 | 0.8 | 1 | 7 | 0.84 |
| Paternal pressure to achieve | 1.6 | 1.0 | 1 | 8 | 0.92 |
| AAI State-of-mind Scales | | | | | |
| Maternal idealization | 3.3 | 1.3 | 1 | 7 | 0.71 |
| Paternal idealization | 2.9 | 1.3 | 1 | 7 | 0.75 |
| Maternal anger | 1.1 | 0.6 | 1 | 7 | 0.85 |
| Paternal anger | 1.2 | 0.8 | 1 | 8 | 0.81 |
| Maternal derogation | 1.1 | 0.4 | 1 | 5 | 0.54 |
| Paternal derogation | 1.1 | 0.4 | 1 | 5 | 0.87 |
| Highest derogation | 1.2 | 0.6 | 1 | 9 | 0.70 |
| Lack of memory | 3.2 | 1.8 | 1 | 9 | 0.93 |
| Metacognitive monitoring | 1.1 | 0.3 | 1 | 3 | 0.29 |
| Passivity of discourse | 2.4 | 1.1 | 1 | 8 | 0.75 |
| Fear of loss of one's child | 1.0 | 0.0 | 1 | 1 | 1.00 |
| Unresolved loss | 1.7 | 1.1 | 1 | 7 | 0.83 |
| Unresolved trauma | 1.1 | 0.6 | 1 | 8 | 0.61 |
| Coherence of transcript | 5.0 | 1.4 | 1 | 8 | 0.84 |
| Coherence of mind | 5.0 | 1.4 | 1 | 8 | 0.85 |

*Note.* All intraclass correlations (ICCs) *p*s < .001, except meta-cognitive monitoring (*p* = .013). *N*s for descriptive data vary from 822 to 857; *n*s for ICCs vary from 170 to 178. The theoretical range for all scales is 1–9.

*loss*), current active resentment toward parents (*mother anger* and *father anger*), and passive or rambling attachment-related discourse (*passivity*). Coders used these state-of-mind scales to classify participants into one of the two major insecure (dismissing, preoccupied) categories. A dismissing state of mind is reflected in any combination of high scores on scales that tap a participant's tendency to idealize parents, derogate them, or show failures of memory (according to the categorical coding system, dismissing adults also occasionally fear the loss of their own [hypothetical] child). Preoccupation is identified through signs of anger and/or passivity. Security is defined by the relative absence of high scores on these indicators as well as evidence that an adult is able to explore his or her thoughts and feelings about childhood experiences without becoming angrily or passively overwhelmed while discussing them. By definition, such an ability to "freely evaluate" one's experiences without becoming emotionally overwrought is reflected in the overall *coherence of mind* and *coherence of transcript* scales. Adults who are able to modify their outlook on their childhood experiences during the AAI as a function of spontaneous reflection are given high scores on *metacognitive monitoring*, another indicator of security.

Additional state-of-mind scales included *unresolved loss* and *unresolved abuse*, which reflect the degree to which the individual's discourse becomes disorganized while discussing loss or abuse experiences, respectively. Participants received a primary *unresolved* classification (irrespective of whether they were otherwise classified as secure, dismissing, or preoccupied) when they scored at, or above the midpoint on either of these scales.

## AAI Scoring—Kobak Method

Using the AAI Q-sort (Kobak, 1993) method, coders characterized each transcript according to 100 descriptors sorted into a forced normal distribution from least to most characteristic, using a computer program modified for the task by the second editor (contact second editor for details). Although not the primary focus of analyses in this Monograph (see Chapter 2), Pearson correlations were computed between each participant's sort and both prototypic secure/insecure and deactivation/hyperactivation sorts (see Kobak, Cole, Ferenz-Gillies, Fleming, & Gamble, 1993). Participants were assigned continuous scores ranging from −1.00 to 1.00 on each construct; higher scores indicate greater resemblance to the prototypically secure and deactivating (dismissing) individual, respectively. Each sort also was compared with a second set of validated prototypes featured more centrally in this volume, allowing for separate continuous ratings of "dismissing" and "preoccupied" dimensions (see Spangler & Zimmermann, 1999).

## DESCRIPTIVE AND RELIABILITY DATA

### Main and Goldwyn Scoring

Descriptive and reliability data for all AAI inferred-experience and state-of-mind scales from the Main and Goldwyn scoring method are shown in Table 1.1. In terms of attachment categories, we found that 60% of the participants were secure (including secure/unresolved) and 40% were insecure. Using a three-way classification scheme in which insecurity was split into types, 60% were secure (including secure/unresolved), 36% were dismissing, and 4% were preoccupied; using a four-way classification method

11

in which those classified as unresolved (regardless of whether they were otherwise classified as secure, dismissing, or preoccupied) were placed in a separate category, 59% were secure, 35% were dismissing, 3% were preoccupied, and 3% were unresolved. Note that, depending on the empirical question being addressed, the size of the sample (which affects the number of cases for the less-frequent classifications) and the need for comparison with extant studies, researchers may choose to use two-, three-, or four-way classifications in their analyses.

Reliability was computed in several ways for 178 (21% of total) cases. First, intraclass correlation coefficients (ICCs) were computed for each of the inferred-experience and state-of-mind dimensions (comparing each coder with a master coder), using a minimum a priori criterion of .6 to designate acceptable reliability (see Table 1.1). Although this criterion was exceeded for most of the scales, two scales failed to meet the minimum criterion (*maternal derogation* and *metacognitive monitoring*). In both cases, variability/range restriction was a problem in that 2 *SD*s of the sample scored between scale points 1 and 2. Also, *fear of loss* had no variability in this sample. Note finally that $\kappa = .90$, $p < .001$ (96% agreement) for *applicable loss?* (yes/no) and $\kappa = .86$, $p < .001$ (98% agreement) for *applicable trauma?* (yes/no). For unresolved scales, not applicable was coded "1" to compute ICCs.

Reliability also was calculated for attachment state-of-mind classifications (categories), using the same 178 cases. For a two-way secure/insecure classification scheme, agreement $= 95\%$, $\kappa = .89$, $p < .001$. For a three-way classification, agreement $= 95\%$, $\kappa = .89$, $p < .001$. For a four-way classification, agreement $= 92\%$, $\kappa = .84$, $p < .001$.

## Kobak Scoring

Descriptive data for the Kobak (1993) Q-set for the four prototype scores were as follows: secure/autonomous $M = .18$, $SD = .39$, range $= -.71$ to .83; deactivation/hyperactivation $M = .14$, $SD = .29$, range $= -.63$ to .69; dismissing $M = -.02$, $SD = .40$, range $= -.72$ to .76; and preoccupied $M = -.23$, $SD = .22$, range $= -.59$ to .78. The percentage of the 178 reliability cases for which reliability was .6 or higher (after Spearman-Brown correction) was 90%. Per convention, a third (and on rare occasions, fourth) coder completed another sort for unreliable cases and data from the two coders with the highest reliability above .6 were averaged and used in analyses (final $M = .77$, $SD = .08$, range $= .60–.93$).

## In-Person Versus Phone Interviews

An analysis of in-person ($n = 679$) vs. phone ($n = 178$) interviews was conducted to evaluate whether the core AAI prototype dimensions drawn from Kobak's (1993) Q-sort—dismissing and preoccupied states of mind—would differ by administration method (see Chapter 2 for rationale for focusing on these two key AAI dimensions). Dismissing scores did not differ by method (In person: $M = -.02$, $SD = .41$; Phone: $M = -.02$, $SD = .39$), $t(855) = -.19$, $p = .85$, $r = -.01$. However, the in-person interviews yielded slightly higher preoccupation scores (In person: $M = -.22$, $SD = .24$; Phone: $M = -.29$, $SD = .15$), $t(855) = 4.74$, $p < .001$, $r = .13$. This result is likely due to the fact that higher scores on the preoccupied dimension are assigned to those individuals who speak at great length about their experiences with caregivers, and we speculate that those being interviewed on the phone may feel less licensed to do so than they would if they were being interviewed in person. That said, the magnitude of this effect was clearly small by conventional standards (i.e., accounting for ~1.7% of the variation in preoccupation) suggesting a minimal effect of the mode of interviewing on AAI state-of-mind data.

## CONCLUSION

Having demonstrated adequate reliability across coders for the Main & Goldwyn and Kobak methods, we proceeded to address the substantive questions outlined in the preceding text. Together, the chapters in this Monograph provide a comprehensive view of adult attachment and address significant questions relevant to attachment theory and research.

## SUPPORTING INFORMATION

Additional supporting information may be found in the online version of this article at the publisher's website:

**Supplement S1.** A Candidate Gene Approach to the Study of the Origins of Adult Attachment Interview States of Mind

## NOTE

1. This Monograph drew primarily on publicly available SECCYD datasets (with the exception of age 18 AAI data and restricted-use molecular-genetic data for the Supplement). That said, the focus of the chapters in this volume required a clear distinction between data acquired from maternal versus paternal caregivers but the standard SECCYD variables beginning at 54 months distinguish between primary caregivers (i.e., mostly maternal figures but some fathers) and secondary caregivers (mostly fathers, but also others, including maternal grandparents). For this reason, all variables labeled mother or maternal-report (mothers'

report about herself or the target participant) and all variables referring to observations of the mother-child interactions in this volume refer to female primary caregivers only (paternal figures were purged from relevant data). Similarly, all variables labeled father or paternal-report (father's report about himself or the target participant) and all variables referring to observations of the father-child interactions in this volume refer to male primary caregivers only (non-paternal figures were purged). Please contact M. Burchinal for details.

# II. THE LATENT STRUCTURE OF THE ADULT ATTACHMENT INTERVIEW: EXPLORATORY AND CONFIRMATORY EVIDENCE

John D. Haltigan, Glenn I. Roisman, and Katherine C. Haydon

In this chapter, we focus on the most fundamental question that can be addressed in relation to the Adult Attachment Interview (AAI). Specifically, we examine what, precisely, the AAI measures. Investigators who use the AAI would note that the protocol is meant to assess adults' current states of mind regarding earlier attachment experiences with primary caregivers. What complicates matters, however, is that such states of mind are actually inferred by coders on the basis of the coherence of adults' discourse about their childhood experiences.

It is the primary thesis of this chapter that coherent discourse has two relatively independent components (Roisman, 2009). First, the coherent speaker is *internally consistent* when he or she discusses childhood attachment experiences during the AAI. Individuals who do not produce internally consistent discourse during the AAI often idealize their caregivers (e.g., are unable to provide specific memories that support their overly positive descriptions of their relationships with parents) or normalize objectively harsh childhood experiences. Second—and distinctively—the coherent speaker is able to discuss his or her early experiences without becoming emotionally overwrought while doing so, as reflected either in passive discussion of childhood memories (e.g., wandering off into irrelevancies) or, more commonly, by becoming actively upset while recounting early life experiences.

Judgments of the kind described immediately above are key to coders' placement of adults into one of the four attachment categories that have served as the primary vehicle by which AAI data have been analyzed over the history of research based on the protocol (George et al., 1984–1998; Main et al., 1985). Specifically, using the standard Main and Goldwyn (1984–1998; Main et al., 2003–2008) coding system for the AAI, a majority of adults are

---

Corresponding author: John D. Haltigan, Faculty of Education, University of Ottawa, Ottawa, Ontario, Canada K1N 6N5, email jhaltiga@uottawa.ca

characterized as *secure-autonomous* (in coding shorthand, the F group) because they coherently describe (i.e., "freely evaluate") their childhood experiences, whether described as supportive or more challenging in nature. In contrast, a large minority of adults are described as *dismissing* (Ds). Dismissing individuals defensively distance themselves from the emotional content of the AAI by normalizing harsh early memories or by idealizing their caregivers, thus failing to produce internally consistent narratives about their early lives. Least common are *preoccupied* (E) adults, who are currently enmeshed or entangled in past experiences with caregivers and are unable to discuss their childhood without becoming overwhelmed by their earlier relationship experiences. In addition to classifying adults into one of these three mutually exclusive groups, coders also categorize individuals as *unresolved* (U) if their discourse becomes psychologically confused while talking about loss or abuse experiences (see Hesse, 2008).

It is important to emphasize, however, that there are at least two sets of assumptions embedded in the Main and Goldwyn coding system. The first assumption, addressed empirically in Chapter 3 of this volume by Fraley and Roisman (see also Roisman et al., 2007), is that individual differences in adult attachment are best conceptualized as categorically rather than continuously distributed. Even more important in our view, however, is the second set of assumptions implicit in the Main and Goldwyn coding system, which are claims regarding the *factor* structure associated with variation in the AAI—that is, the primary axes on which adults vary while talking about their childhood attachment experiences.

## FACTOR ANALYSIS AND THE LATENT STRUCTURE OF THE AAI

Factor analysis is a statistical tool designed to infer the number and nature of latent (i.e., unobserved) variables that account for the variation and covariation among a set of observed measures (i.e., indicators; Brown, 2006). Factor analysis is one of the most commonly used procedures in the development, evaluation, and refinement of psychological measures (Floyd & Widaman, 1995) not only because it provides a mechanism for data reduction, but, perhaps more importantly, because it provides information about the primary individual differences assessed by a given measure. Historically, factor analytic work has proceeded across empirical domains using a two-step process. In the first, exploratory factor analyses are conducted, which allow the researcher to examine how many factors best account for the intercorrelations among a typically much larger set of indicators, such as items on a questionnaire. Although such work is ideally theory-guided, this is not always the case. In the second step, researchers perform confirmatory factor analyses in which this factor structure is evaluated empirically with new data for model fit. In short, exploratory factor analysis is a descriptive, inductive technique to identify the number and nature of the axes on which individuals vary whereas confirmatory factor analysis is empirically grounded and is used to evaluate the tenability of the form and content of the axes of the variation identified in exploratory factor analytic work.

There are at least two reasons why an understanding of the factor structure of the AAI is important. First, we emphasize a purely descriptive purpose. Specifically, Main and Goldwyn's (1984–1998) coding system implies that security in adulthood is a unitary construct that *simultaneously* reflects the capacity to (a) tell an internally consistent narrative about one's childhood experiences (i.e., to "freely evaluate" early attachment experiences) (b) without becoming emotionally entangled while reflecting on past experiences, as reflected either in active or passive preoccupation. In this standard account, insecurity, by contrast, is conceptualized as taking one of the two *mutually incompatible* organized forms described earlier (i.e., dismissing *or* preoccupied states of mind, but not both).

Factor analysis provides an empirical means of distinguishing among different views of what axes of variation are being captured by AAI coders. For example, if the classic view of the conceptualization of the latent structure of the AAI is correct, factor analysis should yield evidence that indicators of dismissing and preoccupied states of mind load on a common factor (with the indicators of preoccupation and dismissing states of mind demonstrating strong negative associations with one another). If instead coders are making two, empirically distinct judgments about how adults vary in terms of their AAI states of mind (i.e., dismissing versus free to evaluate; preoccupied versus not), one would expect instead that the indicators of dismissing and preoccupied discourse should load on separate factors.

Keeping the above applications of factor analysis in mind, it is of interest that, in some contrast to the classic conceptualization of the factor structure of the AAI (reflected in the dashed axes depicted in Figure 2.1), emerging empirical evidence suggests instead that individuals actually vary along two relatively independent axes of variation—one reflecting dismissing states of mind and the other preoccupied states of mind (see solid lines in Figure 2.1). Through the lens of this recent research, security might best be understood as the co-occurrence of relatively low levels of these two empirically distinct (i.e., weakly correlated) insecure states of mind (e.g., Bernier et al., 2004; Larose et al., 2005; Roisman et al., 2007; Haydon et al., 2012).

Apart from accurately describing the key axes on which adults vary on the AAI, a second reason why understanding the factor structure of the AAI is important is because it has implications for hypothesis development and theory testing. For example, as noted in the Introduction of this volume, if researchers find (as they have) that insecure versus secure adults are less likely to provide sensitive care to their children—and if dismissing and preoccupied

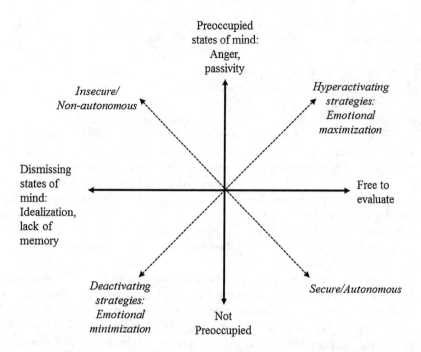

FIGURE 2.1.—The two-dimensional model of individual differences in adult attachment organization (based on Fraley & Spieker, 2003b; see also Kobak et al., 1993). The horizontal and vertical axes represent independent dismissing and preoccupied state-of-mind dimensions; the diagonal axes represent the 45° rotation of these dimensions. More specifically, a continuum of security versus insecurity, as well as a continuum of hyperactivation versus deactivation, can be represented as linear combinations of the dismissing and preoccupied axes.

states of mind are in fact relatively independent empirically—it would be unclear whether such an association is due to individual differences with respect to dismissing attachment, preoccupied attachment, or both (see Whipple et al., 2011). The inability to address such a fundamental issue limits our ability to test theoretical models, develop and refine those models, and enrich our understanding of attachment processes (see Fortuna et al., 2011; Haydon et al., 2011, 2012).

## OVERVIEW OF THE PRESENT ANALYSES

The present chapter reports analyses building on path-finding work focused on the factor structure of the AAI by Bernier and colleagues (Bernier et al., 2004; Larose et al., 2005) as well as our own work in this area based on two large sample studies (Haydon et al., 2012; Roisman et al., 2007). In the first of these investigations (Roisman et al., 2007), we examined the latent structure of individual differences in adult attachment via analysis of the set of rating scales used by AAI coders to index adults' states of mind regarding their childhood attachment experiences, scales that are used to inductively sort participants into attachment categories.[2] Specifically, data reported by Roisman et al. (2007) combined data from three publications (total $N = 504$) drawn from the literature on earned-security (see Chapter 6 of this volume; Roisman & Haydon, 2011).

In the traditional AAI coding system, Main and Goldwyn (1984–1998) contend that a dismissing state of mind is primarily reflected in any combination of high scores on state-of-mind rating scales that tap a participant's tendency to idealize parents (*maternal and paternal idealization*), derogate them (*derogation*), show failures of memory (*lack of memory*), or, more rarely, express unreasonable fears that their [hypothetical] child may die (*fear of loss*). Preoccupation is principally identified through current active resentment toward parents (*mother and father anger*) and/or psychologically confused, rambling attachment-related discourse (*passivity*). Security, in contrast, is defined not only by the relative absence of high scores on these indicators, but by clear signs that an adult is able to explore his or her thoughts and feelings about childhood experiences without becoming angrily or passively caught up while discussing them. By definition, such an ability to "freely evaluate" one's experiences is reflected in the overall *coherence of mind* and *coherence of transcript* scales (scales that tend to be nearly perfectly correlated). Adults who are able to evaluate not only their past experiences but to modify their current outlook on those life events during the interview receive high scores on *metacognitive monitoring*, another indicator of security. Note that participants can also be identified as unresolved—regardless of whether they are otherwise classified as secure, dismissing, or preoccupied—when they score at or above the midpoint on either the *unresolved loss* or *unresolved abuse* scales, which reflect the degree to which their discourse becomes disorganized while discussing loss and/or abuse experiences.

Using principal components analysis (a data reduction tool related but not equivalent to exploratory factor analysis; see Methods and Results section), Roisman et al. (2007) found evidence that two- and three-component solutions accounted for the variation in AAI state-of-mind scales described above reasonably well. The two-component solution suggested that variation in AAI state-of-mind scales could be explained by components reflecting: (1) scales used to differentiate secure from dismissing adults (i.e., mother idealization, father idealization, coherence of mind, lack of memory, and metacognitive monitoring); and (2) scales used to identify both preoccupied and unresolved status (i.e., mother anger, father anger, passivity, unresolved abuse, unresolved loss, fear of loss, and overall derogation). The three-component solution suggested that variation in AAI state-of-mind scales could be explained by components reflecting scales used to differentiate secure from dismissing adults, as in the two-component solution, and an additional set of components that suggested two distinct forms of preoccupied discourse, one involving an active, traumatic enmeshment in earlier experiences (i.e., father and mother anger, derogation, and unresolved trauma) and the other a passive, loss-related preoccupation (i.e., unresolved loss, fear of loss, and passivity). This latter finding of two distinct forms of preoccupied discourse was somewhat surprising given that scholars might reasonably have expected separate preoccupied and unresolved sources of variation paralleling the preoccupied and unresolved classifications that can be assigned using the standard approach to scoring the AAI. Complicating things further, in both the two- and three-factor solutions, two of the scales that (as noted above) are viewed by Main and Goldwyn as evidence of a dismissing state of mind (i.e., derogation and fear of loss) actually loaded with indicators of preoccupation/ unresolved discourse.

In an extension of this work to a larger sample ($N = 842$; Haydon et al., 2012), we examined the latent structure of Kobak's (1993) AAI Q-sort, a coding system designed to capture attachment-related variation in AAI discourse and inferred caregiving experiences dimensionally. Specifically, the AAI Q-sort contains 100 descriptor "cards" or items pertaining to attachment-related states of mind and inferred parental experiences as assessed by the AAI. Items are sorted into a forced quasi-normal distribution across nine piles from most to least characteristic of each participant's narrative. The distribution of participants' items can then be correlated with four prototype sorts that reflect conceptually relevant attachment dimensions, including secure/autonomous, deactivating versus hyperactivating, dismissing, and preoccupied states of mind (Kobak et al., 1993; see also Figure 2.1).

Again using a principal components analysis—this time applied to raw Q-sort data—Haydon et al. (2012) found that a four-component solution best accounted for the variation in the data. Two of these components reflected relatively independent attachment states of mind (dismissing and preoccupied; note that when items that loaded highly and uniquely on each component were composited, they were correlated very strongly with their identically named prototype score) and two additional components reflecting inferred experiences with maternal and paternal caregiving figures (for convergent evidence, see Kobak & Zajac, 2011). We have subsequently validated these scales in a series of studies examining their distinctive predictive significance for a range of important attachment-relevant behaviors (e.g., observed relationship functioning) and cognitions (e.g., attachment word Stroop task performance), as well as self-reported psychopathology (Fortuna et al., 2011; Haydon et al., 2011, 2012; see also Chapter 7).

20

Taken together, the results of these studies, as well as other studies investigating the latent structure of the AAI state-of-mind scales (Bernier et al., 2004; Larose et al., 2005), suggest that the standard coding system for the AAI might subtly misrepresent the main axes of variation captured by the AAI interview protocol. As noted earlier, these studies demonstrate that what is commonly referred to as secure/autonomous states of mind actually blend two *empirically distinct* aspects of attachment-related discourse—variation in the degree to which adults can freely evaluate their childhood experiences or are relatively dismissing of those experiences and variation in preoccupation. The results of these studies also converge with psychometric work on infant attachment based on the SECCYD (Fraley & Spieker, 2003a), which demonstrated that the various behavioral indicators used to assign infants to attachment categories in the Strange Situation procedure loaded on two modestly correlated factors reflecting attachment-related avoidance (i.e., avoidance, contact maintenance, and proximity seeking scales) and anxiety (indicated by resistance and disorganization) rather than a broad dimension of security.

Despite converging evidence from studies of the latent structure of the AAI, prior investigations are limited in that they were exploratory efforts. Indeed, no study has yet used confirmatory factor-analytic methods (Jöreskog, 1969), which permit a more rigorous examination of the model fit of the proposed factor structure to the data, to address the issue of the factor structure of the AAI. In addition, because prior publications in this area used different assessment methods to score the AAI (i.e., the state-of-mind scales drawn from the Main and Goldwyn scoring system in Roisman et al., 2007, versus Kobak's AAI Q-sort method in Haydon et al., 2012) it has not yet been possible to establish the degree to which various approaches for scaling participants on dismissing and preoccupied states of mind are correlated.

Building on prior work, this chapter reports the results of an effort to empirically refine and validate the AAI latent structures described by Roisman et al. (2007) and Haydon et al. (2012) using confirmatory factor analyses (Jöreskog, 1969) of AAI data obtained in a follow-up study of the SECCYD sample at age 18 years. We first present the results of a re-examination of the Roisman et al. (2007) state-of-mind data using exploratory factor analysis. This analysis informed our confirmatory factor analyses of the state-of-mind data in the current study, which are presented subsequently. In a similar fashion, we next present the results of a re-examination of the Haydon et al. (2012) Q-sort data using exploratory factor analysis. These results likewise informed our confirmatory factor analyses of the AAI Q-sort data acquired from members of the SECCYD cohort. Finally, we present correlations among the different options for scaling adults on the dismissing and preoccupied (and inferred experience) scales using the Main and Goldwyn and Kobak methods based on data from the age 18-year follow-up of the SECCYD.

## METHODS AND RESULTS

As a first step in the process of testing a confirmatory factor model of the Main and Goldwyn state-of-mind rating scales, we used the Roisman et al. (2007) data and conducted an exploratory factor analysis on the same state-of-mind rating scales originally included in their principal components analysis. We did so to ensure that our follow-up confirmatory factor analysis was predicated on a method (i.e., exploratory factor analysis) that is also based on the common factor model (Thurstone, 1947). In brief, principal components analysis is not based on the common factor model, which differentiates common and unique (i.e., measurement error) variance. Principal components analysis instead aims to account for the total variance in the observed measures, and is thus regarded as a data reduction tool (Brown, 2006).

Given that Roisman et al. (2007) found evidence for two weakly correlated axes on which adults vary with respect to attachment states of mind (i.e., dismissing and preoccupied) we submitted the Main and Goldwyn state-of-mind indicators to an exploratory factor analysis using maximum likelihood estimation with oblique rotation (direct oblimin) specifying in advance a lower and upper bound of the factor structure at two and three factors, in light of prior evidence (i.e., Roisman et al., 2007, demonstrated that the data from this study fit both a two- and three-factor solution reasonably well). In contrast to the orthogonal (varimax) rotation employed in the Roisman et al. (2007) principal components analysis, we intentionally chose an oblique rotation of the factor model (i.e., which allows derived factors to correlate) in light of the evidence that the dismissing and preoccupied factor scores were modestly correlated.

As was reported in the Roisman et al. (2007) principal components analysis of the same data, in the two-factor model, the AAI scales differentiating secure from dismissing participants (mother idealization, father idealization, coherence of mind, lack of memory, and metacognitive monitoring) loaded on the primary factor, which explained 22.7% of the variation in AAI scores, whereas scales reflecting preoccupation and unresolved loss (coherence of mind, mother anger, passivity, unresolved abuse, father anger, unresolved loss, overall derogation, fear of loss) loaded on a second factor that explained 18.9% of the variation. Aside from coherence of mind, which cross-loaded on both the dismissing and preoccupied factors, there were no other notable cross-loading indicators. In the three-factor model, the third factor accounted for 11.6% of the variance in AAI scores and was predominately defined by indicators that Roisman et al. (2007) described as passive, loss-related preoccupation (fear of loss, passivity, and unresolved loss). Table 2.1 presents the factor pattern loadings from both the two- and three-factor solutions.

TABLE 2.1

FACTOR PATTERN LOADINGS FROM TWO- AND THREE-FACTOR EXPLORATORY FACTOR ANALYSIS (OBLIMIN ROTATION) OF AAI STATE-OF-MIND RATING SCALES FROM ROISMAN ET AL. (2007; $N = 504$)

| AAI State-of-Mind Scale | Two-Factor Solution | | Three-Factor Solution | | |
|---|---|---|---|---|---|
| | 1 | 2 | 1 | 2 | 3 |
| Secure indicators | | | | | |
| Coherence of mind | −.71 | −.64 | −.75 | −.40 | −.36 |
| Metacognitive monitoring | −.42 | −.10 | −.44 | −.09 | .01 |
| Dismissing indicators | | | | | |
| Fear of loss | .03 | .21 | .02 | −.05 | .39 |
| Idealization (father) | .75 | −.16 | .73 | −.28 | .07 |
| Idealization (mother) | .79 | −.14 | .77 | −.21 | .02 |
| Lack of memory | .57 | −.03 | .59 | .01 | −.13 |
| Overall derogation | .08 | .30 | .15 | .51 | −.23 |
| Preoccupied indicators | | | | | |
| Anger (father) | −.20 | .44 | −.14 | .52 | .02 |
| Anger (mother) | −.17 | .51 | −.11 | .48 | .16 |
| Passivity | .12 | .50 | .14 | .22 | .48 |
| Unresolved indicators | | | | | |
| Unresolved abuse | −.05 | .48 | −.01 | .35 | .27 |
| Unresolved loss | −.04 | .30 | −.07 | −.05 | .56 |

*Note.* AAI = Adult Attachment Interview. Indicators are sorted by the AAI categories they best denote conceptually according to Main and Goldwyn (1984–1998). Values in bold are the factors on which each variable loaded most strongly for each solution.

We used these exploratory factor analysis results to specify a confirmatory measurement model that was subsequently evaluated using the AAI state-of-mind data from the SECCYD cohort. In specifying our confirmatory factor model, we elected to focus principally on the two-factor model given its more parsimonious structure. Moreover, in our primary analysis we dropped coherence of mind as a cross-loading indicator of the dismissing and preoccupied factors because it is used by AAI coders as a summary variable (i. e., the coding system forces a unitary structure on this variable by requiring that individuals who score high on either indicators of dismissing or preoccupied states of mind receive low scores on coherence of mind). Given the centrality of coherence of mind in the overall summary scoring of the AAI coding system, however, we also specified an alternative confirmatory model that included coherence of mind as a cross-loader on both the dismissing and preoccupied factors. In all analyses, we dropped indicators that showed very little or no variability in the SECCYD AAI cohort (meta-cognitive monitoring, fear of loss) or loaded weakly on their primary factor in the Roisman et al.

(2007) data, which was defined here as an absolute value of less than or equal to .40 (i.e., derogation, unresolved loss). Thus, the final model included mother idealization, father idealization, and lack of memory as indicators of the dismissing factor. Mother anger, father anger, passivity, and unresolved trauma were indicators of the preoccupied factor.

Confirmatory factor analysis models were estimated in LISREL 8.8 using raw data after multiple imputation via EM algorithm. All indicators were freely estimated and the metric of the latent factors was defined by fixing the variance of the latent factors to 1. In assessing the model fit of all confirmatory factor analyses presented in this report, we drew upon Hu and Bentler (1999), who outline ranges of acceptable fit values for model fit indices. In particular, we followed their advice that adequately fitting models should have a comparative fit index (CFI) value approaching $\geq$.95 and an SRMR cutoff value approaching .08 in order to suggest that there is a relatively good fit between the hypothesized model and the observed data. In light of these criteria, the primary model fit the data reasonably well, CFI = .97; SRMR = .04. The alternative model with coherence of mind as a cross-loader on both the dismissing and preoccupied factors also demonstrated a reasonable fit to the data, albeit slightly less so than the primary model, CFI = .94; SRMR = .05. In an exploratory manner, we examined a confirmatory factor model based on the three-factor solution of the Roisman et al. (2007) data. The fit of this model (CFI = .96; SRMR = .05) was also adequate. Parameter estimates for the models are presented in Table 2.2.

In short, the above analyses provide confirmatory evidence of a two-factor model of the AAI Main and Goldwyn state-of-mind rating scales. Advantages of measuring variation in adult attachment with a focus on these two factors (e.g., using unit weighted composites of relevant indicators), include the absence of cross-loading indicators, with the exception of coherence of mind. That said, the relatively few indicators (i.e., state-of-mind scales) that loaded on each factor and the fact that some of these indicators had to be dropped given their low loadings raises the question of whether a more optimal scoring approach could be derived from another method for coding AAIs. We addressed this issue by performing the same sequence of exploratory and confirmatory factor analyses on data coded using Kobak's AAI Q-sort scoring system.

Paralleling our approach with the Main and Goldwyn state-of-mind scales, in developing our confirmatory model of Kobak's AAI Q-sort dimensions, we returned to the Haydon et al. (2012) data and conducted an exploratory factor analysis using maximum likelihood estimation with oblique rotation (direct oblimin) of the 100 Q-sort cards. We specified an extraction of four factors based on the original PCA conducted by Haydon et al. (2012). The exploratory factor analysis results revealed a dismissing factor that accounted for 25.7% of the variance. The second factor was interpretable as a maternal

24

TABLE 2.2

Unstandardized Loadings (Standard Errors) and Standardized Loadings for Final and Alternative Two- and Three-Factor Confirmatory Models of AAI State-of-Mind Rating Scales From the Age 18 Assessment ($N = 857$)

| AAI State-of-Mind Scale | Dismissing | | Preoccupied | | Active Preoccupation | | Passive Preoccupation | |
|---|---|---|---|---|---|---|---|---|
| | Unstd (SE) | Std | Unstd (SE) | Std | Unstd (SE) | Std | Unstd (SE) | Std |
| Primary model | | | | | | | | |
| Dismissing indicators | | | | | | | | |
|   Idealization (mother) | 1.19 (.05) | .91 | | | | | | |
|   Idealization (father) | .82 (.05) | .66 | | | | | | |
|   Lack of memory | 1.03 (.07) | .57 | | | | | | |
| Preoccupied indicators | | | | | | | | |
|   Anger (mother) | | | .33 (.02) | .57 | | | | |
|   Anger (father) | | | .54 (.03) | .73 | | | | |
|   Passivity | | | .71 (.04) | .65 | | | | |
|   Unresolved abuse | | | .27 (.02) | .44 | | | | |
| Alternative two-factor model | | | | | | | | |
| Dismissing indicators | | | | | | | | |
|   Coherence of mind | −1.41 (.05) | −.98 | | | | | | |
|   Idealization (mother) | .96 (.04) | .74 | | | | | | |
|   Idealization (father) | .75 (.04) | .60 | | | | | | |
|   Lack of memory | 1.36 (.06) | .75 | | | | | | |
| Preoccupied indicators | | | | | | | | |
|   Coherence of mind | | | −.70 (.04) | −.49 | | | | |
|   Anger (mother) | | | .33 (.02) | .56 | | | | |
|   Anger (father) | | | .51 (.03) | .69 | | | | |
|   Passivity | | | .75 (.04) | .68 | | | | |
|   Unresolved abuse | | | .29 (.02) | .46 | | | | |
| Three-factor model | | | | | | | | |
| Dismissing indictors | | | | | | | | |
|   Idealization (mother) | 1.18 (.05) | .91 | | | | | | |
|   Idealization (father) | .83 (.05) | .66 | | | | | | |
|   Lack of memory | 1.03 (.07) | .57 | | | | | | |
| Active preoccupation indicators | | | | | | | | |
|   Anger (mother) | | | | | .34 (.02) | .59 | | |
|   Anger (father) | | | | | .54 (.03) | .73 | | |
|   Derogation (highest) | | | | | .12 (.02) | .20 | | |
| Passive preoccupation indicators | | | | | | | | |
|   Passivity | | | | | | | 1.22 (.13) | 1.11 |
|   Unresolved loss | | | | | | | .33 (.05) | 0.31 |

*Note.* Unstd = unstandardized LISREL lambda coefficients; Std = standardized LISREL lambda coefficients. The alternative two-factor model includes the AAI coherence of mind scale as an indicator of both the dismissing and preoccupied factors. The alternative three-factor model includes the AAI highest derogation scale as an indicator of the active preoccupation factor and the unresolved loss scale as an indicator of the passive preoccupation factor.

inferred experiences factor, accounting for 12.4% of the variance. Finally, factors 3 and 4 assessed inferred paternal experiences (8.2%) and preoccupation (5.5%), respectively. Table 2.3 presents the factor pattern loadings of the 100 Q-sort cards.

As with the Main and Goldwyn AAI state-of-mind confirmatory factor models predicated on the Roisman et al. (2007) exploratory factor analysis, we

TABLE 2.3

FACTOR PATTERN LOADINGS FROM FOUR-FACTOR EXPLORATORY FACTOR ANALYSIS (OBLIMIN ROTATION) OF AAI Q-SORT DATA ($N = 842$) FROM HAYDON ET AL. (2012)

| AAI Q-Sort Items and Card Numbers | Factor 1 | 2 | 3 | 4 |
|---|---|---|---|---|
| 10. Subject recalls specific childhood memories of distress. | **.86** | .10 | −.09 | .00 |
| 19. Responses are superficial and require further probes. | **−.85** | −.02 | .00 | .01 |
| 73. Adjectives supported by vague or shallow memories. | **−.85** | −.01 | −.01 | .00 |
| 74. Memories of childhood are recalled during interview. | **.82** | −.03 | .04 | .00 |
| 84. Is credible and easy to believe. | **.82** | −.09 | .11 | −.27 |
| 1. Parental descriptions are stereotyped. | **−.82** | −.04 | −.02 | −.04 |
| 50. Information about mother is vague, limited, or hard to rate. | **−.81** | .06 | −.02 | .02 |
| 47. Is guarded or threatened by interview questions. | **−.80** | .06 | −.06 | .12 |
| 11. Parental faults or limitations are acknowledged directly. | **.80** | .09 | −.16 | .00 |
| 91. Subject reports negative experience that is not accompanied by feelings of hurt or distress. | **−.79** | .02 | −.01 | −.08 |
| 69. Information about father is vague, limited, or hard to rate. | **−.78** | −.07 | −.07 | .07 |
| 80. Statements about family are vague and poorly developed. | **−.77** | .03 | −.07 | .24 |
| 65. Is able to generalize from personal experience. | **.76** | −.06 | .05 | −.33 |
| 57. Is detached or uninfluenced by childhood experiences. | **−.74** | .08 | −.11 | .07 |
| 93. Depicts parents as perfect or wonderful without convincing reader | **−.73** | .19 | −.16 | .04 |
| 72. Integrates specific memories with more general abstraction. | **.73** | −.02 | .07 | −.44 |
| 46. Subject persistently does not remember. | **−.72** | .01 | −.04 | −.05 |
| 64. Acknowledges setbacks that may have been overcome. | .70 | .12 | −.04 | −.03 |
| 56. Parental shortcomings are implied but not directly acknowledged. | −.69 | .02 | .16 | .11 |
| 100. Presents contradictory descriptions of parents. | −.67 | .16 | −.14 | .20 |
| 38. Shows some reevaluation reappraisal of parental practices. | .66 | .07 | −.07 | −.09 |
| 66. Provides only minimal responses. | −.65 | −.04 | −.02 | −.54 |
| 12. Acknowledges limitations in his or her own view of parents. | .65 | .01 | .01 | −.20 |
| 62. Is able to discuss the influence of "relationships on relationships." | .65 | −.05 | .02 | −.21 |
| 39. Subject values attachment (devalues attachment relationships). | .63 | −.27 | .18 | −.09 |
| 29. Presents an objective and well thought out picture of relationship influences. | .61 | −.10 | .06 | −.42 |
| 54. Is currently angry toward parents. | .59 | .10 | −.01 | .28 |
| 21. Is unaware of violating coherency maxims. | −.58 | .08 | −.03 | .35 |
| 3. Is dissatisfied with parental availability. | .57 | −.02 | −.14 | .14 |
| 71. Relies on others in frustrated or dissatisfied ways. | .56 | −.12 | .13 | .31 |
| 61. Presents self as invulnerable. | −.55 | .25 | −.12 | −.15 |
| 9. Is generally trusting in his or her relationships. | .51 | −.35 | .26 | .04 |
| 35. Is stoic about comfort or support he/she can expect from others. | −.46 | .33 | −.27 | −.10 |
| 53. Describes self as "spoiled" or a "baby" as a child. | −.35 | .25 | −.15 | −.12 |
| 44. Took on precocious caregiving role for parent. | .34 | .27 | −.06 | .20 |
| 27. Is preoccupied with loss of significant others. | .31 | −.03 | .10 | .22 |
| 82. Has fears of abandonment or abuse by parent. | −.28 | −.08 | .16 | −.02 |
| 90. Had a positive turning point in relationship with parent. | .24 | −.22 | .11 | −.22 |
| 28. Has experienced early and prolonged disruption of an attachment relationship. | .12 | .10 | −.12 | .11 |
| 5. Relationship with mother was relaxed and open. | .10 | **−.90** | −.10 | −.01 |

(*Continued*)

TABLE 2.3. (*Continued*)

| AAI Q-Sort Items and Card Numbers | Factor | | | |
|---|---|---|---|---|
| | 1 | 2 | 3 | 4 |
| 85. Mother was psychologically unavailable. | −.07 | **.90** | .04 | −.07 |
| 31. Mother was a competent and supportive confidant. | .12 | **−.88** | −.06 | .02 |
| 41. Mother was patient and tolerant. | .04 | **−.83** | −.05 | −.02 |
| 59. Mother was strict or rigid, intimidated subject. | .07 | **.82** | .07 | −.05 |
| 86. Mother was generally forgiving of mistakes and limitations. | .07 | **−.81** | −.07 | .01 |
| 40. Mother pushed subject toward precocious independence. | .01 | **.78** | .01 | −.16 |
| 95. Mother enjoyed parenting. | −.03 | **−.74** | .05 | .02 |
| 13. Mother called attention to her own needs and concerns. | .11 | **.74** | .05 | .02 |
| 23. Mother relied on subject for affection and support. | .07 | .69 | .02 | .04 |
| 49. Mother was too busy or preoccupied to pay attention to subject. | .04 | .68 | .02 | −.01 |
| 76. Has memories of physical affection from mother. | .24 | −.62 | .01 | .04 |
| 4. Mother emphasized achievement and success at the expense of emotional support. | .07 | .61 | .04 | −.04 |
| 81. Currently maintains a close relationship with mother. | .20 | −.52 | .09 | .02 |
| 67. Mother was incompetent or unable to cope. | .09 | .51 | .08 | .19 |
| 17. Was confident that he/she could rely on parents. | .28 | −.50 | .42 | −.05 |
| 16. Subject fails to depict any relationship in which attachment needs were acknowledged. | −.44 | .47 | −.30 | .14 |
| 14. Mother actively encouraged the subject in developing his or her abilities. | .04 | −.47 | .03 | −.11 |
| 77. Has confidence in mother's well-being and ability to function. | −.04 | −.42 | .01 | −.26 |
| 25. Presents self as actively seeking support. | .31 | −.33 | .17 | −.27 |
| 94. Mother was chronically unhappy with marital or love relationship. | .11 | .25 | −.10 | .09 |
| 37. Subject describes parents with non-attachment related attributes i.e. success, fun. | −.24 | .25 | −.12 | .03 |
| 58. Experienced considerable marital conflict between parents. | .14 | .21 | −.21 | .13 |
| 70. Indications of traumatic experience are present. | .15 | .21 | −.20 | .19 |
| 99. Is free of parental expectations. | −.03 | −.20 | .17 | −.16 |
| 88. Father was chronically unhappy with marital or love relationships. | .07 | .18 | −.12 | .09 |
| 24. Relationship with father was relaxed and open. | .02 | .08 | **.92** | −.06 |
| 60. Father was patient and tolerant. | −.02 | .01 | **.87** | −.04 |
| 87. Father was psychologically unavailable. | −.01 | −.05 | **−.87** | .00 |
| 32. Father was a competent and supportive confidant. | .05 | .04 | **.87** | −.06 |
| 43. Father was strict or rigid, intimidated subject. | .07 | −.02 | **−.83** | −.04 |
| 52. Father was generally forgiving of mistakes. | .04 | .03 | **.81** | .01 |
| 79. Father enjoyed parenting. | −.02 | −.05 | **.79** | .01 |
| 42. Father pushed subject toward precocious independence. | −.02 | .03 | **−.78** | −.10 |
| 15. Father called attention to his own needs and concerns. | .09 | −.03 | **−.77** | .01 |
| 7. Father relied on subject for affection and support. | .07 | −.01 | **−.71** | −.06 |
| 78. Has memories of physical affection from father. | .20 | −.04 | .63 | .06 |
| 51. Father was too busy or preoccupied to pay attention to subject. | −.03 | −.04 | −.63 | −.02 |
| 6. Father emphasized achievement and success at the expense of emotional support. | .01 | .06 | −.60 | −.09 |
| 22. Felt much closer to mother than father as a child. | .05 | −.54 | −.55 | .00 |
| 18. Currently maintains a close relationship with father. | .11 | −.11 | .53 | −.09 |

(*Continued*)

TABLE 2.3. *(Continued)*

| AAI Q-Sort Items and Card Numbers | Factor | | | |
|---|---|---|---|---|
| | 1 | 2 | 3 | 4 |
| 33. Father actively encouraged subject in developing his or her abilities. | .03 | −.07 | .52 | −.10 |
| 68. Father was incompetent or unable to cope. | .14 | −.01 | −.51 | .08 |
| 96. Has confidence in father's well-being and ability to function. | −.10 | .02 | .45 | −.26 |
| 97. Feels responsible for parents' happiness or well-being. | .20 | .03 | .26 | .18 |
| 34. Has experienced the death of a significant attachment figure. | .09 | .07 | .16 | .05 |
| 83. Responds in a clear, well-organized fashion. | .24 | −.04 | .03 | **−.86** |
| 8. Responses maintain focus on interview questions. | −.05 | −.04 | .01 | **−.84** |
| 75. Loses topic during interview, failing to complete thoughts. | −.09 | −.01 | .00 | **.84** |
| 30. Responds in excessive detail about attachment relationships. | −.05 | −.05 | .03 | **.80** |
| 55. Is confused or overwhelmed with information about parents. | −.24 | .06 | −.06 | **.79** |
| 2. Reader must struggle to understand subject's statements. | −.32 | .01 | .01 | **.76** |
| 48. Vacillates between positive and negative attitudes toward parents. | −.30 | −.02 | −.05 | .63 |
| 20. Is conflicted or confused about parents. | −.34 | .17 | −.14 | .56 |
| 89. Belittles or derogates parents in an attempt to dismiss their importance. | −.36 | −.05 | .04 | −.43 |
| 26. Acknowledges own contribution to relationships with parents. | .13 | −.03 | .10 | −.42 |
| 92. Is caught up with analyzing parental shortcomings. | −.04 | .13 | −.12 | .41 |
| 45. Is currently preoccupied with negative experiences with parents. | .07 | .11 | −.11 | .39 |
| 36. Understands parental limitations in light of their own experience. | .34 | −.02 | −.05 | −.35 |
| 98. Is generous or forgiving of faults in parents. | .19 | −.19 | .14 | −.25 |
| 63. Shows continued confusion or disorganization about the loss of a significant other. | .08 | .04 | .06 | .20 |

*Note.* Factor 1 = dismissing; Factor 2 = inferred maternal experiences; Factor 3 = inferred paternal experiences; Factor 4 = preoccupied. Bolded factor loadings reflect items retained for confirmatory analyses (see text). Text in parentheses indicates the low anchor for each card. Item labels have been truncated.

used the exploratory factor analysis results presented immediately above to inform our specification of a confirmatory measurement model of the AAI Q-sort dimensions. In the case of the Q-sort, however, the task was more challenging given the large number of potential indicators as well as the fact that the Q-sort was constructed with cross-loading items (e.g., items intentionally designed to differentiate secure from insecure participants). In addition to the issue of cross-loading, subsets of the Q-sort items contain either similar anchor stems (e.g., information about mother is vague, limited, or hard to rate; information about father is vague, limited, or hard to rate) or use positive and negative framing to measure a given factor (e.g., memories of childhood are recalled during interview; subject persistently does not remember). These measurement nuances suggested to us that it might be necessary to account for method artifact in our confirmatory factor model specification (i.e., shared method variance might give rise to sub-factors within the primary factors). This is an important point, as failure to appropriately correlate item residuals (i.e., in our case, to account for method artifact) could lead to a misspecification of the factorial structure of the proposed confirmatory model and subsequent substantive misinterpretation of the observed latent structure. With these considerations in mind, an initial confirmatory factor model was first tested on the Haydon et al. (2012) data and then optimized (again using confirmatory factor analysis) on the same data based on consideration of a priori as well as empirically based criteria noted below. Finally, we examined whether this more optimal solution could be cross-validated using the AAI data from the age 18 follow-up of the SECCYD.

In specifying our initial confirmatory factor model, we included Q-sort indicators that loaded greater than or equal to .7 on their primary factor (i.e., from the initial exploratory factor analysis) with no cross-loaders (the .7 loading criterion is a widely used rule of thumb; note that loadings can be loosely interpreted as how highly correlated the indicator is with the factor). This decision rule left 17 cards as indicators of the dismissing factor, six for the preoccupied factor, nine for maternal experiences, and 10 for paternal experiences (see Table 2.4). The model was estimated using LISREL version 8.8 using raw data with full information maximum-likelihood estimation (the AAI Q-sort system produces no missing data). All indicators were freely estimated and the metric of the latent factors was defined by fixing the variance of the latent factors to 1. Inspection of model fit revealed that the model fit the data reasonably well, CFI = .94; SRMR = .09. (Parameter estimates for this model are available from the authors.)

We next sought to refine this model through the use of both a priori conceptual as well empirical criteria (i.e., inspection of the modification indices). Specifically, only modification indices with high values (i.e., greater than 100) were considered. These modification indices included both those that allowed items to load on more than one factor (i.e., cross-loaders) or suggested correlating indicator residuals. We only freed a parameter suggested by the modification indices if the following criteria were met: (a) the correlated residuals were from items from the same factor and (b) the cross-loading items were those the three authors had independently identified a priori as theoretically likely cross-loaders (most commonly because the intent of the item was to scale participants on a broad security/insecurity dimension, which would result in the relevant items cross-loading on both the dismissing and preoccupied factor).

This approach to model re-specification led to the modeling of 14 correlated indicator residuals (card 30/card 75; card 31/card 85; card 32/card 87; card 43/card 32; card 43/card 60; card 46/card 73; card 46/card 74; card 57/card 65; card 65/card 73; card 65/card 80; card 69/card 50; card 73/card 19; card 74/card 73; and card 91/card 10) and three cross-loading items (cards 65, 72, and 84; see Table 2.3 for item content) relevant to the dismissing and preoccupied factors. The re-specified model resulted in an

## TABLE 2.4

Unstandardized Loadings (Standard Errors) and Standardized Loadings for Four-Factor Confirmatory Model of AAI Q-Sort Data From the Age 18 Assessment ($N = 857$)

| Q-Sort Item (Card) Number | Dismissing | | Preoccupied | | Maternal Experiences | | Paternal Experiences | |
|---|---|---|---|---|---|---|---|---|
| | Unstd (SE) | Std | Unstd (SE) | Std | Unstd (SE) | Std | Unstd (SE) | Std |
| 1 | 1.72 (.07) | .70 | | | | | | |
| 10 | −1.86 (.07) | −.77 | | | | | | |
| 11 | −1.33 (.07) | −.59 | | | | | | |
| 19 | 2.08 (.08) | .80 | | | | | | |
| 46 | 1.95 (.08) | .76 | | | | | | |
| 47 | 1.71 (.07) | .75 | | | | | | |
| 50 | 1.75 (.06) | .80 | | | | | | |
| 57 | 1.36 (.05) | .75 | | | | | | |
| 65 | −1.46 (.06) | −.70 | −0.44 (.05) | −.21 | | | | |
| 69 | 1.63 (.06) | .75 | | | | | | |
| 72 | −1.30 (.06) | −.66 | −0.55 (.05) | −.28 | | | | |
| 73 | 2.05 (.07) | .80 | | | | | | |
| 74 | −2.21 (.07) | −.84 | | | | | | |
| 80 | 1.63 (.07) | .72 | | | | | | |
| 84 | −1.64 (.06) | −.75 | −0.59 (.05) | −.27 | | | | |
| 91 | 1.56 (.07) | .73 | | | | | | |
| 93 | 1.28 (.06) | .71 | | | | | | |
| 2 | | | 1.68 (.07) | .74 | | | | |
| 8 | | | −1.57 (.06) | −.81 | | | | |
| 30 | | | 1.06 (.05) | .65 | | | | |
| 55 | | | 1.15 (.05) | .71 | | | | |
| 75 | | | 1.50 (.05) | .82 | | | | |
| 83 | | | −1.55 (.05) | −.87 | | | | |
| 5 | | | | | 1.70 (.05) | .89 | | |
| 13 | | | | | −0.98 (.06) | −.53 | | |
| 31 | | | | | 1.65 (.06) | .85 | | |
| 40 | | | | | −1.37 (.06) | −.69 | | |
| 41 | | | | | 1.48 (.05) | .86 | | |
| 59 | | | | | −0.85 (.04) | −.61 | | |
| 85 | | | | | −1.62 (.05) | −.85 | | |
| 86 | | | | | 1.06 (.04) | .74 | | |
| 95 | | | | | 1.07 (.04) | .75 | | |
| 7 | | | | | | | 0.66 (.03) | .70 |
| 15 | | | | | | | 0.83 (.04) | .60 |
| 24 | | | | | | | −1.97 (.06) | −.89 |
| 32 | | | | | | | −1.72 (.06) | −.83 |
| 42 | | | | | | | 1.37 (.06) | .73 |
| 43 | | | | | | | 1.02 (.05) | .64 |
| 52 | | | | | | | −0.98 (.04) | −.70 |
| 60 | | | | | | | −1.43 (.05) | −.80 |
| 79 | | | | | | | −1.15 (.04) | −.82 |
| 87 | | | | | | | 1.89 (.06) | .85 |

*Note.* Unstd = unstandardized LISREL lambda coefficients; Std = standardized LISREL lambda coefficients. Dashed lines are provided to help facilitate factor-to-item correspondence. Bolded Q-sort items denote items that were allowed to load on both the dismissing and preoccupied factors. As noted in the text, the model from which these parameter estimates were derived included 14 sets of intercorrelated error terms (residuals) among manifest Q-sort indicator cards.

improvement in model fit: CFI = .96, SRMR = .08. As such, this model was retained and applied to the AAI data from the SECCYD cohort. Parameter estimates for the model as applied to these data are presented in Table 2.4. The model fit the data reasonably well (CFI = .95; SRMR = .09) thus providing confirmatory evidence for a four-factor latent structure of Kobak's AAI Q-sort.

## DISCUSSION

The aim of this chapter was to present confirmatory factor analytic evidence of the latent structure of adult attachment based on AAI data from the SECCYD cohort. For both the standard Main and Goldwyn state-of-mind scale scoring approach as well as Kobak's Q-sort approach we developed confirmatory models by revisiting large data sets that used these coding methods (Haydon et al., 2012; Roisman et al., 2007) and by conducting exploratory factor analyses that provided empirical model-building information. The resultant models for both approaches to scoring AAIs were then applied to data from the SECCYD cohort, providing confirmatory evidence that adults vary on two empirically distinctive state-of-mind dimensions: dismissing and preoccupied.

A question that follows from these results concerns which of the several available methods for scaling participants on dismissing and preoccupied states of mind is optimal (e.g., composites derived from Main & Goldwyn's state-of-mind scales, the Kobak Q-sort dismissing and preoccupied prototype scores, or composites based on the select Q-sort cards). As can be seen in Table 2.5, the associations among these three different approaches to scaling participants on dismissing and preoccupied states of mind converge quite well with one another in the present study, with correlations ranging from .60 to .93 between approaches for scaling participants on the same dimension (relevant associations are underlined; mean $r = .88$ for dismissing, mean $r = .73$ for preoccupied). Nonetheless, it is noteworthy that the operational definition for which we have advocated elsewhere (i.e., Haydon et al., 2011, 2012)—the use of the prototype scores derived from the Q-sort system—correlated quite well with both our empirically driven approach to scaling participants on the dismissing and preoccupied dimensions using Q-sort items as well as the dismissing and preoccupied scales derived from the Main and Goldwyn state-of-mind scales. Similarly, both approaches available for scaling participants on maternal and paternal caregiving experiences (the use of select items from the Kobak Q-sort or the compositing of relevant scales from the Main and Goldwyn system, see [2]), converged well with $r$s ≈ .80 (also underlined in Table 2.5). In short, one comprehensive strategy to analyzing AAI data (which we have used elsewhere; Haydon et al., 2012) involves the use

31

TABLE 2.5

ASSOCIATIONS BETWEEN AAI Q-SORT PROTOTYPE AND SCALED COMPOSITES AND MAIN AND GOLDWYN AAI STATE-OF-MIND AND INFERRED-EXPERIENCE SCALED COMPOSITES FROM THE AGE 18 ASSESSMENT (RANGE $N$ = 826–857)

| | Main and Goldwyn Scaled Composite Scores | | | | Kobak Q-Sort Prototypes | | | | Kobak Q-Sort Scaled Composite Scores | | | |
|---|---|---|---|---|---|---|---|---|---|---|---|---|
| | Ds | E | Mom | Dad | Ds | E | Secure | Deact. | Ds | E | Mom | Dad |
| Dismissing MG | — | | | | | | | | | | | |
| Preoccupied MG | -.19** | — | | | | | | | | | | |
| Mom MG | .34** | .26** | — | | | | | | | | | |
| Dad MG | .22** | .29** | .42** | — | | | | | | | | |
| Dismissing QP | .85** | -.10** | .47** | .35** | — | | | | | | | |
| Preoccupied QP | -.04 | .77** | .44** | .38** | .07* | — | | | | | | |
| Secure QP | -.78** | -.16** | -.55** | -.41** | -.94** | -.39** | — | | | | | |
| Deactivation QP | .79** | -.46** | .23** | .15** | .87** | -.41** | -.67** | — | | | | |
| Dismissing QS | .86** | -.28** | .26** | .14** | .93** | -.18** | -.81** | .92** | — | | | |
| Preoccupied QS | .11** | .61** | .26** | .24** | .18** | .81** | -.45** | -.23** | .02 | — | | |
| Mom QS | .33** | .28** | .79** | .26** | .48** | .49** | -.57** | .22** | .24** | .29** | — | |
| Dad QS | .27** | .26** | .33** | .80** | .43** | .41** | -.47** | .20** | .20** | .24** | .28** | — |

*Note.* Ds = dismissing; E = preoccupied; Mom = maternal inferred experiences; Dad = paternal inferred experiences; Secure = secure/autonomous; Deact. = deactivation; QS = Kobak Q-sort scaled composite scores; QP = Kobak Q-sort prototype scores; MG = Main and Goldwyn scaled composite scores; Item content for the various composites are as follows (higher scores on all composites reflect higher levels of dismissing and preoccupied states of mind and higher levels of negative inferred maternal and paternal experiences; Q-sort cards and Main and Goldwyn inferred-experience scales were reversed as necessary; see Table 2.3 for Q-sort card description): Q-sort scaled dismissing [cards 1, 10, 11, 19, 46, 47, 50, 57, 69, 73, 74, 80, 91, 93]; Q-sort scaled preoccupied [cards 2, 8, 30, 55, 75, 83]; Q-sort scaled maternal [cards 5, 13, 31, 40, 41, 59, 85, 86, 95]; Q-sort scaled paternal [cards 7, 15, 24, 32, 42, 43, 52, 60, 79, 87]; MG scaled dismissing [mother idealization, father idealization, lack of memory]; MG scaled preoccupied [mother anger, father anger, passivity, unresolved abuse]; MG scaled maternal [mother loving, mother reject, mother neglect]; MG scaled paternal [paternal loving, paternal reject, paternal neglect].

* $p < .05$.

** $p < .01$.

of the dismissing and preoccupied prototype scores (drawn from the Q-sort) combined with the maternal and paternal inferred-experience scales based on compositing relevant items from the sort.

It is also the case that the dismissing and preoccupied scales converge with standard categorical coding using the Main and Goldwyn classifications. Specifically, Table 2.6 reports means and standard deviations for the various state-of-mind and inferred-experiences composites described above by attachment classification (secure vs. insecure, including unresolved secures; dismissing vs. secure vs. preoccupied; and dismissing vs. secure vs. preoccupied vs. unresolved). Simple effect size calculations reveal that the dimensions described above differentiate the standard classic AAI categories quite well. For example, the difference between dismissing versus secure and dismissing versus preoccupied groups (three-way coding) on the dismissing prototype Q-sort dimension reflected effect sizes greater than $rs = \sim.8$. Similarly, the difference between preoccupied versus secure and preoccupied versus dismissing groups (three-way coding) on the preoccupied prototype Q-sort dimension reflected effect sizes greater than $rs = .9$. Nonetheless, it should be kept in mind that, as discussed above, the use of the standard classifications (and, indeed, the Kobak security and deactivation prototype scores) requires accepting some restrictive and empirically unsupported assumptions about the latent structure of adult attachment (e.g., by assigning a participant to the dismissing classification, the analyst ignores the fact that the very same individual could be simultaneously elevated on preoccupation).

One final issue under-emphasized in this analysis—but of some importance—is our observation that there may be no empirical distinction between indicators of preoccupation and unresolved discourse. One possibility is that the more normative risk cohorts that have been the focus of work on the latent structure of the AAI (including data from the SECCYD AAI cohort) have obscured empirical divergence between indicators of unresolved and preoccupied discourse. Another possibility, however, is that no such distinction exists empirically, a possibility consistent with Fraley and Spieker's (2003a) demonstration that resistance and disorganization also load on a common factor in infancy.

In summary, this report is the first to empirically specify and validate models of the factor structure pertinent to the two primary scoring approaches to the AAI. In so doing, the results of analyses reported in this chapter provide confirmatory factor analytic evidence for the existence of two modestly correlated dismissing and preoccupied dimensions that (together with assessments of inferred maternal and paternal experiences) capture a good deal of the variation in participants' coded discourse during the AAI. Importantly, however, these results do not address the question of whether individual differences in adult attachment are categorically or continuously distributed (Fraley & Spieker, 2003a; Fraley & Waller, 1998;

## TABLE 2.6

MEANS (AND SDs) OF AAI Q-SORT PROTOTYPE AND SCALED COMPOSITES AND MAIN AND GOLDWYN AAI STATE-OF-MIND AND INFERRED-EXPERIENCE SCALED COMPOSITES BY AAI TWO-, THREE-, AND FOUR-WAY ATTACHMENT CLASSIFICATIONS FROM THE AGE 18 ASSESSMENT (RANGE $N$ = 826–857)

| | AAI Two-Way Classification | | AAI Three-Way Classification | | | AAI Four-Way Classification | | | |
|---|---|---|---|---|---|---|---|---|---|
| | Secure | Insecure | Secure | Dismissing | Preoccupied | Secure | Dismissing | Preoccupied | Unresolved |
| Dismissing MG | 2.48 (0.66) | 4.19 (1.08) | 2.46 (0.67) | 4.44 (0.85) | 2.54 (0.84) | 2.48 (0.66) | 4.46 (0.85) | 2.60 (0.90) | 2.78 (1.12) |
| Preoccupied MG | 1.41 (0.33) | 1.57 (0.77) | 1.42 (0.34) | 1.36 (0.39) | 3.34 (1.00) | 1.41 (0.33) | 1.34 (0.33) | 3.06 (0.69) | 2.68 (1.45) |
| Mom MG | 2.73 (0.81) | 3.58 (0.89) | 2.74 (0.81) | 3.55 (0.86) | 3.92 (1.02) | 2.73 (0.81) | 3.55 (0.84) | 3.93 (0.91) | 3.61 (1.24) |
| Dad MG | 3.37 (1.07) | 4.13 (1.01) | 3.37 (1.07) | 4.07 (0.97) | 4.76 (0.99) | 3.37 (1.07) | 4.07 (0.96) | 4.70 (0.87) | 4.26 (1.42) |
| Dismissing QP | −0.29 (0.22) | 0.37 (0.26) | −0.29 (0.22) | 0.44 (0.18) | −0.05 (0.20) | −0.29 (0.22) | 0.44 (0.18) | −0.06 (0.21) | 0.01 (0.38) |
| Preoccupied QP | −0.30 (0.17) | −0.14 (0.26) | −0.29 (0.17) | −0.22 (0.16) | 0.47 (0.15) | −0.30 (0.17) | −0.23 (0.15) | 0.47 (0.14) | 0.17 (0.27) |
| Secure QP | 0.46 (0.19) | −0.23 (0.21) | 0.46 (0.19) | −0.25 (0.19) | −0.23 (0.17) | 0.46 (0.19) | −0.25 (0.20) | −0.23 (0.18) | −0.07 (0.36) |
| Deactivation QP | −0.00 (0.21) | 0.34 (0.28) | −0.01 (0.21) | 0.43 (0.13) | −0.32 (0.18) | −0.00 (0.21) | 0.44 (0.13) | −0.32 (0.18) | −0.10 (0.32) |
| Dismissing QS | 4.15 (1.15) | 6.72 (1.42) | 4.13 (1.15) | 7.14 (0.86) | 3.90 (0.89) | 4.15 (1.15) | 7.18 (0.82) | 3.92 (0.86) | 4.43 (1.70) |
| Preoccupied QS | 2.65 (1.20) | 3.88 (1.61) | 2.68 (1.21) | 3.49 (1.13) | 7.19 (1.41) | 2.65 (1.20) | 3.46 (1.11) | 7.22 (1.35) | 5.21 (1.89) |
| Mom QS | 3.53 (1.16) | 4.80 (1.28) | 3.54 (1.16) | 4.75 (1.27) | 5.46 (1.29) | 3.53 (1.16) | 4.74 (1.27) | 5.44 (1.17) | 4.92 (1.40) |
| Dad QS | 4.41 (1.34) | 5.54 (1.07) | 4.42 (1.33) | 5.50 (1.07) | 6.05 (0.83) | 4.41 (1.34) | 5.46 (1.06) | 6.01 (0.78) | 5.97 (1.27) |

*Note.* Mom = maternal inferred experiences; Dad = paternal inferred experiences; MG = Main & Goldwyn scaled composite; QP = Kobak Q-sort prototype; QS = Kobak Q-sort scaled composite.

Rosiman et al., 2007). It is this issue that is addressed by Fraley and Roisman in Chapter 3.

## NOTE

2. As described in Chapter 1, in addition to assessing adults' coherence of discourse regarding childhood experiences using the state-of-mind rating scales, Main and Goldwyn's AAI coding system uses nine-point scales to rate aspects of the inferred nature of participants' childhood experiences with caregivers. Nonetheless, in the analysis reported in the chapter—as in all prior studies focused on the latent structure of the AAI—we excluded the ten inferred-experience scales of the AAI (i.e., maternal and paternal love, rejection, neglect, pressure to achieve, and role reversal) from consideration because insecurity is intentionally confounded with low levels of love and high levels of rejection, neglect, pressure to achieve, and/or reversal in the Main and Goldwyn scoring system. Specifically, participants can only be coded as insecure if their inferred-experience ratings suggest low quality early experiences, although secure participants can vary freely on these scales. (Importantly, inferred experiences and states of mind are not intentionally confounded in this way using Kobak's AAI Q-set and thus relevant items were included in these analyses). Nonetheless, in the interest of providing direction to investigators who might wish to use the inferred-experience dimensions of the Main and Goldwyn system, we conducted exploratory factor analyses (maximum likelihood estimation, direct oblimin rotation) of these 10 scales, which revealed evidence for two factors underlying them—maternal experience (mother loving, mother rejection, mother neglect) and paternal experience (father loving, father rejection, father neglect). The pressure to achieve and role reversal scales did not load very well on either factor and, indeed, the factor structure specified above was especially clear when these scales were dropped.

# III. CATEGORIES OR DIMENSIONS? A TAXOMETRIC ANALYSIS OF THE ADULT ATTACHMENT INTERVIEW

*R. Chris Fraley and Glenn I. Roisman*

Haltigan, Roisman, and Haydon (this volume) demonstrated that the state-of-mind rating scales used in the AAI have a robust two-factor structure. The first factor appears to reflect variation in dismissing strategies, whereas the second factor reflects variation in preoccupation. As Haltigan et al. stated, however, the existence of an empirically replicable latent structure begs the question of how individuals are distributed with respect to that structure. It could be the case that the factors uncovered in Chapter 2 represent latent classes within a multivariate space. It is also possible, however, that these factors represent continuous or graded variation between persons. This would suggest that people vary in the degree to which their attachment systems are organized in dismissing and preoccupied ways.

The objective of this chapter is to address empirically the types versus dimensions question with respect to individual differences in the AAI. This chapter is designed to build upon an article published by Roisman et al. (2007) in two ways. First, since the publication of that article, substantial progress has been made in understanding the latent structure of AAI ratings (e.g., Chapter 2 of this volume; Haydon et al., 2011, 2012; Roisman et al., 2007). As such, we are in a stronger position than we were before to target the specific domains that underlie variation in AAI ratings and to address the types versus dimensions question with respect to those domains. Second, by drawing upon AAI data collected at age 18 years from 857 adolescents who had participated in the SECCYD, we are able to address the types versus dimensions question with the largest sample available to date.

Corresponding author: R. Chris Fraley, Department of Psychology, University of Illinois at Urbana-Champaign, Champaign, IL 61820, email: rcfraley@uiuc.edu

## WHAT IS TAXOMETRIC ANALYSIS AND WHY DOES IT MATTER?

In psychology, individual differences are often regarded as reflections of variation in latent dimensions or continua. For example, researchers in developmental psychology studying symptoms of psychopathology often assume that variation in, for example, externalizing problems reflects variation in degree rather than variation in kind. As such, researchers often assign numeric values to individuals to represent their standing on the latent dimension of interest. However, there are many constructs in psychology that have been treated in a categorical fashion. For example, attachment security has often been conceptualized as a categorical variable (e.g., Ainsworth et al., 1978). As such, researchers have focused historically on assigning individuals to groups for the purpose of assessment and data analysis rather than locating individuals quantitatively in a multi-dimensional space.

Unfortunately, questions about types and dimensions in psychology have often been resolved via fiat and convenience. One reason for this is that, until recently, the methodological tools available did not provide a way for researchers to determine whether a construct had a categorical or continuous latent distribution. Commonly used typological methods, such as cluster analysis and latent class or profile analysis, reveal groupings in data regardless of whether natural groupings actually exist. For example, if data generated from a dimensional model are submitted to cluster analysis, clusters or groupings will always be found (Fraley & Waller, 1998). Moreover, factor analysis, although often regarded as a dimensional tool, only reveals latent sources of variability responsible for covariation among measurements; it is agnostic, however, with respect to the distribution of those individual differences. To answer the types versus dimensions question appropriately, *structure uncovering* methods (i.e., methods that are able to reveal the actual distributional structure of a construct) are needed, rather than *structure imposing* ones (i.e., methods that force a structure onto the data).

Fortunately, Meehl and his colleagues developed a suite of techniques that allow researchers to determine whether individual differences in a latent variable represent naturally occurring categories or continuous variation (i.e., the *taxonicity* debate; Meehl, 1973, 1995; Meehl & Yonce, 1996; Waller & Meehl, 1998). The techniques developed by Meehl and his colleagues are being used increasingly by psychologists to resolve debates about taxonicity in a number of domains, such as psychopathology and personality (e.g., Haslam, 2011; Haslam, Holland, & Kuppens, 2012; Ruscio, Haslam, & Ruscio, 2006). For example, Waller, Putnam, and Carlson (1996) used these techniques to demonstrate that pathological dissociation—a disorder characterized by feelings of depersonalization and memory lapses for everyday experiences—has a categorical distribution, whereas absorption—a tendency to become overly absorbed in an experience—has a continuous distribution.

Understanding whether variation reflected in the AAI is categorical or continuous can have significant implications for empirical research. For example, it has been extensively documented that imposing a categorical structure on dimensional data can attenuate predictive validity (MacCallum, Zhang, Preacher, & Rucker, 2002). Cohen (1983), for instance, noted that when categorical models are used to represent continuous variation, 36% of the reliable variance is lost. Moreover, for researchers interested in studying the continuity of attachment across time, the use of categories can lead to underestimates of stability. For example, if the true test-retest stability is high ($r = .90$) across two time points, the expected stability for categorical measures (i.e., two-category secure vs. insecure) can be as low as $\kappa = r = .71$ (see Fraley & Waller, 1998).

It has also been demonstrated that the use of inappropriate measurement systems can impair statistical power—the probability of correctly rejecting a null hypothesis when there really is an effect. It is well known that statistical power is partly a function of measurement precision or reliability (Cohen, 1988). If individual differences are continuously distributed but are modeled categorically, then measurement precision is reduced and the ability to detect true effects is compromised. The consequences of this problem were quantified by Fraley and Spieker (2003a), who simulated infant attachment data using a two-dimensional model across a variety of effect sizes using a modest sample size that is characteristic of much research on adult attachment. Using these simulated data, they tested the statistical significance of parameters from (a) a continuous two-dimensional model, (b) a two-category (secure–insecure) model, and (c) a three-category model. The resulting power curves over a range of effect sizes ($R^2$s from 1% to 99%) for the three kinds of models revealed that the statistical power was poor when the effects to be detected were weak and high when the effects to be detected were high. In between these two extremes, however, there were marked differences in the power curves for the different kinds of analysis. For example, if the true model explained 25% of the variance, then the statistical power of the two-dimensional model was 80%, but the power of the two-category model was only 50%. These findings suggest that, given the typical sample size used in attachment research—and assuming the true effects to be sizable—researchers have only a 50–50 chance of discovering the real developmental implications of adult attachment patterns by using categorical measurement models. If the kinds of individual differences captured by the AAI are truly continuous, using a dimensional measurement model would likely improve the empirical yield of developmental research on adult attachment.

Up to this point we have highlighted the way in which the inappropriate use of categorical models for studying continuous phenomena can impede psychological research. We should emphasize, however, that when categorical models are appropriate, taxometric methods can be valuable for estimating base rates of category membership and improving assessment methods. Unfortunately, categorical boundaries for hypothesized categorical variables are often delineated on the basis of arbitrary, yet reified, conventions. Taxometric methods have the potential to solve the classification problem in multiple domains by providing a rational and systematic approach to the problem (Meehl, 1995).

## OVERVIEW OF THE PRESENT INVESTIGATION

The objective of the present investigation was to use taxometric techniques to address the types versus dimensions question with respect to individual differences in the AAI. We conducted taxometric analyses on the rating scales used for the AAI, based on the sample of 857 adolescents in the current study. This sizable sample provided us with a unique opportunity to test rigorously the latent distribution of adult attachment patterns.

We examined the types versus dimensions question using the rating systems developed by Main and Goldwyn. In the Main and Goldwyn system, researchers are principally concerned with *states of mind* with respect to attachment (see Chapter 1). As such, we target states of mind in our primary analysis, using indicators selected from the factor analytic work reported in Chapter 2. However, because the *inferred-experience* scales are sometimes used in attachment research, particularly in research on earned security (see Chapter 6), we also examine the types versus dimensions question with respect to these indicators. The debate over the significance of the earned-versus continuous-secure distinction rests on the assumption that child-hood experiences with caregivers (at least as recalled and reported retrospectively) become organized in the mind in qualitatively distinct ways, leading some people to view their early experiences favorably and others less favorably. These data offer a rare opportunity to test this assumption.

## METHODS

### Taxometric Procedures

To address the types versus dimensions question, we used three taxometric procedures developed by Meehl and his colleagues: MAXCOV-HITMAX (MAXCOV; Meehl, 1973; Meehl & Yonce, 1996), MAMBAC (Meehl & Yonce, 1994), and L-Mode (Waller & Meehl, 1998). MAXCOV is one of the most widely used taxometric methods for addressing questions about taxonicity (for a detailed overview of MAXCOV see Meehl, 1973, or Waller & Meehl, 1998). In MAXCOV, one examines the covariance between two indicators of a latent construct as a function of a third indicator. The function characterizing these conditional covariances is called a MAXCOV function and its shape depends on the categorical status of the latent variable under investigation. For example, if the latent variable is categorical with a base rate of .5, the MAXCOV curve tends to have a mountain-like peak. In samples in which the base rate is less than .5, the peak will be shifted to the right; in samples in which the base rate is larger than .5, the peak will be shifted to the left. If the latent variable is continuous, however, the MAXCOV curve will tend to resemble a flat line (see Fraley & Spieker, 2003a, for graphical illustrations).

MAMBAC (Meehl & Yonce, 1994) is a related taxometric procedure that is based on computing the mean difference between cases located above versus below a sliding cut score. Specifically, for any pair of indicators, one indicator is designated as the "input" and the other as the "output" indicator. The cases are then sorted from lowest to highest along the input indicator and, at various regions along that input variable, cases are split into two groups with respect to the output indicator and the mean difference between those two groups is saved. The MAMBAC function is the plot of those conditional mean differences across varying values of the input variable. Importantly, when the latent variable is categorical, the function will be peaked. In contrast, when the latent variable is continuous, the function characterizing the ordered mean differences will be concave.

The L-Mode procedure (Waller & Meehl, 1998) is based on examining the distribution of factor score estimates for the first factor extracted from a principal axis factor analysis of the indicators of a taxon. When the data are generated by a latent categorical model, the distribution of factor scores will be bimodal, with the location of the modes and their relative heights providing information about the base rate of the latent class. In contrast, when the data are generated by a latent dimensional model, the distribution of factor scores will be uni-modal.

Although researchers have evaluated the output of taxometric methods historically by studying the shape of taxometric functions subjectively, Ruscio, Ruscio, and Meron (2007) have developed useful tools for comparing quantitatively the empirical functions against those expected under categorical and dimensional models. In the present report we focus on their *Comparison Curve Fit Index* (CCFI) as a way of determining whether the data are more compatible with a categorical or dimensional model. The CCFI can range from 0 to 1, with values of 0 being most compatible with a dimensional model and values of 1 being most consistent with a categorical model. Although there are no strict cutoffs in how to interpret the CCFI, Ruscio et al.

recommended that CCFI values falling between .40 and .60 be interpreted with caution because they do not clearly rule out one model in favor of the other (Ruscio et al., 2007). Importantly, the CCFI can be computed separately on the basis of the output of MAXCOV, MAMBAC, and L-Mode analyses. Thus, when multiple taxometric procedures are used, the average CCFI across those procedures can be interpreted as a robust way of evaluating the evidence (see Ruscio, Walters, Marcus, & Kaczetow, 2010). Recent simulation studies indicate that thresholds of .45 and .55 for the average CCFI perform comparatively well in discriminating latent dimensions from latent types (Ruscio et al., 2010).

### Simulation of Taxonic and Dimensional Comparison Data

The interpretation of taxometric results is not clear-cut when indicators are skewed, as is the case for indicators of attachment used in this report (see Roisman et al., 2007, and descriptive data in Chapter 1 of the Monograph). For example, when indicators are skewed, the resulting MAXCOV curves will be consistent with those expected when there is a low base-rate category—even if the data were generated by a dimensional model (see Ruscio et al., 2006). To aid in drawing valid inferences, it is helpful to evaluate taxometric output with respect to output that would be expected both in categorical and dimensional situations in which skew is present. To do so, we simulated skewed data under categorical and dimensional models using the R routines developed by Ruscio et al. (2006). Specifically, we simulated data for hypothetical individuals by generating scores in which the latent variable was either continuously distributed or categorical. Importantly, however, the simulated data were constructed to have distributional properties similar to those of the empirical data (i.e., similar means, $SD$s, skews, and inter-item covariances). In short, this method allows us to capture the surface-level statistical properties of the observed variables (i.e., their means, standard deviations, skew, and inter-item correlations) while allowing us to vary the latent structure that generated them (i.e., categorical vs. continuous; Hankin, Fraley, Lahey, & Waldman, 2005; Roisman et al., 2007; Ruscio, Ruscio, & Keane, 2004). For the purposes of simulating categorical data, we used base rates derived from the empirical estimates in the current analyses rather than theoretically derived base rate values.

As might be expected, simulated curves generated under each model within each procedure can vary from one simulation to the next because of random sampling errors. To quantify this variation, we simulated data under each kind of model (dimensional and categorical) 100 times to approximate sampling distributions for the functions expected under each model for MAXCOV, MAMBAC, and L-Mode. In the analyses that follow, we illustrate the average empirical functions (denoted as connected points in the figures), as well the middle 50% of expected functions (solid gray area). This latter region captures the range of taxometric functions that are expected 50% of the time under each theoretical model given sampling error.

## RESULTS

We present the results of two sets of analyses below. The first set focuses on the Main and Goldwyn state-of-mind indicators (dismissing and preoccupied). Next we examine indicators of inferred experiences, studying the negativity of maternal and paternal inferred experiences separately. In each case, the indicators used to examine each attachment-related construct were selected on the basis of the factor analytic results reported in Chapter 2. Recall from Chapter 1 that, in addition to having the Main and Goldwyn indicators, we also had data from the Kobak Q-sort system. Although the mathematical foundation for taxometric analyses is worked out well for situations in which there are mean-level differences between people (as in with the Main and Goldwyn indicators), the Q-sort procedure itself imposes statistical constraints on the data that remove these differences. Specifically, the mean value for each person across the 100 cards is 0.00 and the $SD$ of his or her scores is 1.00. As such, there are no mean-level differences across individuals in a Q-sort with respect to the full 100 cards (see Waller & Meehl, 1998, Ch. 6). Thus, our analysis focuses exclusively on indicators from the Main and Goldwyn system.

### States of Mind

#### Dismissing
To examine whether variation in dismissing states of mind was more compatible with a categorical or dimensional model, we conducted taxometric analyses on the following rating scales: mother idealization, father idealization, and lack of memory. Recall from Chapter 2 that these three variables are the strongest indicators of dismissing states of mind. Thirty-two cases contained missing data. As such, the analyses were based on 825 of the 857 cases available for analysis. The CCFI values from each analysis, along with the categorical base rate estimates from each analysis, are summarized in Table 3.1.

The averaged empirical MAXCOV curve was most similar to that expected under a dimensional model as opposed to a categorical one (see upper row of Figure 3.1). The empirical curve falls within the region expected if the data were generated from a dimensional model but deviates markedly from what would be expected under a categorical model. The CCFI value was .19,

TABLE 3.1

TAXOMETRIC BASE RATE ESTIMATES AND MODEL FIT INDICES BASED ON MAXCOV, MAMBAC, AND L-MODE ANALYSES

| | M | SD | CCFI |
|---|---|---|---|
| States of mind | | | |
| Dismissing | | | |
| MAXCOV | .28 | .13 | .19 |
| MAMBAC | .40 | .09 | .47 |
| L-Mode | .57 | — | .33 |
| | | | Average = .33 |
| Preoccupied | | | |
| MAXCOV | .04 | .01 | .50 |
| MAMBAC | .08 | .06 | .37 |
| L-Mode | .57 | — | .51 |
| | | | Average = .46 |
| Inferred experience | | | |
| Maternal experience | | | |
| MAXCOV | .16 | .06 | .24 |
| MAMBAC | .23 | .05 | .56 |
| L-Mode | .57 | — | .39 |
| | | | Average = .40 |
| Paternal experience | | | |
| MAXCOV | .34 | .24 | .14 |
| MAMBAC | .24 | .11 | .62 |
| L-Mode | .53 | — | .38 |
| | | | Average = .38 |

*Note.* M = average category base rate estimate within a taxometric analysis; SD = standard deviation of base rate estimates within a taxometric analysis; CCFI = comparison curve fit index. L-Mode base rates are based on two estimates; therefore a standard deviation of those estimates is not reported. The average reported in the CCFI column represents the average CCFI value for those indicators across the three taxometric analyses.

indicating that, on average, the data were most compatible with a dimensional model of individual differences. The averaged empirical MAMBAC function was more ambiguous. As can be seen in the middle row of Figure 3.1, the empirical MAMBAC function has a U-shape, with a higher elevation on the right side—a pattern most compatible with data generated under a dimensional model with skewness. The CCFI value, however, was .47, indicating that the MAMBAC analyses were largely ambiguous with respect to the latent distribution of dismissing attachment. As can be seen in the lower row of Figure 3.1, the empirical L-mode function is most compatible with what would be expected under a dimensional versus categorical model. The CCFI based on this analysis was .33. The average CCFI values across these three taxometric procedures was .33. Overall, then, taxometric analyses of dismissing attachment are indicative of an underlying dimension rather than underlying categories.

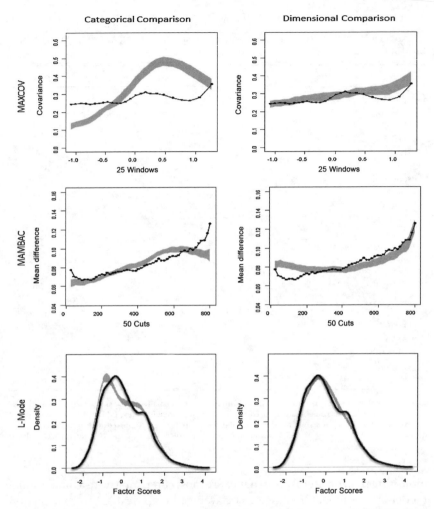

FIGURE 3.1.—Taxometric functions for indicators of dismissing states of mind. The dark line in each panel represents the empirical function. The shaded region represents the range of values that would be expected 50% of the time under categorical (left column) or dimensional (right column) models.

### Preoccupied

To examine whether variation in preoccupied states of mind was more compatible with a categorical or dimensional model, we conducted taxometric analyses on the following rating scales: mother anger, father anger, passivity, and unresolved abuse. We focused on these four indicators in particular based on the factor analytic results summarized in Chapter 2. Thirty-two cases contained missing data. Thus, the analyses were based on 825

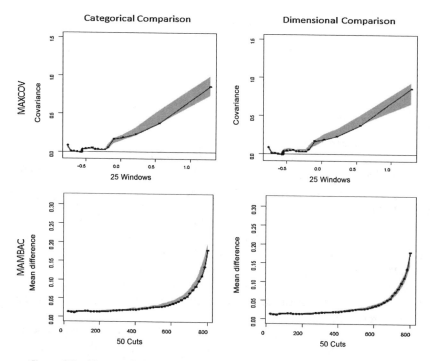

FIGURE 3.2.—Taxometric functions for indicators of preoccupied states of mind. The dark line in each panel represents the empirical function. The shaded region represents the range of values that would be expected 50% of the time under categorical (left column) or dimensional (right column) models. The L-Mode functions are not depicted because the L-mode analyses did not produce interpretable results.

of the 857 cases available for analysis. The CCFI values from each analysis, along with the categorical base rate estimates from each analysis, are summarized in Table 3.1.

The results of these analyses suggested that it was not possible to distinguish between categorical and dimensional hypotheses (see Figure 3.2). For example, the top row of Figure 3.2 shows the averaged empirical MAXCOV function for indicators of preoccupation. Notice that the empirical MAXCOV curve falls well within the range of values that would be expected under both categorical and dimensional models. The second row of Figure 3.2 reveals a similar degree of ambiguity. The CCFI values were .50 for the MAXCOV analyses and .37 for the MAMBAC analyses. Although the MAMBAC CCFI value is less than .40—suggesting a dimensional interpretation—the average of the two CCFI values was .44, which is within the range of values that are best interpreted as dimensional per Ruscio et al.'s (2010) thresholds. Although we also used L-Mode, the factor score densities were exceptionally noisy. Thus, we did not place any interpretive weight on those

45

analyses. For the sake of completeness, however, we note that the CCFI based on the L-Mode analysis was .51 and the average CCFI based on all three methods was .46, which falls within the ambiguous range [.45–.55] according to Ruscio et al.'s thresholds.

## Inferred Experiences

### Maternal Experiences

To examine whether variation in inferred maternal experience was more compatible with a categorical or dimensional model, we conducted taxometric analyses on the following rating scales: mother loving (reversed), mother rejection, and mother neglect (see footnote 2). Three cases contained missing data; thus the analyses were based on 854 of the 857 cases available for analysis. The CCFI values from each analysis, along with the category base-rate estimates from each analysis, are summarized in Table 3.1.

The averaged empirical MAXCOV curve was most similar to that expected under a dimensional model as opposed to a categorical one (see upper row of Figure 3.3). The empirical curve falls within the region expected if the data were generated from a dimensional model but deviates markedly from what would be expected under a categorical model. The CCFI value was .24, indicating that, on average, the data were most compatible with a dimensional model of individual differences. The averaged empirical MAMBAC function was more ambiguous. As can be seen in the middle panel of Figure 3.3, the empirical MAMBAC function has a U-shape, with a higher elevation on the right side—a pattern compatible with data generated under a dimensional model with skewness. The CCFI value, however, was .56, indicating that the MAMBAC analyses were largely ambiguous. As can be seen in the lower row of Figure 3.3, the empirical L-Mode function is most compatible with what would be expected under a dimensional versus categorical model. The CCFI value was .39. The average CCFI values across these three taxometric procedures was .40, suggesting dimensionality.

### Paternal Experiences

To examine whether variation in inferred paternal experience was more compatible with a categorical or dimensional model, we conducted taxometric analyses on the following rating scales: father loving (reversed), father rejection, and father neglect. Thirty-five cases contained missing data; thus the analyses were based on 822 of the 857 cases available for analysis. The CCFI values from each analysis, along with the base rate estimates from each analysis, are summarized in Table 3.1.

The averaged empirical MAXCOV curve was most similar to that expected under a dimensional model as opposed to a categorical one (see upper row of Figure 3.4). The empirical curve falls within the region expected if the data

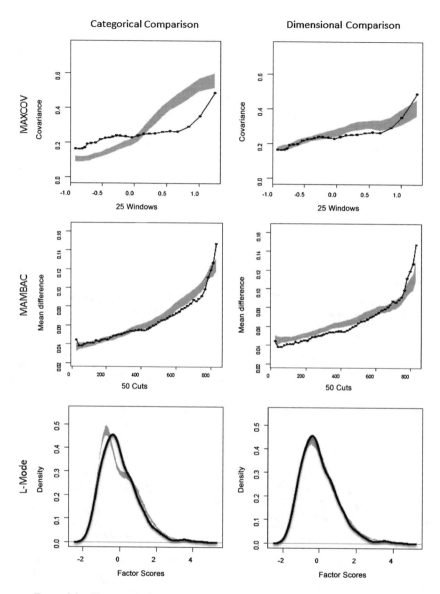

FIGURE 3.3.—Taxometric functions for indicators of inferred maternal experience. The dark line in each panel represents the empirical function. The shaded region represents the range of values that would be expected 50% of the time under categorical (left column) or dimensional (right column) models.

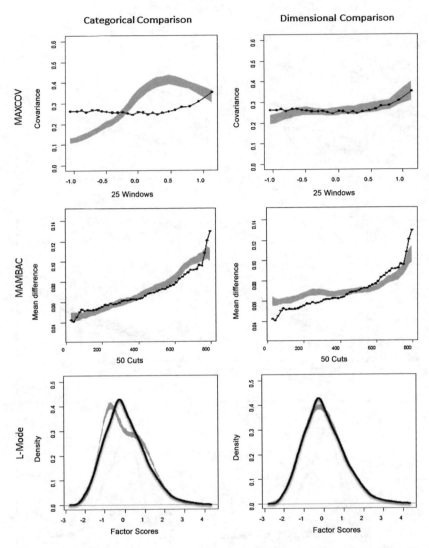

FIGURE 3.4.—Taxometric functions for indicators of inferred paternal experience. The dark line in each panel represents the empirical function. The shaded region represents the range of values that would be expected 50% of the time under categorical (left column) or dimensional (right column) models.

were generated from a dimensional model but deviates from what would be expected under a categorical model. The CCFI value was .14, indicating that, on average, the data were highly compatible with a dimensional model of individual differences. The averaged empirical MAMBAC function was somewhat more compatible with a categorical model. As can be seen in the

48

middle panel of Figure 3.4, the empirical MAMBAC function falls within the region expected by both models, but adheres a bit more closely to that expected under a categorical model. The CCFI value was .62, indicating that the MAMBAC analyses were more indicative of types than dimensions. As can be seen in the lower row of Figure 3.4, the empirical L-Mode function is most compatible with what would be expected under a dimensional versus categorical model. The CCFI value was .38. The average CCFI values across these three taxometric procedures was .38. Overall, then, taxometric analysis of inferred paternal experience are most indicative of an underlying dimension rather than underlying categories.

## DISCUSSION

This chapter reports the largest empirical examination to date of the latent structure of the AAI (George et al., 1984–1996). Our taxometric analyses suggest that the primary distinction made by AAI coders between secure and dismissing states of mind within the Main and Goldwyn coding system is more consistent with an underlying dimensional rather than categorical model. In contrast, our taxometric analyses of the indicators of preoccupation were indeterminate, a problem encountered in Roisman et al. (2007) as well, which led to the speculation that one reason why the analyses of preoccupied attachment were ambiguous may have been due to the relatively low sample size employed in those analyses ($N = 504$). The sample size of the present study was larger, suggesting that the ambiguity might lie elsewhere. As can be seen in Figure 3.2, given the amount of skew that characterizes the indicators of preoccupation, it might simply be impossible to distinguish between categorical and dimensional models in this domain.

Given the ambiguity that exists regarding the latent distribution of preoccupation, should researchers treat variation in preoccupation as continuous or categorical? There are costs associated with each decision. In a situation in which the latent variable is truly continuous, but people are assigned to categories, the researcher is restricting existing variation (some portion of which reflects true score variation) artificially. In a sense, the researcher is throwing away information that is potentially useful for understanding attachment organization. In contrast, in a situation in which the latent variable is truly categorical, but people are given continuous scores, the researcher is treating continuous variation (some portion of which is irrelevant for classification) as diagnostically meaningful. This can lead to a situation in which researchers reify individual differences between people that, in fact, are not relevant for understanding their true attachment status.

Which of these costs is more substantial? In our opinion, it would be more harmful for the field if researchers discarded continuous information that might be relevant for understanding attachment organization than if they used continuous information, some portion of which might turn out to be irrelevant for understanding attachment organization. Moreover, if future research uncovers evidence that disambiguates the latent distribution of preoccupation, it will be easier for researchers to use continuous scores to assign people to categories (if compelling evidence for taxonicity is found) than to use category assignments to rescale people along a continuous dimension (if compelling evidence of dimensionality is found).

We also examined the inferred-experience scales within the Main and Goldwyn system. These analyses suggest that the quality of caregiving experiences, as recalled by participants and scored by trained observers, is continuously distributed. It does not appear to be the case that there are subsets of individuals who have qualitatively different experiences, as is often assumed in research on earned security (see Chapter 6, this volume).

In conclusion, it is becoming clear that the variation underlying measures of both infant (Fraley & Spieker, 2003a) and romantic (Fraley & Waller, 1998) attachment security is distributed continuously and not categorically as was once widely assumed. The current taxometric analysis adds to this growing literature, demonstrating that secure versus dismissing discourse in the AAI in particular reflects a *dimension* of variability. Although the value of attachment theory does not hinge on the categorical status of measures of security (Fraley & Spieker, 2003b; Waters & Beauchaine, 2003), we believe that wider adoption of coding procedures that map on to the natural variability reflected in such measures can only serve to strengthen the literature on attachment by addressing the fundamental questions of Bowlby's (1969/1982) theory with the greatest measurement precision possible.

# IV. STABILITY OF ATTACHMENT SECURITY FROM INFANCY TO LATE ADOLESCENCE

Ashley M. Groh, Glenn I. Roisman, Cathryn Booth-LaForce, R. Chris Fraley, Margaret T. Owen, Martha J. Cox, and Margaret R. Burchinal

The first section of this Monograph emphasized methodological issues concerning the AAI (George et al., 1984–1996). From this point forward, we turn our attention to continuity and change in attachment security over time, and the antecedents of variation in adult attachment more generally. According to attachment theory, individuals develop internalized representations of their early attachment-relevant experiences with primary caregivers. Such representations are argued to have their roots in the attachment relationships that individuals share with their primary caregivers in early childhood (Bowlby, 1969/1982; Main et al., 1985). Thus, an important question concerns the degree to which attachment variation is stable over time. Accordingly, we begin this section by quantifying the degree of stability in attachment security from infancy to late adolescence, leveraging three measures of mother-child attachment security acquired from the SECCYD in early childhood.

In infancy, individual differences in attachment are often measured using the Strange Situation procedure (Ainsworth et al., 1978), a laboratory procedure designed to activate infants' attachment behavioral system via a series of increasingly stressful separations from and subsequent reunions with their primary caregivers. In brief, infants are classified as *secure* in the Strange Situation procedure when their separation distress is effectively relieved upon their caregiver's return. Infants are classified as insecure if they either ignore their primary caregiver upon reunion (i.e., *insecure-avoidant*) or simultaneously seek, yet resist, their caregiver upon reunion (i.e., *insecure-resistant*). Finally, infants who exhibit a momentary breakdown of one of these organized strategies are classified as *disorganized* (Main & Solomon, 1990).

---

Corresponding author: Ashley M. Groh, Center for Developmental Science, University of North Carolina at Chapel Hill, Chapel Hill, NC 27599-8115, email agroh@unc.edu

The quality of a child's attachment relationship with primary caregivers is theorized to shape the kind of attachment representation the child develops (Bowlby, 1969/1982). Moreover, it is assumed that these representations are relatively stable over time—provided there are not substantial changes in the caregiving environment. Thus, it might be expected that individual differences in infant attachment would be associated with individual differences in adult attachment as measured by the AAI. Specifically, we might expect that infants classified as secure in the Strange Situation procedure would be eventually classified as *secure-autonomous* with respect to the AAI, infants classified as insecure-avoidant in the Strange Situation procedure, *insecure-dismissing* with respect to the AAI, and infants classified as insecure-resistant in the Strange Situation procedure, *insecure-preoccupied* with respect to the AAI (Waters, Hamilton, & Weinfield, 2000). Although it is possible that disorganized infants would go on to be *unresolved* with respect to loss and/or trauma in adulthood, adults can only be classified as unresolved if they have experienced a significant death or a traumatic experience. Therefore, Main (2001) speculated that disorganization in infancy is likely to be associated with increased risk for insecurity in adulthood generally.

Because investigating links between infant and adult attachment requires prospective data, it was not until the beginning of the 21st century that researchers were able to address questions related to the stability of attachment from infancy to adulthood. More specifically, beginning in 2000, data from a number of longitudinal studies became available (Hamilton, 2000; Lewis, Feiring, & Rosenthal, 2000; Waters, Merrick, Treboux, Crowell, & Albersheim, 2000; Weinfield, Sroufe, & Egeland, 2000). However, due to the small sample size of many of these investigations, there is at present a relatively limited corpus on which to estimate the stability of attachment security. In fact, as of 2011, only about 785 participants had been studied across *all* investigations of the stability of attachment security from infancy to young adulthood (Roisman & Haydon, 2011). In contrast, the present study draws on a much larger single sample ($N = 857$).

Additionally, the extant longitudinal studies have produced mixed findings, with some studies reporting statistically significant stability in security from infancy to adulthood (Hamilton, 2000; Main, 2000, 2001; Main, Hesse, & Kaplan, 2005; Waters, Merrick, et al., 2000) and others not finding such stability (Lewis et al., 2000; Weinfield et al., 2000; Zimmerman, Fremmer-Bombik, Spangler, & Grossmann, 1997; for a meta-analysis, see Fraley, 2002). Although the apparent discrepancy among these findings can be explained in a number of ways, one explanation that has emerged in the literature is that attachment security might be expected to be less stable in cohorts that are at higher risk for experiencing life stress and thus experience more profound changes in the caregiving environment (Waters, Weinfield, & Hamilton, 2000), a topic addressed in Chapter 5 of this volume.

## DISORGANIZATION

The disorganization coding system (Main & Solomon, 1990) was developed after infant attachment assessments were administered in many of the key longitudinal studies of attachment (for a review see Grossmann, Grossmann, & Waters, 2005; Roisman & Haydon, 2011). Consequently, the majority of investigations of attachment stability over the first two decades of life have focused on the stability of the organized (secure, insecure-avoidant, insecure-resistant) classifications. In fact, only two investigations of the stability of disorganization have been conducted to date. Specifically, in the high-risk Minnesota Longitudinal Study of Risk and Adaptation (Sroufe et al., 2005) sample, infants classified as disorganized were more likely than their non-disorganized counterparts to be found insecure (vs. secure) in adulthood (Weinfield et al., 2004). Additionally, in the only study of the stability of disorganized attachment in a normative-risk sample, infants classified as disorganized were more likely to be insecure in adulthood (Main, 2001). Although findings from these investigations provide tentative evidence for the stability of infant disorganization from infancy to adulthood, they await test for replication.

## CATEGORICAL VERSUS CONTINUOUS ASSESSMENTS OF ATTACHMENT

The extant literature on the stability of attachment has focused almost exclusively on the concordance between infant and adult attachment classifications. However, some researchers have used dimensional methods for characterizing individual differences in attachment. For example, Richters, Waters, and Vaughn (1988) conducted a multiple discriminant function analysis of the four Strange Situation procedure interactive behavioral scales (contact maintenance, proximity seeking, avoidance, resistance) used to inform classification coding and found that the data could be reduced to a single security dimension. This security dimension (often used in combination with the subsequently developed disorganization scale) has been used increasingly in analyses instead of classifications (e.g., Luijk et al., 2011). Fraley and Spieker (2003a) conducted factor and taxometric analyses of the four Strange Situation procedure interaction behavioral scales to investigate both the latent structure and the taxonicity of variation in infant attachment. Findings from their analyses suggest that variation in infant attachment is most accurately represented by two weakly correlated dimensions, one representing proximity seeking versus avoidant strategies and the other angry and resistant strategies. As described in Chapters 2 and 3 (this volume), similar findings have emerged from factor and taxometric analyses of adult attachment as measured by the AAI.

53

Although these findings suggest that variation in attachment might be best represented continuously, no study to date has investigated the stability of attachment from infancy to late adolescence using these dimensional systems.

## THE ATTACHMENT Q-SORT AND MODIFIED STRANGE SITUATION PROCEDURE

The Attachment Q-sort (Waters & Deane, 1985) and the modified Strange Situation procedure (Cassidy et al., 1992) are well-validated behavioral assessments of the quality of children's early attachment relationships with their primary caregivers. However, most studies of attachment stability from early childhood to adulthood have used the Strange Situation procedure and few studies have investigated attachment stability with the Attachment Q-sort or the modified Strange Situation procedure. The Attachment Q-sort is a measure of children's secure base behavior with their primary caregiver as observed through naturalistic observations and can be used to create a continuous measure of children's security. Currently, only one investigation (Bahadur, 1998) has examined the stability of attachment using the Attachment Q-sort, and results revealed little stability ($r = .02$) in attachment security from 1 to 30 years of age. However, the validity of these Attachment Q-sort data may be questionable due to the non-traditional coding method used. More specifically, the Attachment Q-sort in the Bahadur (1998) study was completed by using information from mother interviews and taped observations of mother-child interactions, rather than using naturalistic observation.

Similar to the Strange Situation procedure, the modified Strange Situation procedure is a laboratory procedure developed for preschool-aged children in which the child's attachment system is activated through a series of separations from and reunions with the primary caregiver. In the modified Strange Situation procedure, children who resume comfortable interactions with their primary caregiver upon reunion are classified as *secure*; children who maintain extreme neutrality toward their caregiver upon reunion are classified as *insecure-avoidant*; children who exhibit fussy, helpless, petulant, and/or resistant behavior upon reunion are classified as *insecure-resistant*; and children who are controlling or exhibit combinations of avoidant and resistant behavior upon reunion are classified as insecure-controlling/insecure-other, referred to here as *disorganized*. In addition to being classified into one of these categories, children are also rated on a 9-point security scale. To date, no study has investigated the stability of attachment from childhood, as measured with the modified Strange Situation procedure, to late adolescence. According to attachment theory, children's attachment representations may not consolidate until early childhood (Bowlby, 1969/

1982). As such, it is important to investigate not only the stability of attachment from infancy to adulthood, but also from early childhood to adulthood.

## SUMMARY AND OVERVIEW

In this chapter, we present the largest sample investigation of the stability of attachment from the first 3 years of life to late adolescence to quantify more precisely the stability of attachment security during this period. To address lingering questions concerning the stability of security and disorganization, we include a focus on attachment disorganization as well as the organized attachment categories. Following mounting evidence suggesting that variation in attachment may be best represented dimensionally, we also provide, whenever possible, analyses that examine the stability of attachment measured both categorically and dimensionally. Finally, we include measurement of mother-child attachment three times in the infancy/preschool period (Strange Situation procedure at 15 months, Attachment Q-sort at 24 months, and modified Strange Situation procedure at 36 months). This allows us to examine questions related to the stability of attachment within the early childhood years, as well as from early childhood to late adolescence, using a variety of well-validated early attachment assessments both singly and in the form of a composite measure of early security.

## METHOD

### Adult Attachment Interview

For analyses involving three-way classifications (*dismissing* [Ds], *secure-autonomous* [F], *preoccupied* [E]), if participants were classified as *unresolved* (U) as their primary classification, then their secondary, organized classification (dismissing, secure-autonomous, preoccupied) was used in analyses. For analyses involving secure versus insecure classifications, if participants were coded as dismissing, preoccupied, or unresolved (including unresolved/secure-autonomous), they were classified as insecure. Following results from Chapters 2 and 3 of this volume, the dismissing and preoccupied prototype scores reflected *dismissing* and *preoccupied* states of mind. (Stability estimates using the scale composite dismissing and preoccupied dimensions identified in Chapter 2 were nearly identical to the findings reported below based on the prototype scores; for additional information see General Discussion of this volume).

### Strange Situation Procedure

Infant–mother attachment security was assessed at 15 months in 1,195 dyads using the Ainsworth et al. (1978) Strange Situation procedure. Each Strange Situation procedure was scored using the standard classifications of *secure* (B), *insecure-avoidant* (A), *insecure-resistant* (C), *disorganized* (D), and *unclassifiable* (U). Intercoder agreement (before consensus) for the five-category classification system was 83% ($\kappa = .69$). For the purpose of this chapter, disorganized and unclassifiable categories were combined into one disorganized/unclassifiable (D/U) category. All infants coded as disorganized or unclassifiable were also classified with the best-fitting alternative organized classification (avoidant, secure, or resistant), which was used in analyses involving three-way classifications (avoidant, secure, resistant). For analyses involving secure versus insecure classifications, participants coded as avoidant, resistant, or disorganized/unclassifiable were classified as insecure. (For further information on Strange Situation scoring, see NICHD ECCRN, 1997).

Four 7-point interactive behavior scales in the two reunion episodes (Episodes 5 and 8) of the Strange Situation procedure were coded: proximity/contact seeking, contact maintenance, avoidance, and resistance. Intercoder agreement for the four scales, across the two episodes, determined by Pearson correlation ranged from .83 to .94. Coders also rated the degree of disorganization for the entire Strange Situation procedure on a 9-point scale (Main & Solomon, 1990). Intercoder agreement determined by Pearson correlation was .72. These scales were used to create both (a) Fraley and Spieker's (2003a) *proximity seeking* and *resistance* scales and (b) Richters's *security scale* (Richters et al., 1988) using a simplified method developed by Van IJzendoorn and Kroonenberg (1990). The *disorganization* dimension that complements Richters's security scale is the 9-point disorganization scale rated by Strange Situation procedure coders. For eight participants, Episode 8 data were missing because the Strange Situation procedure was terminated early due to infant distress. For Fraley and Spieker's proximity seeking and resistance scales, scores for these participants were created by adjusting averages according to the reduced number of data points. For Richters's security, the scale was created by replacing the missing Episode 8 data with Episode 5 data (see, e.g., Luijk et al., 2011).

### Attachment Q-Sort

Child-mother attachment security was assessed at 24 months in 1,197 dyads using the Attachment Q-sort procedure (Waters & Deane, 1985) based on a 2-hr home observation. Following the visit, the observer sorted the 90 items of the Q-sort into nine piles ranging from least to most characteristic for each participant. The score for each item, based on its placement in the distribution, was correlated with the Security Criterion Sort to yield a security score for each participant. Inter-observer reliability determined by ICC was .96. (For further information on Attachment Q-sort scoring, see McCartney, Owen, Booth, Clarke-Stewart, & Vandell, 2004).

### Modified Strange Situation Procedure

Child-mother attachment security was assessed at 36 months in 1,150 dyads using the modified Strange Situation procedure developed by Cassidy et al. (1992). Each modified Strange Situation procedure was scored using the standard classifications of *secure* (B), *insecure-avoidant* (A), *insecure-resistant* (C), and insecure-controlling/insecure-other, referred to here as *disorganized* (D). In addition, coders rated global security on a 9-point scale, ranging from (1) highly insecure to (9) highly secure. Inter-coder agreement (before consensus) for the four-category classification system was 75.7% ($\kappa = .58$). For the global rating of security, the average Pearson correlation between paired coders was .73. All children coded as disorganized were also classified with the best-fitting alternative organized classification (avoidant, secure, or resistant), which was used for analyses involving three-way classifications (avoidant, secure, resistant). For analyses involving secure versus insecure classifications, participants coded as avoidant, resistant, or disorganized were classified as insecure. (For further information see NICHD ECCRN, 2001).

### Proportion of Times Secure

A summary score reflecting the proportion of times the child was coded secure across the early attachment assessments (Strange Situation procedure, Attachment Q-sort, and modified Strange Situation procedure) was estimated for this chapter and those that follow. For the Strange Situation procedure, a secure versus insecure (avoidant, resistant, disorganized/unclassifiable) variable was created. For the Attachment Q-sort, children whose Q-sorts were correlated at .30 or above with the criterion sort were classified as secure (vs. insecure; Waters, 2003). For the modified Strange Situation procedure, a secure versus insecure (avoidant, resistant, disorganized) variable was also computed. If data were available on two or more early attachment assessments, we created a *proportion of times secure* variable by taking the number of times the child was classified secure for each available attachment assessment and dividing it by the total number of attachment assessments available for that child.

## RESULTS

### Intercorrelations Among 15-Month, 24-Month, and 36-Month Attachment Measures

Intercorrelations among the 15-month Strange Situation procedure, 24-month Attachment Q-sort, and 36-month modified Strange Situation procedure attachment dimensions are reported in Table 4.1 for all

*57*

TABLE 4.1

INTERCORRELATIONS AMONG 15-MONTH, 24-MONTH, 36-MONTH, AND 18-YEAR
ATTACHMENT DIMENSIONS

| Variable | 1 | 2 | 3 | 4 | 5 | 6 |
|---|---|---|---|---|---|---|
| 1. Fraley & Spieker Proximity Seeking (SSP) | | | | | | |
| 2. Fraley & Spieker Resistance (SSP) | .19*** | | | | | |
| 3. Richters's Security (SSP) | .46*** | −.56*** | | | | |
| 4. Disorganization (SSP) | −.12*** | .62*** | −.24*** | | | |
| 5. Security (AQS) | .06 | .00 | .04 | .03 | | |
| 6. Security (MSSP) | .08** | −.03 | .07** | −.04 | .17*** | |
| 7. Dismissing Prototype (AAI) | −.02 | −.01 | −.02 | .01 | −.17*** | −.05 |
| 8. Preoccupied Prototype (AAI) | −.05 | .03 | −.03 | .09** | −.08* | −.11*** |

*Note.* SSP = Strange Situation procedure; AQS = attachment Q-sort; MSSP = modified Strange Situation procedure; AAI = Adult Attachment Interview; $n$ (SSP) = 1,191; $n$ (SSP and AQS) = 1,143; $n$ (SSP and MSSP) = 1,097; $n$ (AQS and MSSP) = 1,114; $n$ (SSP and AAI) = 819; $n$ (AQS and AAI) = 821; $n$ (MSSP and AAI) = 795.
*$p < .05$.
**$p < .01$.
***$p < .001$.

participants for whom attachment data were available for a given assessment (e.g., Strange Situation procedure) or assessment pair (e.g., correlation between Attachment Q-sort and modified Strange Situation procedure security). As would be expected, 15-month Richters security, disorganization, Fraley and Spieker proximity seeking, and Fraley and Spieker resistance were significantly intercorrelated (mean $r = |.44|$, range $= |.12|$–$|.62|$, all $ps < .001$). The association between 24- and 36-month attachment dimensions was somewhat stronger ($r = .17$, $p < .001$) than associations among 15- and 24-month (mean $r = .03$, range $= .00$–.06; and 15- and 36-month (mean $r = |.06|$, range $= |.03|$–$|.08|$) attachment dimensions. Additionally, we examined associations among the 15-, 24-, and 36-month attachment assessments using the standard categorical (i.e., secure vs. insecure) approach to operationalizing security at 15 and 36 months. Similar to the data presented in Table 4.1, 24-month Attachment Q-sort and 36-month modified Strange Situation procedure security were somewhat more strongly associated ($r = .13$, $p < .001$) than were 15-month Strange Situation procedure and 24-month Attachment Q-sort security ($r = .04$, $p = .18$), but not 15-month Strange Situation procedure and 36-month modified Strange Situation procedure security ($r = .06$, $p = .05$).

## Stability of Attachment From Strange Situation at 15 Months to AAI at 18 Years

### Dimensions

Correlations between 15-month Strange Situation procedure and 18-year AAI attachment dimensions were computed for all participants for whom both 15-month and 18-year attachment data were available (see Table 4.1). Disorganization at 15 months was significantly associated with 18-year preoccupied states of mind ($r = .09$, $p < .01$). However, 15-month Fraley and Spieker proximity seeking, Fraley and Spieker resistance, and Richters's security were not significantly associated with preoccupied states of mind (mean $r = |.03|$, range $= |.03|-|.05|$). Strange Situation procedure dimensions at 15 months were not significantly associated with 18-year dismissing states of mind (mean $r = |.02|$, range $= |.01|-|.02|$).

### Categories

Concordance between 15-month and 18-year attachment classifications was examined using Chi-square analyses[3] in the 819 participants for whom both 15-month and 18-year attachment data were available (see Table 4.2). At 15 months, four-way, three-way, and two-way attachment classifications were not significantly associated with four-way, three-way, or two-way AAI categories, respectively. Similarly, Strange Situation procedure 15-month disorganized/unclassifiable status was not associated with either unresolved status[4] or secure versus insecure status on the AAI at age 18 (see Table 4.2 for effect sizes).

### Stability of Attachment From Attachment Q-Sort at 24 Months to AAI at 18 Years

#### Dimensions

Correlations between 24-month Attachment Q-sort security and 18-year AAI dismissing and preoccupied states of mind were computed for all participants for whom 24-month and 18-year data were available (see Table 4.1). Attachment Q-sort security was significantly and negatively associated with both 18-year dismissing ($r = -.17$, $p < .001$) and preoccupied ($r = -.08$, $p < .05$) states of mind.

#### Categories

Associations between 24-month Attachment Q-sort security and 18-year attachment classifications were examined in the 821 participants for whom both 24-month and 18-year attachment data were available. Using a one-way ANOVA, 24-month Attachment Q-sort security scores differed significantly by AAI four-way categories, $F(3, 817) = 7.35$, $p < .001$, with the mean for secure-autonomous greater than for dismissing and unresolved, but not preoccupied (secure-autonomous: $M = .33$, $SD = .20$, $n = 487$; dismissing: $M = .27$, $SD = .21$, $n = 284$; unresolved: $M = .22$, $SD = .20$, $n = 24$; preoccupied: $M = .28$, $SD = .19$, $n = 26$; secure-autonomous vs. dismissing: $t[817] = 4.17$, $p < .001$, $r = .14$; secure-autonomous vs. unresolved: $t[817] = 2.60$, $p < .01$, $r = .27$; secure-autonomous vs. preoccupied: $t[817] = 1.25$, $p = .21$, $r = .13$). Attachment Q-sort scores also differed significantly by three-way AAI classifications, $F(2, 818) = 9.55$, $p < .001$, with the mean for secure-autonomous greater than for dismissing, but not preoccupied (secure-autonomous:

## TABLE 4.2

ASSOCIATIONS BETWEEN FOUR-WAY, THREE-WAY, TWO-WAY, DISORGANIZED/UNRESOLVED, AND DISORGANIZED/INSECURE ATTACHMENT CLASSIFICATIONS MEASURED AT 15 MONTHS AND 18 YEARS

| | Adult Attachment Classification (AAI) | | | | |
|---|---|---|---|---|---|

*Four-Way Classifications*[a]

| Infant Attachment Classification (SSP) | Dismissing (Ds) | Secure (F) | Preoccupied (E) | Unresolved (U) | Total |
|---|---|---|---|---|---|
| Avoidant (A) | 41 | 63 | 2 | 4 | 110 |
| Secure (B) | 165 | 304 | 14 | 14 | 497 |
| Resistant (C) | 23 | 36 | 1 | 3 | 63 |
| Disorganized/Unclassifiable (D/U) | 52 | 86 | 7 | 4 | 149 |
| Total | 281 | 489 | 24 | 25 | 819 |

*Three-Way Classifications*[b]

| Infant Attachment Classification (SSP) | Dismissing (Ds) | Secure (F) | Preoccupied (E) | Total |
|---|---|---|---|---|
| Avoidant (A) | 48 | 79 | 4 | 131 |
| Secure (B) | 201 | 347 | 23 | 571 |
| Resistant (C) | 42 | 70 | 5 | 117 |
| Total | 291 | 496 | 32 | 819 |

*Two-Way Classifications*[c]

| Infant Attachment Classification (SSP) | Secure (F) | Insecure (Not-F) | Total |
|---|---|---|---|
| Secure (B) | 304 | 193 | 497 |
| Insecure (Not-B) | 185 | 137 | 322 |
| Total | 489 | 330 | 819 |

*Disorganized/Unresolved Classifications*[d]

| Infant Attachment Classification (SSP) | Not-Unresolved (Not-U) | Unresolved (U) | Total |
|---|---|---|---|
| Not-Dis./Unclass. (Not-D/U) | 649 | 21 | 670 |
| Dis./Unclass (D/U) | 145 | 4 | 149 |
| Total | 794 | 25 | 819 |

*Disorganized/Insecure Classifications*[e]

| Infant Attachment Classification (SSP) | Secure (F) | Insecure (Not-F) | Total |
|---|---|---|---|
| Not-Dis./Unclass. (Not-D/U) | 403 | 267 | 670 |
| Dis./unclass (D/U) | 86 | 63 | 149 |
| Total | 489 | 330 | 819 |

*Note.* SSP = Strange Situation procedure; AAI = Adult Attachment Interview; Dis = disorganized; Unclass. = unclassifiable.
[a]$\chi^2[9, n = 819] = 4.36$, Monte-Carlo $p = .89$, Monte-Carlo CI .88–.90, $r = .01$.
[b]$\chi^2[4, n = 819] = 0.39$, Monte-Carlo $p = .98$, Monte-Carlo CI .98–.99, $r = .01$.
[c]$\chi^2[1, n = 819] = 1.12$, $p = .29$, $r = .04$.
[d]$\chi^2[1, n = 819] = 0.08$, Exact $p = .81$, $r = .01$.
[e]$\chi^2[1, n = 819] = 0.30$, $p = .58$ $r = .02$.

$M=.33$, $SD=.20$, $n=495$; dismissing: $M=.27$, $SD=.21$, $n=292$; preoccupied: $M=.27$, $SD=.20$, $n=34$; secure-autonomous vs. dismissing: $t[818]=4.23$, $p<.001$, $r=.14$; secure-autonomous vs. preoccupied: $t[818]=1.75$, $p=.08$, $r=.15$). Using independent samples $t$-tests, significant differences in 24-month Attachment Q-sort security scores were found for AAI secure versus insecure status, $t(819)=4.55$, $p<.001$, $r=.14$ (with the mean for secure greater than insecure [secure: $M=.33$, $SD=.20$, $n=487$; insecure: $M=.27$, $SD=.21$, $n=334$]), and for AAI unresolved versus not-unresolved status,[5] $t(819)=2.03$, $p<.05$, $r=.21$ (with the mean for unresolved less than not-unresolved [unresolved: $M=.22$, $SD=.20$, $n=24$; not-unresolved: $M=.31$, $SD=.21$, $n=797$]).

### Stability of Attachment From Modified Strange Situation Procedure at 36 Months to AAI at 18 Years

#### Dimensions
Correlations between 36-month modified Strange Situation procedure security and 18-year AAI dismissing and preoccupied states of mind were computed for all participants for whom both 36-month and 18-year attachment data were available. As shown in Table 4.1, 36-month security was significantly associated with 18-year preoccupied states of mind ($r=-.11$, $p<.001$) but not with 18-year dismissing states of mind ($r=-.05$, $p=.14$).

#### Categories
Concordance between 36-month modified Strange Situation procedure and 18-year AAI attachment classifications was examined using Chi-square analyses drawing on the 795 participants for whom both 36-month and 18-year attachment data were available (see Table 4.3). At 36 months, four-way, three-way, and two-way attachment classifications were not associated significantly with four-way, three-way, or two-way AAI categories, respectively, and disorganized status was not associated significantly with secure versus insecure status on the AAI (see Table 4.3 for effect sizes). However, disorganized status was associated significantly with unresolved status on the AAI ($r=.10$, $p<.01$).[6]

### Stability of Attachment From Early Childhood Security Composite to AAI at 18 Years

Correlations between the proportion of times participants were classified as secure in early childhood and 18-year dismissing and preoccupied states of mind were computed for the 825 participants for whom data were available from two or more early attachment assessments and for whom 18-year attachment data were available. As expected, proportion of times secure in early childhood was significantly and negatively associated with both 18-year

TABLE 4.3

ASSOCIATIONS BETWEEN FOUR-WAY, THREE-WAY, TWO-WAY, DISORGANIZED/UNRESOLVED, AND
DISORGANIZED/INSECURE ATTACHMENT CLASSIFICATIONS MEASURED AT 36 MONTHS AND 18 YEARS

| | Adult Attachment Classification (AAI) | | | | |
|---|---|---|---|---|---|
| *Four-Way Classifications*[a] | | | | | |
| 36-Month Attachment | Dismissing | Secure | Preoccupied | Unresolved | |
| Classification (MSSP) | (Ds) | (F) | (E) | (U) | Total |
| Avoidant (A) | 11 | 23 | 3 | 1 | 38 |
| Secure (B) | 169 | 294 | 14 | 11 | 488 |
| Resistant (C) | 54 | 80 | 2 | 3 | 139 |
| Disorganized (D) | 41 | 76 | 4 | 9 | 130 |
| Total | 275 | 473 | 23 | 24 | 795 |

| | | | | |
|---|---|---|---|---|
| *Three-Way Classifications*[b] | | | | |
| 36-Month Attachment | Dismissing | Secure | Preoccupied | |
| Classification (MSSP) | (Ds) | (F) | (E) | Total |
| Avoidant (A) | 21 | 32 | 5 | 58 |
| Secure (B) | 189 | 342 | 22 | 553 |
| Resistant (C) | 74 | 106 | 4 | 184 |
| Total | 284 | 480 | 31 | 795 |

| | | | |
|---|---|---|---|
| *Two-Way Classifications*[c] | | | |
| 36-Month Attachment | Secure | Insecure | |
| Classification (MSSP) | (F) | (Not-F) | Total |
| Secure (B) | 294 | 194 | 488 |
| Insecure (Not-B) | 179 | 128 | 307 |
| Total | 473 | 322 | 795 |

| | | | |
|---|---|---|---|
| *Disorganized/Unresolved Classifications*[d] | | | |
| 36-Month Attachment | Not-Unresolved | Unresolved | |
| Classification (MSSP) | (Not-U) | (U) | Total |
| Not-disorganized (Not-D) | 650 | 15 | 665 |
| Disorganized (D) | 121 | 9 | 130 |
| Total | 771 | 24 | 795 |

| | | | |
|---|---|---|---|
| *Disorganized/Insecure Classifications*[e] | | | |
| 36-Month Attachment | Secure | Insecure | |
| Classification (MSSP) | (F) | (Not-F) | Total |
| Not-Dis./Unclass. (Not-D/U) | 397 | 268 | 665 |
| Dis./Unclass (D/U) | 76 | 54 | 130 |
| Total | 473 | 322 | 795 |

*Note.* MSSP = modified Strange Situation procedure; AAI = Adult Attachment Interview.
[a] $\chi^2[9, n = 795] = 13.78$, Monte-Carlo $p = .14$, Monte-Carlo CI .13–.14, $r = .03$.
[b] $\chi^2[4, n = 795] = 6.83$, Monte-Carlo $p = .15$, Monte-Carlo CI .14–.15, $r = .06$.
[c] $\chi^2[1, n = 795] = 0.29$, $p = .59$, $r = .02$.
[d] $\chi^2[1, n = 795] = 8.09$, $p < .01$, $r = .10$.
[e] $\chi^2[1, n = 795] = 0.07$, $p = .79$, $r = .01$.

dismissing ($r = -.11$, $p < .01$) and preoccupied ($r = -.13$, $p < .001$) states of mind on the AAI.

## DISCUSSION

In this chapter we describe the largest and most comprehensive investigation to date of the stability of individual differences in attachment security from early childhood to late adolescence. Overall, findings from this study provided evidence for weak stability in attachment security ($r = .12$)[7] and disorganization. As discussed below, this study also addressed three outstanding issues in the literature: the stability of early disorganization, the stability of attachment security measured dimensionally versus categorically, and the stability of attachment security as measured by a variety of early behavioral assessments.

### Disorganization

In prior studies, infant disorganization was found to be relatively stable from infancy to late adolescence. However, these findings were based on an at-risk sample (Weinfield et al., 2004) and a relatively small, low-risk sample ($N = 42$; Main, 2001). In this chapter, we drew on assessments of disorganization at ages 15 and 36 months to investigate the stability of early disorganization measured in both infancy and early childhood to late adolescence. We found significant but weak stability in 15-month attachment disorganization when measured dimensionally with the Strange Situation procedure to preoccupied states of mind in adulthood. Also, we found that children who were classified as disorganized at 36 months with the modified Strange Situation procedure were more likely to be unresolved (vs. resolved) with respect to loss and/or trauma in late adolescence. Although disorganization at 15 and 36 months was associated differentially with preoccupied and unresolved states of mind in adulthood, these findings converge with evidence from Chapter 2 (this volume) that indicators of preoccupied and unresolved states of mind load on a single factor and, together with prior evidence (Main, 2001; Weinfield et al., 2004), suggest that disorganization measured in both infancy and early childhood shows relatively weak stability to late adolescence.

### Categorical Versus Continuous Assessments of Attachment

Recent evidence suggests that variation in attachment may be more accurately represented by dimensions rather than categories (Fraley & Spieker, 2003a; Chapter 3, this volume), but the majority of research on the stability of attachment security has focused on categories. In this chapter we investigated the stability of attachment security from infancy to late adolescence both categorically and dimensionally. We found that—contrary to prior findings from smaller studies of attachment stability in normative samples (Hamilton, 2000; Main, 2000, 2001; Main et al., 2006; Waters, Merrick, et al., 2000)—attachment security measured both dimensionally and categorically was not especially stable from infancy to late adolescence in the present study. It is noteworthy that findings tended to converge with those from the Minnesota study (Weinfield et al., 2004), despite the fact that the Minnesota study comprises a high-risk sample.

### The Attachment Q-Sort and Modified Strange Situation Procedure

Although a variety of well-validated early behavioral measures of attachment variation have been developed, relatively few studies have investigated the stability of attachment from early childhood to adulthood with measures of early attachment security other than the Strange Situation procedure. Because attachment representations may not consolidate until early childhood or later (Bowlby, 1969/1982)—a claim supported by our findings that 24-month attachment security was more strongly associated with 36-month attachment security than it was with 15-month attachment security—we investigated attachment stability from early childhood to late adolescence by using the Attachment Q-sort and the modified Strange Situation procedure and by using the proportion of times secure composite that drew on the three early attachment assessments in the SECCYD. In contrast to our findings that attachment security was not significantly stable from 15 months to late adolescence, we found slightly stronger (although in absolute terms still weak) stability in attachment security from 24 months, as measured with the Attachment Q-sort, and from 36 months, as measured with the modified Strange Situation procedure, to late adolescence. Moreover, we found weak stability in attachment security from across early childhood (i.e., proportion of times secure in early childhood) into late adolescence.

Several limitations of this work should be noted. First, measures of father-child attachment security were not included in the SECCYD (see Zimmerman et al., 1997; Steele & Steele, 2005) and it may be the case that the quality of the child's early attachment security with both mother and father, rather than security with the mother alone, is more predictive of states of mind with respect to attachment in late adolescence.

Second, this study is not well positioned to examine *mechanisms* of attachment stability. Specifically, some developmental scholars conceptualize developmental outcomes (such as security at 18 years) to be a function of an individual's developmental history (e.g., Sroufe, Egeland, & Kreutzer, 1990). This perspective implies that security early in life should predict security later in life above and beyond security assessed in the interim. Examining this prediction (that Fraley [2002] labeled the *prototype hypothesis* to distinguish it from the prediction of developmental models that do not make this assumption) requires a larger number of data points sampled across developmental periods than were included in this investigation.[8] Although these data cannot be used to examine mechanisms of attachment stability, they would seem to undermine the most literal interpretation of the prototype hypothesis given that individual differences in attachment security were not significantly stable from 15 months to 18 years. On the other hand, the relative lack of stability in attachment from 15 months to 24 and 36 months suggests that the Strange Situation procedure data may be anomalous in this study or that there may be greater consolidation in attachment in the early childhood years. In addition, the stability findings from both 24 months and 36 months to 18 years would seem to offer more support for the prototype hypothesis, especially in light of our findings that estimates of attachment stability from these two methods to AAI security were relatively comparable, as well as findings that these estimates were comparable to the stability of attachment from 24 to 36 months.

Finally, although it is generally assumed that attachment security should be relatively stable across time due to the transactional nature of parent-child interactions and the information processing biases that characterize working models, it is also acknowledged that security can change in lawful ways when the caregiving environment changes. In Chapter 5, Booth-LaForce et al. examine sources of continuity and change in attachment security from early childhood to late adolescence to investigate whether instability of attachment is a predictable (Waters et al., 2000) or stochastic (Lewis et al., 2000) developmental phenomenon.

## NOTES

3. Exact $p$-values were calculated for $2 \times 2$ tables and Monte Carlo estimates of $p$-values; CIs were calculated based on 10,000 samples for larger tables with cell counts less than 5.

4. We investigated whether infants classified as disorganized were more likely to be classified as unresolved if they experienced a loss and/or traumatic experience, using logistic regression. Disorganization status ($b = .15$, Wald $\chi^2 = .07$, $p = .79$, odds ratio $= 1.16$), experience of loss/trauma ($b = -18.00$, Wald $\chi^2 = .00$, $p = 1.0$, odds ratio $= .00$), and their interaction ($b = -.15$, Wald $\chi^2 = .00$, $p = 1.00$, odds ratio $= .86$) were not significantly associated with unresolved status. Weinfield et al. (2004) found that in the subsample of adults who had experienced a loss or traumatic experience, infant disorganization was associated with unresolved trauma, but not unresolved loss. Thus, we examined correlations between infant disorganization, unresolved loss, and unresolved trauma. In contrast with Weinfield et al. (2004) findings, we found that infant disorganization was significantly associated with unresolved loss ($r[548] = .12$, $p < .01$), but not unresolved trauma ($r[62] = .08$, $p = .55$).

5. We investigated whether AQS security was associated with unresolved status if children experienced a loss and/or traumatic experience, using logistic regression. AQS security ($b = -1.70$, Wald $\chi^2 = 3.35$, $p = .07$, odds ratio $= .18$), experience of loss/trauma ($b = -18.52$, Wald $\chi^2 = .00$, $p = 1.0$, odds ratio $= .00$), and their interaction ($b = 1.70$, Wald $\chi^2 = .00$, $p = 1.00$, odds ratio $= 5.47$) were not significantly associated with unresolved status.

6. We investigated whether children classified as disorganized were more likely to be classified as unresolved if they experienced a loss and/or traumatic experience, using logistic regression. Disorganization status ($b = -1.10$, Wald $\chi^2 = 6.27$, $p = .01$, odds ratio $= .33$) was significantly associated with unresolved status. However, experience of loss/trauma ($b = -18.93$, Wald $\chi^2 = .00$, $p = 1.0$, odds ratio $= .00$) and the interaction between disorganization status and experience of loss/trauma ($b = 1.10$, Wald $\chi^2 = .00$, $p = 1.00$, odds ratio $= 2.99$) were not significantly associated with unresolved status.

7. Estimate derived from average of associations between proportion of times secure and AAI dismissing/preoccupied state-of-mind scales.

8. Although the Kerns Security Scale (Kerns, Klepac, & Cole, 1996) and the Behavioral Systems Questionnaire (BSQ; Furman & Wehner, 1999) are self-report assessments of attachment security administered in the SECCYD, they were not included in the current report because there is little evidence linking these measures to the early attachment assessments included in this study and evidence suggests that, with respect to the BSQ, variation in attachment as assessed by this measure is associated with experience, but not state-of-mind, scales of the AAI (Furman & Simon, 2004). Therefore, the current study focused on attachment measures traditionally included in investigations of attachment stability (see Fraley, 2002).

# V. CAREGIVING AND CONTEXTUAL SOURCES OF CONTINUITY AND CHANGE IN ATTACHMENT SECURITY FROM INFANCY TO LATE ADOLESCENCE

*Cathryn Booth-LaForce, Ashley M. Groh, Margaret R. Burchinal,*
*Glenn I. Roisman, Margaret T. Owen, and Martha J. Cox*

In Chapter 4 (this volume), Groh et al. examined the stability of attachment security from infancy through late adolescence in a number of ways, and found evidence of significant but relatively weak stability of individual differences in security over the first two decades of life. We now focus our attention on identifying caregiving and contextual sources of variation that might contribute to the continuity and discontinuity in attachment security that we identified during this period, in order to examine whether such change is lawful.

According to attachment theory, children's early experiences with primary caregivers form the basis for the development of a secure or insecure attachment relationship, as well as a more generalized internal working model of attachment. This model is reinforced under conditions of relative stability in parent-child relationship quality over time. Updates to the model are hypothesized to occur with developmental change, but its relative stability is theorized to be ensured by the increasing automatization of caregiver-child interaction patterns as well as the child's positive or negative perceptual biases arising from these habitual patterns (Bowlby, 1969/1982). Nonetheless, under stressful life circumstances and/or changing parent-child relationship quality, attachment security is less likely to be stable. That is, stressors that alter habitual patterns, the child's expectation of the parent's availability, or the parent's actual availability and sensitivity may serve as agents of change toward insecurity. Similarly, improvements in caregiving quality and/or life circumstances would be expected to modify security in a positive direction (Waters, Weinfield, et al., 2000).

Corresponding author: Cathryn Booth-LaForce, University of Washington, Box 357920, Seattle, WA 98195-7920, email: ibcb@uw.edu

Although few studies have examined the stability of attachment from infancy through late adolescence/early adulthood, these studies have begun to identify aspects of the caregiving environment that promote stability or lead to change (Beijersbergen et al., 2012; Hamilton, 2000; Lewis et al., 2000; Main et al., 2005; Van Ryzin et al., 2011; Waters, Merrick, et al., 2000; Weinfield et al., 2000, 2004). Consistent with the idea that security may be less stable under stressful life circumstances, both proximal and distal factors have been investigated as sources of lawful change in attachment security over time, with considerable variability in the specific predictors found to be relevant. One such distal factor is the relatively high- or low-risk nature of the sample under investigation. In this regard, Fraley (2002) provided meta-analytic evidence that attachment security was less stable in samples considered to be at higher risk ($r = .27$) than those at lower risk ($r = .48$). Although Fraley's meta-analysis included both shorter and longer-term longitudinal studies, these data are nonetheless relevant in the present context.

Other more specific stressful life circumstances have been investigated as possible sources of attachment discontinuity. For example, Main et al. (2005) found that trauma directly experienced by the participant (e.g., death of a parent or parent figure) was linked with negative deflections in attachment security. Similarly, in the at-risk sample from the Minnesota Longitudinal Study of Risk and Adaptation, Weinfield et al. (2004) found that mothers' stress from life events was higher among children who transitioned from secure to insecure compared with those who were stably secure from infancy to late adolescence. Similar results linking stressful life experiences with changes in attachment security have been obtained in other studies (Hamilton, 2000; Van Ryzin et al., 2011; Waters, Merrick, et al., 2000).

At a more proximal level, changes in caregiving quality or in the psychological or physical availability of the parent may contribute to attachment discontinuity. For example, parental depression has long been known to be a factor affecting the quality of caregiving (National Research Council and Institute of Medicine, 2009); therefore, changes in depression over time could be a source of positive or negative change in attachment security. In fact, Weinfield et al. (2000) found that mothers of children who switched from secure to insecure between infancy and late adolescence were more often depressed than were mothers of those who were stably secure. However, in a later report that included more participants from the same sample, these results were not replicated (Weinfield et al., 2004). Another important contextual variable may be the physical availability of the father in the home, which has been implicated as a factor affecting the short-term stability of attachment security (e.g., Egeland & Farber, 1984). That said, in a longer-term study, Lewis et al. (2000) found that changes in attachment security over time were unrelated to divorce.

Perhaps more importantly, the stability and/or change in the quality of the mother-child relationship from infancy to late adolescence has been targeted as a theoretically potent source of possible continuity or discontinuity in attachment security (Bowlby 1969/1982; Lewis et al., 2000; Sroufe, 1983; Thompson, 1999). Several relatively short-term longitudinal analyses have tested this idea directly, and have found that changes in the quality of caregiving were associated with expected changes in attachment security (Egeland & Farber, 1984; Frodi, Grolnick, & Bridges, 1985; NICHD ECCRN, 2006). In the longer-term attachment studies, only two have directly tested the role of caregiving quality in changes from security to insecurity, or vice versa, from infancy to adolescence. Although Weinfield et al. (2004) found that mother-child interactive quality in early childhood did not predict such changes, more recent evidence from the same sample suggests that the quality of mother-child interactions was associated with complementary stability/change in the quality of attachment security from infancy to adulthood (Van Ryzin et al., 2011). Similarly, Beijersbergen et al. (2012) found that consistently secure participants, compared with those who changed from secure to insecure, had more sensitive mothers at 12 months of age, and a trend toward greater sensitivity at Age 14. Compared with the consistently insecure participants, those who changed from insecure to secure had more sensitive mothers at both 12 months and 14 years.

Taken together, research from longitudinal investigations of attachment security has begun to identify theoretically relevant aspects of the caregiving environment that contribute to stability and change in attachment security. However, there is considerable variability across studies in the predictors that have been investigated and findings from studies including the same predictors have not always converged. In the present study we investigated key sources of continuity and change from mother-child attachment security in early childhood (at 15, 24, and 36 months) to state of mind regarding attachment in late adolescence. Given the opportunity provided by the large longitudinal SECCYD sample that included assessments over time of important potential sources of change and continuity in attachment security, we were uniquely positioned to address this question. Moreover, although the SECCYD did not recruit a high-risk sample at birth, the relative socio-demographic breadth of the sample compared with the more uniform low-risk attachment samples studied by most other investigators is a clear advantage. Analyses included comparisons of those who changed from secure to insecure versus those who were stably secure; those who changed from insecure to secure versus those who were stably insecure, and (for reference) those who were stably secure versus those who were stably insecure. On the basis of theory and extant empirical evidence, we included, as predictors, assessments over time of observed maternal and paternal sensitivity, presence of the father in the home, maternal and paternal depression, and number of negative life events.

## METHODS

### Attachment Measures

Participants were designated as secure or insecure in early childhood, and secure or insecure in late adolescence. These categories were used, rather than attachment dimension scores, due to ease of comparison with prior studies, analytic considerations, and interpretability.

#### Early Attachment Security

Security status in early childhood was determined based on the proportion of times the child was classified as secure on the early attachment assessments (Strange Situation procedure, Attachment Q-sort, and modified Strange Situation procedure; see Chapter 4 for an overview of assessments). First, a secure versus insecure variable for each attachment assessment was developed based on the operationalization of security used in Chapter 4. For the Strange Situation at 15 months, a secure versus insecure variable was created. For the Attachment Q-sort at 24 months, children whose Q-sorts were correlated at .30 or above with the criterion sort were classified as secure (vs. insecure; Waters, 2003). For the modified Strange Situation at 36 months, a secure versus insecure variable also was computed. Next, if data were available on two or more early attachment assessments, the proportion of times the child was coded as secure was determined by taking the number of times the child was classified secure for each available attachment assessment and dividing it by the total number of attachment assessments available for that child, which resulted in the following categories: secure on all assessments, secure on most assessments, secure on one assessment/insecure on one assessment, insecure on most assessments, and insecure on all assessments. This distribution informed the final early security variable, with the *secure* group comprising children who were secure on all or 2/3 of the attachment assessments and the *insecure* group comprising those who were insecure on all assessments, insecure on 2/3 of the assessments, or insecure on one assessment/secure on one assessment (if only two were available). Children in this latter group were classified as insecure rather than secure because by including them as insecure, the resulting percentage of children in the early childhood insecure group (37%) was closest to the percentage of insecurity found in each early attachment assessment considered individually (Strange Situation = 39% insecure; Attachment Q-sort = 44% insecure; modified Strange Situation = 39% insecure).

### Adult Attachment Security

Following Chapter 4, individuals who were coded as secure in late adolescence on the AAI were included in the *secure* group. The *insecure* group comprised individuals who were coded dismissing, preoccupied, or unresolved (e.g., unresolved/secure).

### Attachment Groups

Participants were grouped according to stability and change in their early childhood and adult attachment status. Overall, 330 (40%) were stably secure, 142 (17%) were stably insecure, 160 (20%) changed from insecure in early childhood to secure at 18 years, and 193 (23%) changed from secure to insecure.

### Demographic Covariates

A set of demographic covariates was used in all models: child race/ethnicity (1 = White, non-Hispanic, 0 = other), child gender (1 = male, 0 = female), maternal and paternal years of education, and family income. Family income was measured as an income-to-needs ratio (total family income divided by the year-specific poverty threshold for the appropriate family size), calculated separately at 1, 6, 15, 24, 36, and 54 months; Grades 1, 3, 5, and 6; and age 15.

### Maternal and Parental Sensitivity

Early maternal sensitivity was assessed in the context of mother-child interactions that were videotaped during 15-min semi-structured play procedures at 6, 15, 24, 36, and 54 months; Grades 1, 3, and 5; and age 15. At each assessment point, the study children were videotaped while engaging in tasks at the zone of proximal development while primary caregivers provided assistance at the younger ages; at older ages (Grade 3 and older), joint tasks, including discussion tasks, were used. Tasks were designed to be developmentally appropriate. Measures of paternal sensitivity were added to the SECCYD common protocol beginning at age 54 months. Paternal sensitivity assessments from 54 months through age 15 were conducted in parallel fashion to those described above for maternal sensitivity for the same time frame. Psychometric properties for composite measures of observed maternal and paternal sensitivity at each assessment point were adequate (for more information see Belsky et al., 2007; NICHD ECCRN 2001, 2004, 2008). Internal consistencies of the sensitivity composite measures for mothers averaged .79 (range .70–.85) and for fathers averaged .78 (range .71–.82) across assessments.

### Father Absence

Primary caregivers indicated whether the study child's father was living in the home at each assessment wave through age 15 (1, 3, 6, 9, 12, 15, 24, 36, 42, 50, 54, 60, 66 months; Kindergarten-Fall [F], Kindergarten-Spring [S]; Grades 1F, 1S, 2F, 2S, 3, 4, 5, 6, 7; ages 14 and 15). A proportion score was created indicating the total number of contacts with the family during which the father was not living in the home, divided by number of assessments.

### Maternal and Paternal Depression

Self-reported maternal and paternal depressive symptoms were assessed using the 20-item Center for Epidemiologic Studies–Depression Scale (CES-D; Radloff, 1977). CES-D reports from the mother were obtained from assessments at 1, 6, 15, 24, 36, and 54 months; Grades 1, 3, 5, and 6; and age 15. CES-D reports from the father were acquired at 54 months; Grades 1, 3, 5, and 6; and age 15. (Note that mothers' and fathers' reports of depressive symptoms on the CES-D were acquired at age 18. However, we excluded these reports from the current chapter to ensure that all predictors of change temporally preceded the age 18 AAI assessment). For mothers' scores, alphas averaged .90 (range = .88–.91; for fathers' scores, alphas averaged .87 (range = .86–.88).

### Negative Life Events

Mothers completed the Life Experiences Survey (LES; Sarason, Johnson, & Siegel, 1978) at 54 months and Grades 3 and 5. This 57-item questionnaire asks mothers to identify from a list those life events that have happened to them over the past year, and to rate, on a 7-point scale (from +3 = very positive to 0 = neutral, to −3 = very negative) the impact the event has had on their lives. Events include routine happenings (e.g., "child started school") to major events (e.g., major change in financial status) to catastrophic events (e.g., death of a parent). This measure provides an overview of the stressful events that have befallen the study child's family and may have an impact on the child's well-being, as well as on the quality of parenting. The total number of negative life events was summed at each assessment age.

## RESULTS

The analyses were designed to determine whether stability or change in attachment status from early childhood to late adolescence varied as a function of level or change in parental sensitivity and indicators of family stress, in addition to (and net of) demographic characteristics. The early childhood (1–36 months) period was considered separately from the later

(54 months–15 years) period for two reasons. First, the early childhood period corresponded with the times during which early attachment security was assessed (15, 24, 36 months), which allowed us to separate out the importance of factors occurring contemporaneously with the early assessments from those occurring in the intervening period between the early childhood and late adolescent attachment assessments. Second, fathers began participating in the study when their children were 54 months of age. Therefore, the 54 months–15 years time frame allowed to us evaluate maternal and paternal predictors during the same period.

*Data Reduction*

Indices of level and change were computed using unconditional hierarchical linear models (HLM) that estimated a separate intercept and slope with respect to age for each individual. Age was centered at 54 months so the intercept represented the level at the 54-month assessment. The estimated slopes described the individual's linear change from 54 months to 15 years. Intercepts and slopes were computed for the following characteristics: family income/needs ratio (54 months–15 years); maternal sensitivity (54 months–15 years); paternal sensitivity (54 months–15 years); maternal depressive symptoms (54 months–15 years); paternal depressive symptoms (54 months–15 years); and negative life events (54 months-Grade 5). We also examined level and change during early childhood for family income/needs (1–36 months), maternal sensitivity (6–36 months), and maternal depressive symptoms (1–36 months). The proportion of assessments during which the father did not live in the household was computed for the early childhood (1–36 months) and the later assessment periods (54 months–15 years). A square root transformation was applied to depressive symptoms due to skew in those variables.

The results from these HLM analyses are displayed in Table 5.1, showing the estimated random variances for the intercepts and slopes and the estimated population intercepts and slopes from the HLM analysis. All estimated random variance terms were statistically different from zero, demonstrating adequate individual differences to warrant use of the intercepts and slopes from the individual growth curves as predictors in subsequent analyses. The estimated population intercepts and slopes are shown in the rows under the heading "fixed effects."

*Descriptive Statistics*

The sample sizes, means, and standard deviations for the estimated indices of level and change for the selected covariates and predictors are shown in Table 5.2 for the four early-childhood by late-adolescent attachment

73

## TABLE 5.1

### HLM Results: Estimating Indicators of Level and Change in Selected Family Characteristics

| | | M. sens. 6-36 Months | M sens. 54 Months-15 Years | P. sens. 54 Months-15 years | M. dep. 1-36 Months (sqrt) | M. dep. 54 Months-15 Years (sqrt) | P. dep. 54 Months-15 Years (sqrt) | Income 1-36 Months | Income 54 Months-15 Years | Negative Life Events 54 Months-G5 |
|---|---|---|---|---|---|---|---|---|---|---|
| **Variance components** | | | | | | | | | | |
| Intercept | var | 0.421*** | 0.514*** | 0.249*** | 0.993*** | 1.136*** | 0.898*** | 0.731*** | 0.609*** | 4.934*** |
| Time | var | 0.003 | 0.002*** | 0.001* | 0.025*** | 0.003*** | 0.004*** | 0.019*** | 0.002*** | 0.077*** |
| Intercept, time | cov | -0.012 | -0.024*** | -0.008* | 0.016 | -0.008 | -0.006 | -0.038*** | -0.007** | -0.252** |
| **Population parameters** | | | | | | | | | | |
| Intercept | B | 5.350*** | 5.669*** | 5.878*** | 2.860*** | 2.615*** | 2.468*** | 0.789*** | 0.999*** | 3.363*** |
| | (se) | (0.025) | (0.026) | (0.024) | (0.031) | (0.039) | (0.039) | (0.024) | (0.024) | (0.100) |
| Time | B | 0.128*** | -0.045*** | -0.052*** | -0.079*** | 0.009* | 0.015** | 0.073*** | 0.027*** | -0.039 |
| | (se) | (0.012) | (0.003) | (0.004) | (0.012) | (0.012) | (0.005) | (0.007) | (0.002) | (0.020) |

*Note.* M. sens. = maternal sensitivity; P. sens. = paternal sensitivity; M. dep. = maternal depression; P. dep. = paternal depression; G = grade.

*$p < .05$.
**$p < .01$.
***$p < .001$.

TABLE 5.2

DESCRIPTIVE STATISTICS FOR ATTACHMENT GROUPS

| | Insecure/Insecure | | | Insecure/Secure | | | Secure/Insecure | | | Secure/Secure | | |
|---|---|---|---|---|---|---|---|---|---|---|---|---|
| | N | Mean/Prop | SD | N | Mean/Prop | SD | N | Mean/Prop | SD | N | Mean/Prop | SD |
| Child race-White, non-Hispanic | 142 | 0.65 | | 160 | 0.79 | | 193 | 0.76 | | 330 | 0.85 | |
| Male | 142 | 0.52 | | 160 | 0.47 | | 193 | 0.61 | | 330 | 0.41 | |
| Maternal education | 142 | 13.42 | 2.40 | 160 | 14.51 | 2.42 | 193 | 14.63 | 2.12 | 330 | 15.08 | 2.42 |
| Paternal education | 129 | 13.67 | 2.28 | 154 | 14.45 | 2.49 | 187 | 14.81 | 2.60 | 321 | 15.26 | 2.62 |
| Income/needs 54 months–15 years: intercept | 142 | 0.70 | 0.79 | 159 | 0.97 | 0.75 | 193 | 1.09 | 0.65 | 330 | 1.19 | 0.65 |
| Income/needs 54 months–15 years: time slope | 142 | 0.02 | 0.04 | 159 | 0.03 | 0.03 | 193 | 0.02 | 0.04 | 330 | 0.03 | 0.04 |
| Prop 1–36 months Father absent | 142 | 0.27 | 0.40 | 160 | 0.13 | 0.29 | 193 | 0.14 | 0.32 | 330 | 0.09 | 0.27 |
| Prop 54 months–15 years Father absent | 142 | 0.44 | 0.45 | 160 | 0.24 | 0.40 | 193 | 0.32 | 0.41 | 330 | 0.17 | 0.34 |
| M sensitivity 6–36 months: intercept | 142 | 5.06 | 0.63 | 160 | 5.38 | 0.51 | 193 | 5.44 | 0.46 | 330 | 5.57 | 0.44 |
| M sensitivity 6–36 months: slope | 142 | 0.13 | 0.01 | 160 | 0.13 | 0.01 | 193 | 0.13 | 0.01 | 330 | 0.12 | 0.01 |
| M sensitivity 54 months–15 years: intercept | 140 | 5.28 | 0.66 | 160 | 5.73 | 0.53 | 190 | 5.73 | 0.53 | 330 | 5.91 | 0.49 |
| M sensitivity 54 months–15 years: time slope | 140 | -0.03 | 0.03 | 160 | -0.05 | 0.03 | 190 | -0.05 | 0.02 | 330 | -0.05 | 0.02 |
| P sensitivity 54 months–15 years: intercept | 110 | 5.76 | 0.34 | 139 | 5.88 | 0.40 | 175 | 5.84 | 0.41 | 297 | 5.99 | 0.34 |
| P sensitivity 54 months–15 years: slope | 110 | -0.05 | 0.01 | 139 | -0.05 | 0.01 | 175 | -0.05 | 0.01 | 297 | -0.05 | 0.01 |
| M depression (sqrt) 54 months–15 years: intercept | 140 | 2.83 | 0.88 | 160 | 2.66 | 0.94 | 190 | 2.50 | 0.89 | 330 | 2.51 | 0.97 |
| M depression (sqrt) 54 months–15 years: time slope | 140 | 0.01 | 0.02 | 160 | 0.01 | 0.02 | 190 | 0.01 | 0.02 | 330 | 0.01 | 0.02 |
| P depression (sqrt) 54 months–15 years: intercept | 115 | 2.77 | 0.82 | 141 | 2.48 | 0.90 | 178 | 2.51 | 0.84 | 302 | 2.31 | 0.78 |
| P depression (sqrt) 54 months–15 years: time slope | 115 | 0.02 | 0.03 | 141 | 0.01 | 0.03 | 178 | 0.02 | 0.03 | 302 | 0.02 | 0.03 |
| Neg life events 54 months-G5: intercept | 142 | 3.19 | 1.58 | 160 | 3.34 | 1.68 | 193 | 3.41 | 1.61 | 330 | 3.42 | 1.68 |
| Neg life events 54 months-G5: time slope | 142 | -0.06 | 0.11 | 160 | -0.04 | 0.11 | 193 | -0.02 | 0.10 | 330 | -0.04 | 0.12 |

*Note.* Prop = proportion; M = maternal; P = paternal; Neg = negative; G = grade.

75

## TABLE 5.3

### Correlations Among Predictor Variables

| | M Ed. | P Ed | Income Level 54 Months-15 Years | Income Slope 54 Months-15 Years | Father Absent 1-36 Months | Father Absent 54 Months-15 Years | M.sen. Level 6-36 Months | M sen Slope 6-36 Months | M sen Level 54 Months-15 Years | M sen Slope 54 Months-15 Years | P sen Level 54 Months-15 years | P sen Slope 54 Months-15 Years | M dep Level 54 Months-15 Years | M dep Slope 54 Months-15 Years | P dep Level 54 Months-15 Years | P dep Slope 54 Months-15 Years | Neg.ev Level 54 Months-G5 | Neg.ev Slope 54 Months-G5 |
|---|---|---|---|---|---|---|---|---|---|---|---|---|---|---|---|---|---|---|
| Maternal education | 1.00 | | | | | | | | | | | | | | | | | |
| Paternal education | 0.66 | 1.00 | | | | | | | | | | | | | | | | |
| Income/needs 54 months-15 years intercept | 0.61 | 0.60 | 1.00 | | | | | | | | | | | | | | | |
| Income/needs 54 months-15 years: time slope | 0.01 | 0.06 | -0.09 | 1.00 | | | | | | | | | | | | | | |
| Father absent-prop. (1-36 months) | -0.33 | -0.29 | -0.49 | 0.14 | 1.00 | | | | | | | | | | | | | |
| Father absent-prop. (54 months-15 years) | -0.33 | -0.32 | -0.49 | 0.08 | 0.68 | 1.00 | | | | | | | | | | | | |
| M sensitivity 6-36 months: intercept | 0.50 | 0.48 | 0.51 | 0.02 | -0.38 | -0.36 | 1.00 | | | | | | | | | | | |
| M sensitivity 6-36 months: slope | -0.43 | -0.40 | -0.42 | 0.03 | 0.30 | 0.26 | -0.87 | 1.00 | | | | | | | | | | |
| M sensitivity 54 months-15 years: intercept | 0.45 | 0.39 | 0.47 | 0.03 | -0.37 | -0.34 | 0.65 | -0.48 | 1.00 | | | | | | | | | |
| M sensitivity 54 months-15 years: time slope | -0.37 | -0.33 | -0.41 | -0.01 | 0.32 | 0.29 | -0.58 | 0.42 | -0.89 | 1.00 | | | | | | | | |
| P sensitivity 54 months-15 years: intercept | 0.26 | 0.31 | 0.23 | 0.09 | -0.09 | -0.11 | 0.34 | -0.26 | 0.99 | -0.29 | 1.00 | | | | | | | |
| P sensitivity 54 months-15 years: slope | -0.09 | -0.13 | -0.10 | -0.06 | 0.03 | 0.03 | -0.20 | 0.14 | -0.19 | 0.17 | -0.60 | 1.00 | | | | | | |
| M depression(sqrt) 54 months-15 years: intercept | -0.30 | -0.28 | -0.40 | -0.09 | 0.24 | 0.28 | -0.31 | 0.23 | -0.30 | 0.25 | -0.14 | 0.05 | 1.00 | | | | | |
| M depression(sqrt) 54 months-15 years: time slope | -0.04 | -0.02 | -0.06 | -0.16 | 0.01 | 0.02 | -0.07 | 0.04 | -0.06 | 0.04 | -0.01 | -0.01 | 0.19 | 1.00 | | | | |
| P depression(sqrt) 54 months-15 years: intercept | -0.17 | -0.20 | -0.24 | -0.14 | 0.10 | 0.15 | -0.17 | 0.09 | -0.17 | 0.15 | -0.20 | 0.09 | 0.25 | 0.06 | 1.00 | | | |
| P depression(sqrt) 54 months-15 years: time slope | -0.08 | -0.12 | -0.11 | -0.10 | 0.04 | 0.05 | -0.09 | 0.08 | -0.10 | 0.08 | -0.10 | -0.02 | 0.13 | 0.12 | 0.24 | 1.00 | | |
| Neg life events 54 months-G5: intercept | 0.05 | 0.01 | -0.07 | -0.04 | -0.01 | 0.08 | 0.10 | -0.10 | 0.06 | -0.08 | 0.04 | -0.05 | 0.33 | 0.05 | 0.11 | 0.03 | 1.00 | |
| Neg life events 54 months-G5: time slope | 0.02 | 0.04 | 0.01 | -0.10 | -0.03 | -0.05 | 0.02 | -0.02 | -0.01 | 0.01 | 0.02 | -0.03 | -0.03 | 0.13 | 0.03 | 0.08 | -0.23 | 1.00 |

*Note.* Prop = proportion; M = maternal; P = paternal; Neg = negative; Ed = education; sen = sensitivity; dep = depression; Neg ev = negative life events.

groups. As expected, the stably insecure group tended to be the most disadvantaged economically and educationally, have lower levels of parental sensitivity, and higher levels of parental depressive symptoms, whereas the stably secure group tended to be the most advantaged, have higher levels of parental sensitivity and lower levels of parental depressive symptoms.

The correlations among these variables and the other demographic variables of interest in the inferential analyses are shown in Table 5.3. As expected, parental education, income levels, and father absence were highly correlated. Similarly, the summary scores describing early childhood and later experiences tended to be highly correlated for proportion of time father was absent ($r = .68$) and level of maternal sensitivity ($r = .65$). The indices of level and change also were highly correlated for maternal sensitivity during early childhood ($r = -.87$) and later years ($r = -.89$) and for paternal sensitivity during later years ($r = -.60$).

*Multinomial Analyses*

The inferential analyses evaluated whether level and change in parental sensitivity and indicators of family stress, net of demographic characteristics, predicted whether the participants showed continuity or change in their attachment status from early childhood through late adolescence. Multinomial analyses were conducted, using the stably secure group as the reference group. Follow-up comparisons of the secure-to-insecure group with the stably secure group, and of insecure-to-secure group with the stably insecure group were examined when the overall Chi-square test was statistically significant for a predictor. Models were fit hierarchically. The covariates (site, child race/ethnicity, gender, maternal education, paternal education, income/needs level and change) were included in all models. Added to this base model were hypothesized explanatory characteristics that varied in terms of their proximity to the child: (1) maternal sensitivity, (2) paternal sensitivity, (3) father absence, (4) maternal and paternal depressive symptoms, and (5) negative life events. The early childhood (through 36 months) and later years (54 months–15 years) were considered separately. For maternal depressive symptoms, note that the very high correlation between the estimated intercept from the early-childhood and later periods ($r = .72$) led us to include only the intercept and slope from the latter (54 months–15 years) in the analyses. Similarly, we included income/needs only for this later period due to the very high correlation between the early-childhood and later-childhood intercepts ($r = .83$). Our rationale for these choices was that the primary focus was on continuity and change during the time between the early and AAI attachment assessments.

The hierarchical models are shown in Table 5.4. The first model focused on maternal sensitivity as a predictor. Both the intercept and slope from

TABLE 5.4

HIERARCHICAL MULTINOMIAL REGRESSION RESULTS: PREDICTING CONTINUITY AND CHANGE IN
ATTACHMENT STATUS

| Predictor | $\chi^2(3, 785)$ | II Versus SS B (se) | SI Versus SS B (se) | II Versus IS B (se) |
|---|---|---|---|---|
| Model 1 | | | | |
| Child race | 1.77 | −0.20 (0.33) | −0.31 (0.29) | −0.37 (0.35) |
| Gender | 14.40** | 0.41 (0.25) | 0.78*** (0.20) | 0.23 (0.28) |
| M education | 1.61 | −0.05 (0.07) | −0.02 (0.06) | −0.10 (0.08) |
| P education | 2.22 | −0.02 (0.07) | −0.01 (0.05) | 0.05 (0.08) |
| Income-level 54 months–15 years | 0.98 | −0.14 (0.27) | 0.12 (0.22) | −0.00 (0.29) |
| Income-change 54 months–15 years | 2.63 | −0.02 (0.12) | −0.08 (0.10) | −0.26 (0.14) |
| M sensitive level 6–36 months | 12.98** | −1.63** (0.56) | −1.03* (0.50) | −0.92 (0.57) |
| M sensitive change 6–36 months | 8.72* | −0.57* (0.25) | −0.43* (0.22) | −0.42 (0.27) |
| M sensitive level 54 months–15 years | 24.73*** | −1.62*** (0.48) | −1.52*** (0.39) | −1.65*** (0.50) |
| M sensitive change 54 months–15 years | 14.34** | −0.32 (0.25) | −0.80*** (0.22) | −0.38 (0.25) |
| Model 2 | | | | |
| P sensitive level 54 months–15 years | 5.22 | −0.63 (0.50) | −0.67 (0.37) | 0.13 (0.55) |
| P sensitive change 54 months–15 years | 5.08 | 0.15 (0.16) | −0.06 (0.12) | 0.36* (0.18) |
| Model 3 | | | | |
| Father absent 1–36 months | 1.56 | −0.53 (0.57) | −0.47 (0.55) | −0.02 (0.67) |
| Father absent 54 months–15 years | 17.28*** | 1.09* (0.45) | 1.53*** (0.39) | 0.61 (0.51) |
| Model 4 | | | | |
| M Depression level 54 months–15 years | 6.16 | −0.14 (0.16) | −0.22 (0.13) | −0.26 (0.18) |
| M Depression change 54 months–15 years | 3.22 | 0.03 (0.13) | 0.12 (0.11) | 0.21 (0.14) |
| P Depression level 54 months–15 years | 8.95* | 0.56** (0.19) | 0.21 (0.14) | 0.21 (0.20) |
| P Depression change 54 months–15 years | 3.82 | −0.17 (0.14) | 0.01 (0.11) | 0.05 (0.16) |
| Model 5 | | | | |
| Negative events level 54 months-G5 | 2.74 | −0.09 (0.10) | 0.02 (0.07) | −0.00 (0.10) |
| Negative events change 54 months-G5 | 13.08** | −0.20 (0.14) | 0.29** (0.11) | −0.28 (0.16) |

Note. M = maternal; P = paternal; G = grade; II = stably insecure; SS = stably secure; SI = change from secure to insecure; IS = change from insecure to secure. IS versus SS was omitted from this table because it was not a comparison of interest; none of the predictors was significant for this comparison. Analyses included data-collection site as a covariate.
*$p < .05$.
**$p < .01$.
***$p < .001$.

analyses of maternal sensitivity at 6–36 months and 54 months–15 years were included in the analysis as four separate variables. Results indicated that all four added to the model: Early maternal sensitivity intercept $\chi^2$ (3, $n = 785$) = 12.98, $p < .01$; early maternal sensitivity slope $\chi^2$ (3, $n = 785$) = 8.72, $p < .05$; later maternal sensitivity intercept $\chi^2$ (3, $n = 785$) = 24.73, $p < .001$; and later maternal sensitivity slope $\chi^2$ (3, $n = 785$) = 14.34, $p < .01$. Examination of the coefficients for maternal sensitivity in early childhood indicated that, compared with the stably secure group, mothers in the stably insecure and secure-to-insecure groups showed lower levels and greater decreases in maternal sensitivity during this period. The coefficients for maternal sensitivity between 54 months and 15 years indicated that the secure-to-insecure group showed lower levels and larger decreases in maternal sensitivity compared with the stably secure group. Additionally, the stably insecure group had mothers with lower levels of maternal sensitivity between 54 months and 15 years than did the stably secure group, and the stably insecure group also had mothers with lower maternal sensitivity than did the insecure-to-secure group. Note also that gender was a significant covariate, $\chi^2$ (3, $n = 785$) $= 14.40$, $p < .01$, with more girls in the secure-to-insecure group than the stably secure group.

The second model added observations of paternal sensitivity between 54 months and 15 years of age, using the estimated intercepts and slopes from the HLM analysis. A missing-value dummy variable was included indicating that the child was not observed with his/her father, which allowed the inclusion of that child's data in the overall analysis while omitting the case from the estimation of the coefficients for paternal sensitivity level or change. Neither the level nor change in paternal sensitivity differentially predicted attachment group.

The third model added the proportion of assessment points during which the father was absent from the child's household in early childhood (1–36 months) or later (54 months–15 years). The father's absence in later years, but not during early childhood, was a significant predictor of attachment group, $\chi^2$ (3, $n = 785$) $= 17.28$, $p < .001$. The stably insecure children lived with their fathers proportionately less often than did children in the stably secure group, and the secure-to-insecure children also lived with their fathers proportionately less often than did the children in the stably secure group.

The fourth model added the intercepts and slopes from analyses of maternal and paternal reports of depressive symptoms between 54 months and 15 years, along with a missing value dummy variable to allow the inclusion of children whose fathers did not provide information about depressive symptoms. The father's reported level of depressive symptoms was a significant predictor of attachment group, $\chi^2$ (3, $n = 785$) $= 8.95$, $p < .05$. Fathers in the stably insecure group reported significantly more symptoms than did fathers in the stably secure group.

The final model added negative life events. Again, the intercepts and slopes from HLM analyses of mothers' reports of events from 54 months to Grade 5 were added to the model. Change over time in negative life events was a significant predictor of attachment group, $\chi^2$ (3, $n = 785$) $= 13.08$, $p < .01$. Mothers in the secure-to-insecure group reported a larger increase in negative life events over time than did mothers in the stably secure group.

Table 5.5 provides the chi-square tests and coefficients for each of the predictors from the final model when all predictors were considered simultaneously. As shown, the same factors that we observed in the hierarchical

## TABLE 5.5

FINAL MODEL MULTINOMIAL REGRESSION RESULTS: PREDICTING CONTINUITY AND CHANGE IN ATTACHMENT STATUS

| Predictor | $\chi^2(3,721)$ | II Versus SS<br>$B$ (se) | SI Versus SS<br>$B$ (se) | II Versus IS<br>$B$ (se) |
|---|---|---|---|---|
| Race/ethnicity (White/nonHisp. = 1) | 2.15 | −0.24 (0.35) | −0.32 (0.31) | −0.25 (0.38) |
| Gender (male = 1) | 15.23** | 0.50 (0.27) | 0.83*** (0.21) | 0.23 (0.29) |
| M education | 2.17 | −0.06 (0.08) | −0.02 (0.06) | −0.13 (0.08) |
| P education | 2.22 | 0.02 (0.07) | −0.01 (0.06) | 0.13 (0.09) |
| Income- level 54 months–15 years | 1.98 | 0.01 (0.32) | 0.27 (0.25) | 0.03 (0.33) |
| Income-change 54 months–15 years | 1.34 | 0.02 (0.14) | 0.02 (0.11) | −0.29 (0.16) |
| M sensitive level 6–36 months | 10.26* | −1.60** (0.60) | −0.96 (0.53) | −0.76 (0.61) |
| M sensitive change 6–36 months | 6.29 | −0.54* (0.27) | −0.39 (0.23) | −0.31 (0.29) |
| M sensitive level 54 months–15 years | 20.18*** | −1.48** (0.51) | −1.39** (0.43) | −1.74** (0.55) |
| M sensitive change 54 months–15 years | 11.98** | −0.33 (0.26) | −0.74** (0.23) | −0.40 (0.27) |
| P sensitive level 54 months–15 years | 4.47 | −0.52 (0.54) | −0.47 (0.39) | −0.08 (0.60) |
| P sensitive change 54 months–15 years | 4.29 | 0.12 (0.17) | −0.03 (0.13) | 0.33 (0.19) |
| Father absent 1–36 months | 1.48 | −0.69 (0.60) | −0.52 (0.57) | 0.08 (0.71) |
| Father absent 54 months–15 years | 17.34*** | 1.06* (0.47) | 1.64*** (0.41) | 0.43 (0.54) |
| M depression level 54 months–15 years | 6.17 | −0.12 (0.17) | −0.24 (0.14) | −0.32 (0.20) |
| M depression change 54 months–15 years | 3.54 | 0.07 (0.13) | 0.09 (0.11) | 0.23 (0.15) |
| P depression level 54 months–15 years | 9.01* | 0.57** (0.19) | 0.22 (0.15) | 0.25 (0.20) |
| P depression change 54 months–15 years | 3.58 | −0.16 (0.14) | −0.01 (0.11) | 0.04 (0.16) |
| Negative events level 54 months-G5 | 2.74 | −0.09 (0.10) | 0.02 (0.07) | −0.00 (0.10) |
| Negative events change 54 months-G5 | 13.08** | −0.20 (0.14) | 0.29** (0.11) | −0.28 (0.16) |

*Note.* M = maternal; P = paternal; G = grade; II = stably insecure; SS = stably secure; SI = change from secure to insecure; IS = change from insecure to secure. IS versus SS was omitted from this table because it was not a comparison of interest; none of the predictors was significant for this comparison. Analyses included data-collection site as a covariate.
*$p < .05$.
**$p < .01$.
***$p < .001$.

analyses differentiated the attachment groups: Gender $\chi^2$ (3, $n = 785$) = 15.23, $p < .01$; level of maternal sensitivity 6–36 months, $\chi^2$ (3, $n = 785$) = 10.26, $p < .05$; level of maternal sensitivity 54 months–15 years, $\chi^2$ (3, $n = 785$) = 20.18, $p < .001$; change over time in maternal sensitivity 54 months–15 years, $\chi^2$ (3, $n = 785$) = 11.98, $p < .01$; father absence 54 months–15 years, $\chi^2$ (3, $n = 785$) = 17.34, $p < .001$; level of father's depressive symptoms 54 months–15 years, $\chi^2$ (3, $n = 785$) = 9.01, $p < .05$; and increases in the number of negative life events between 54 months and Grade 5, $\chi^2$(3, $n = 785$) = 13.08, $p < .01$. Overall, the results suggest that factors that differentiated the secure-to-insecure and stably secure groups included gender (more likely to be girls), lower levels and greater decline in maternal sensitivity between 54 months and 15 years, lower likelihood of living with the father during this period, and a larger increase in negative life events over time. The results also indicated that the one factor differentiating the stably insecure group from the insecure-to-secure group was a higher level of maternal sensitivity in the latter group between 54 months and 15 years. Finally, factors that distinguished stably insecure and stably secure groups included lower levels of maternal sensitivity both in early childhood and in later years, higher likelihood of having the father absent from 54 months to 15 years, and higher levels of paternal depressive symptoms during this same period.

## DISCUSSION

Sources of within-person change and continuity in attachment security over time have long been of interest to both attachment theorists and researchers. In particular, changes from security to insecurity, or the reverse, are theorized to be lawfully connected with declining (or improving) aspects of parental availability and sensitivity, as well as changes in life circumstances that would affect these aspects of parenting (Bowlby, 1969/1982; Sroufe, 1983; Waters, Weinfield, et al., 2000). Although limited evidence exists from both short-term longitudinal work (Egeland & Farber, 1984; Frodi et al., 1985; NICHD ECCRN, 2006) and longer-term studies (Beijersbergen et al., 2012; Hamilton, 2000; Main et al., 2005; Waters, Merrick et al., 2000; Weinfield et al., 2004) to support these hypothesized sources of lawful change in attachment security, the present results provide relevant evidence from the largest long-term longitudinal study of attachment to date. Specifically, when we compared study participants who remained secure between early childhood and age 18 years with those who changed from secure to insecure, we found that in the intervening period those who became insecure experienced lower levels and a greater decline in maternal sensitivity, they were less likely to be living with their fathers, and their mothers reported a larger increase in negative life events over time. Comparison of those who were stably insecure and those who changed from insecure in early childhood to secure in late adolescence also supported the lawful discontinuity model in that those who became secure experienced a higher level of maternal sensitivity in the intervening years.

As pointed out by Waters, Weinfield, et al. (2000), it is also important to be able to explain *continuity* in attachment security over time. That is, intervening parenting quality and life circumstances should be consistent with continuous security or insecurity. Although most of the work in this area has concentrated on change rather than continuity, we addressed both issues. We found that study participants who were stably insecure, compared with those who were stably secure, experienced less maternal sensitivity from 6 to 36 months, as well as 54 months to age 15. Additionally, from 54 months to 15 years, fathers were less likely to be present in the home, and the level of paternal depressive symptoms was greater.

Taken together, these results support attachment theory as well as provide a stronger empirical basis for confirming some of the findings from the limited number of smaller studies investigating sources of change in attachment security from infancy through late adolescence. In a number of these studies, stressful life events were found to forecast a change from security to insecurity (Hamilton, 2000; Main et al., 2005; Van Ryzin et al., 2011; Waters, Merrick, et al., 2000; Weinfield et al., 2004), similar to the present results. Additionally, we confirmed the central role of maternal sensitivity as a factor in predicting both positive and negative changes in attachment security, which converges with evidence from prior research (Beijersbergen et al., 2012; Van Ryzin et al., 2011; but see Weinfield et al., 2004). It is noteworthy that both the number and the strength of our findings regarding maternal sensitivity align with the reported links in the literature between sensitivity and security (De Wolff & Van IJzendoorn, 1997), and also align with the idea that the most proximal variable of interest—the ongoing quality of the mother-child relationship—may serve as a significant modifier of early mother-child attachment security (Bowlby 1969/1982; Lewis et al., 2000; Sroufe, 1983; Thompson, 1999).

Importantly, a particular strength of our study compared with others is that we were able to include multiple measures of paternal sensitivity and availability, which have rarely been included in such research (but see Grossmann, Grossmann, & Kindler, 2005). Our rationale was that in the early years, the child's attachment security in relation to the primary caregiver is considered to be central, but with maturity, it is the state of mind regarding attachment rather than the quality of a specific caregiving relationship that appears to be critical. Presumably, attachment states of mind develop in the context of early mother-child attachment security but are influenced by relationships beyond infancy, including the father-child relationship (Bretherton, 2005). Therefore, we deemed it important to include assessments of paternal sensitivity, paternal depressive symptoms, and father absence from the home (and ideally we would have had an assessment of father-child attachment security). We found that neither the level nor the change over time in paternal sensitivity was related to changes in attachment security from early childhood (measured in relation to the mother) to late adolescence. However, those who changed from secure to insecure had fathers who were absent a greater proportion of the time than did those who were stably secure. Additionally, the level of both paternal depressive symptoms and the amount of father absence forecast stable insecurity compared with stable security. Altogether, these results suggest to us that the actual or perceived availability of the father, as opposed to the quality of the father's interaction with the child, may have particular significance, at least in terms of stability and change in mother-child attachment over time. That is, it is possible that the father's absence or unavailability has a more indirect impact on the child's security through the effects of such unavailability on the mother's ability to provide sensitive caregiving to her child under stressful circumstances. Although we did not test this model directly, it is worth consideration in future analyses. Future large-scale research also is necessary to examine whether changes in father-child attachment from infancy are forecast by changes in paternal sensitivity over time, a question that goes beyond the data collected in the context of the SECCYD.

Although almost all of the results of this study were in alignment with theoretical expectations, we did find one unexpected result—namely, those who changed from secure to insecure were more likely to be girls, compared with those who were stably secure. We do not have an unequivocal explanation for this finding, but one factor may be that fathers were absent more in the group that became insecure, and girls may be especially vulnerable to father absence in terms of their risk for a variety of deleterious outcomes (see Belsky, Steinberg, & Draper, 1991).

*Strengths and Limitations*

One of the strengths of the present study we have noted in prior chapters is that it contains long-term longitudinal attachment data on a larger number of participants than in any other existing study or, indeed, in all of the other longitudinal studies combined, thereby giving us greater power to detect sources of change and continuity in attachment security over time. Additionally, we were able to take advantage of a wealth of relevant data from the SECCYD to capture both distal and proximal influences on continuity and change. An additional advantage was that all of the predictors of interest were assessed at least three times (and usually many more) in the intervening period between the early childhood and the adult attachment assessments, allowing us to gauge the effects of both level and change in these variables with development. Finally, as noted previously, we were able to include significant information about fathers as well as mothers, which provided a more complete picture of ongoing influences on attachment security than in other studies.

Despite these strengths, there are a number of limitations. First, although the present sample is socioeconomically broad, it was not designed to be high-risk. Therefore, comparing our results with those from higher-risk samples could be problematic. For example, we were not able to evaluate more extreme factors that would be expected to affect attachment security, such as child maltreatment or parental substance abuse. Regardless, our findings were not inconsistent with those from higher-risk samples. An additional limitation is that we did not disaggregate the negative life events score into specific sources of life stress, which may have resulted in an underestimate of the impact of specific events. Further, we did not account for a variety of possible sources of change and continuity in attachment security, such as the quality of close relationships with friends and romantic partners, but chose to focus instead on a more limited but theoretically central set of possible influences. A more comprehensive approach may have yielded different results.

## CONCLUSIONS

Even in the face of these limitations, it is clear that the results of this study contribute significantly to the current literature on lawful change and continuity in attachment security, as well as supporting central tenets of attachment theory. Whereas in this chapter we investigated the impact of actual parental unavailability and lack of sensitivity, in Chapter 6 Roisman et al. explore these actual experiences in relation to the adolescents' perceptions of them. Specifically, Chapter 6 addresses the actual and inferred parenting experiences of those classified as *earned-secure* on the AAI—that is, those who describe below-average childhood experiences with their care-givers, but do so in a coherent manner.

# VI. EARNED-SECURITY IN RETROSPECT: DEPRESSIVE SYMPTOMS, FAMILY STRESS, AND MATERNAL AND PATERNAL SENSITIVITY FROM EARLY CHILDHOOD TO MID-ADOLESCENCE

*Glenn I. Roisman, John D. Haltigan, Katherine C. Haydon, and Cathryn Booth-LaForce*

The gold standard for examining attachment-related change is to do so using prospective data (see Chapter 5). In the absence of such data, however, there is a tradition of using the Adult Attachment Interview (AAI; George et al., 1984–1996) to identify an *earned-secure* group containing participants who produce coherent (i.e., secure) discourse during the AAI but describe relatively unsupportive experiences with one or more primary caregivers during the interview. The major assumption that guides such work, of course, is that such adults actually *encountered* difficult early experiences with primary caregivers and/or had insecure attachments in childhood (see Roisman & Haydon, 2011, for a review).

Early research using a variety of such retrospective operationalizations of attachment-related resilience (see Methods Section) offers evidence that such individuals—like adults who meet criteria for the secure group generally—provide sensitive caregiving to their children (Pearson et al., 1994; Phelps, Belsky, & Crnic, 1998; Saunders, Jacobvitz, Zaccagnino, Beverung, & Hazen, 2011) and share high-quality relationships with their romantic partners (Paley, Cox, Burchinal, & Payne, 1999). However, consistent with the idea that there may be a "price paid" for having struggled through early interpersonal challenges, studies in this area also offer evidence that those who meet criteria for earned-secure attachment status report levels of internalizing distress comparable to or in excess of those typical of individuals in the insecure group (Pearson et al., 1994; Roisman et al., 2002, 2006).

Prospective studies of earned-security take decades and a great deal of human and financial resources to complete successfully. Therefore, a valid

---

Corresponding author: Glenn I. Roisman, Institute of Child Development, University of Minnesota, Minneapolis, MN 55455, email: roism001@umn.edu

*retrospective* assessment of attachment-related resilience would provide a cost-effective means to address crucial questions about the kinds of developmental experiences that might allow adults with difficult early histories to flourish in the years of maturity. Unfortunately, however, the validity of retrospective assessments of earned-security began to be called into question with the publication of Roisman et al.'s (2002) examination of the early histories of such adults within the Minnesota Longitudinal Study of Risk and Adaptation (Sroufe et al., 2005).

Roisman et al. (2002) began by replicating evidence that individuals who met criteria for earned-secure status, retrospectively defined, resolve conflict effectively with their romantic partners despite simultaneously reporting relatively high levels of internalizing symptomatology as young adults (as had been shown in prior studies). However, more importantly, this study was also able to provide what no prior investigation could—the first test of the validity of the earned-secure sub-classification by way of observational data on young adult participants' actual (i.e., observed) experiences with maternal caregivers when the target participants were infants, children, and adolescents. Interestingly—and inconsistent with the view that individuals with earned-secure status experience pervasively negative childhood experiences—such adults were shown in Roisman et al. (2002) to have experienced relatively high-quality maternal caregiving experiences in the years prior to maturity. This publication, based on prospective, longitudinal data from the Minnesota study, was important in raising doubts about the validity of Pearson et al. (1994) retrospective "diagnosis" of earned-security as it failed to provide evidence either that individuals who met criteria for earned-secure status as adults (again, based on retrospective reports about difficult experiences with primary caregivers) either overcame insecure maternal attachments in infancy or otherwise insensitive maternal caregiving in childhood and/or adolescence.

Roisman et al. (2002) presented something of a paradox: If earned-secures actually benefit from supportive early experiences, why do individuals in this group recall relatively negative childhood experiences as adults? One possibility (originally suggested by Phelps et al., 1998) is that the internalizing distress reported by those in the earned-secure group—rather than being a consequence of having overcome negative early attachment-related experiences—might instead play a role in biasing recall of early life events. Consistent with this hypothesis, Roisman et al. (2006) discovered that the valence (but not coherence) of secure adults' narratives about their childhood experiences could be experimentally manipulated using a mood induction procedure.

Above and beyond the value of testing whether the Roisman et al. (2002) results are replicable generally, several important questions remain regarding the developmental origins of retrospectively defined earned-security, which the current chapter sought to address using data from the SECCYD. First, as

Roisman et al. (2002) noted, lacking father-child observational data on the majority of the Minnesota study participants, it was impossible to know whether the supportive maternal care observed among those in the earned-secure group in that investigation took place within the context of a more generally supportive family dynamic in childhood or if it was compensatory—leaving open the possibility that the retrospectively defined earned-secure group actually did, on average, experience poorer quality (i.e., less sensitive) relationships with paternal figures in childhood relative to their counterparts in the continuous-secure group.

Second, Roisman et al. (2002) demonstrated that, despite providing above-average care to their children, the mothers of participants in the earned-secure group reported relatively high levels of depressive symptomatology when their children were young. This finding is also in need of testing for replication as well as examined in relation to whether it extends or not to paternal caregivers. Also, the proper interpretation of this finding would benefit from additional contextualization. As noted earlier, we have typically interpreted the relatively negative depictions provided about their early experiences by those in the earned-secure group as attributable to current and/or chronic mood-related biases, and the depressive symptomatology among their caregivers as additional evidence for familial loading for such symptomatology (e.g., Roisman & Haydon, 2011). However, a non-mutually exclusive alternative is that participants who meet retrospective criteria for earned-secure status benefit from average or higher quality parenting in the context of a broader suite of family stressors. To address this possibility, in this analysis we examined family income-to-needs ratio and father absence in addition to maternal and paternal depressive symptomatology.

Third, some scholars have argued that the original, most commonly used criteria for earned-secure status (i.e., Pearson et al., 1994) are too liberal as they require only evidence in adults' AAI narratives that one primary caregiver provided below average care ($<5$ on the 9-point loving scale and $\geq 5$ on parental rejection, neglect, pressure to achieve, and/or role reversal). Motivated in part by this concern, Main and Goldwyn (1984–1998; see also Main et al., 2003–2008) developed more conservative (yet still retrospective) criteria for assessing earned-secure status. Specifically, they suggest, first, that earned-security should reflect negative experiences with *both* primary caregivers and, second, that such experiences should be highly aversive ($\leq \sim 3$ on the 9-point maternal *and* paternal loving scales). That said, Main and Goldwyn's restrictive criteria require relatively large samples to identify participants who meet criteria for their groups. Moreover, their approach would seem inconsistent with evidence indicating that AAI inferred experiences: (a) are caregiver-specific, not caregiver-general (Chapter 2, this volume) and (b) may well be distributed continuously and not categorically in the population (Chapter 3, this volume; Roisman et al., 2007).

To address these outstanding issues, the core analyses in this chapter compare Pearson's (and Main and Goldwyn's) earned-secure group to participants who met criteria for the insecure and continuous-secure groups. We began by examining the replicability of prior evidence that the earned-secure group (and their caregivers) experience relatively high levels of internalizing symptoms (and possibly other family stressors) by leveraging the multi-informant data available in the SECCYD from infancy to late adolescence. Next, we examined antecedents of earned-security in early mother-child attachment security as well as maternal and paternal sensitivity, observed within and across early childhood, grade school, and adolescence.

Two distinct accounts have emerged in the literature about what one might expect to discover about the observed sensitive caregiving experienced in the years prior to maturity by adults who are retrospectively categorized into the earned-secure group. The hypothesis that motivated work in this area is that the early histories of these participants should be marked by notable and (in the case of the Main and Goldwyn definition) pervasive (i.e., maternal *and* paternal) below-average parenting. The major alternative hypothesis derives from the findings presented by Roisman et al. (2002) based on the Minnesota cohort, which would instead lead to the expectation that those defined using retrospective criteria into the earned-secure group should have experienced levels of early sensitive caregiving comparable to their level of security on the AAI—irrespective of how positively or negatively adults described their early experiences as young adults. In other words, the Roisman et al. (2002) analysis leads to the somewhat paradoxical expectation that those with earned-secure status are likely to have experienced average to above-average sensitivity from maternal and paternal caregivers in childhood.[9]

After presenting analyses based on the Pearson and Main and Goldwyn categories, we introduce an alternative approach to examining the correlates of earned-security that leverages the four AAI dimensions described in Chapter 2 of this volume—dismissing and preoccupied states of mind and maternal and paternal inferred experiences. Specifically, we use a regression-based approach to test two competing models regarding the parenting experienced by those who meet retrospective criteria for earned-secure status in childhood. (Chapter 7 of this volume elaborates on this approach to study the antecedents of AAI dimensions more generally).

On the one hand, depicted in Figure 6.1 on the left-panel is a prototypical illustration of the basic prediction of a model that assumes that those with earned-secure status are accurately and representatively reporting about their early or later experiences with caregivers (Model 1). Model 1 predicts that the association between antecedent sensitivity and adult security will be approximately zero for those who report that their experiences were difficult, but that the association will be notable for those who report that their earlier experiences were supportive (i.e., a significant [in]security in adulthood by

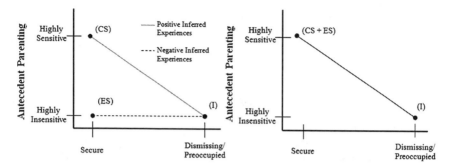

FIGURE 6.1.—The left-hand panel (Model 1 in text) depicts a prototypical interaction plot of simulated data consistent with the assumption that individuals with earned-secure status (retrospectively defined) accurately and representatively report about their childhood and/or adolescent parenting experiences with primary caregivers. The right-hand panel, by contrast, illustrates the main effect (only) prediction, based on the findings from Roisman et al. (2002) that adults who are prototypically secure would be expected to have experienced sensitive caregiving irrespective of whether they describe their early experiences as difficult or supportive (Model 2 in text). Although all variables are distributed continuously above, we use the following three prototypes to anchor readers' interpretation of the interaction plots: CS = continuous-secure group; ES = earned-secure group; I = insecure group.

inferred experiences interaction in the retrodiction of observed quality caregiving).

To elaborate, note in the left panel of Figure 6.1 that those high on security and high on positive inferred experiences are predicted to have had sensitive caregivers (top left). Similarly, those high on insecurity and high on positive inferred experiences are expected to be low on early observed sensitivity (bottom right; the latter individuals are likely to score high on *idealization* of caregivers and thus low on coherence). However, Model 1 diverges notably in its predictions regarding those high on negative inferred experiences. Specifically, those high on security and high on negative childhood inferred experiences are young adults who (the model predicts) actually overcame the early negative experiences they describe in their AAI narratives (i.e., their childhood caregiving is observed to be insensitive). Further, those who are highly insecure (preoccupied or dismissing) and report negative childhood experiences would be predicted to have experienced insensitive parenting in childhood.

In contrast, the data from Roisman et al. (2002) suggest (more parsimoniously) that there should be a main effect of antecedent sensitivity on adult security that is not (strongly) moderated by inferred-experience ratings. In other words, adults who can be characterized as prototypically secure would be expected to have experienced sensitive caregiving

89

irrespective of whether such adults describe their early experiences as difficult or supportive (Model 2, right panel of Figure 6.1).

## METHOD

### Earned- and Continuous-Secure Groups

#### Pearson Groups

After identifying individuals who met criteria for secure ($n = 516$) and insecure ($n = 341$) status, the secure group was further divided into retrospectively defined earned- and continuous-secure groups by following the procedure developed by Pearson et al. (1994). As in previous research on earned security, participants who met criteria for earned-secure status were those who produced coherent discourse during the AAI but whose mother and/or father received scores below 5 on the loving scale and whose mother and/or father received a score of 5 or higher on the rejecting, neglecting, pressure to achieve, and/or role reversal inferred-experience scales. (Participants who met criteria for unresolved/secure status, $n = 8$, were set aside as in prior studies in this literature, although $Ms$ and $SDs$ for this group are presented in relevant tables). The final number of participants in the earned- and continuous-secure groups by this definition was 74 and 434 individuals, respectively.

A set of two-tailed planned comparisons was conducted to examine whether those with earned-secure status reported significantly poorer childhood experiences than did those in the continuous-secure group and had a significantly higher coherence of mind rating than did those in the insecure group. Consistent with previous research, results of planned comparisons in general provided evidence that the Pearson system appropriately differentiated the three security groups with respect to the inferred early experience and narrative coherence ratings. Specifically, results of planned comparisons revealed that those with earned-secure status had significantly poorer inferred-experience ratings than did those in the continuous-secure group (see Table 6.1), $t (93) = 6.15$, $p < .001$ for maternal love; $t (97) = 10.48$, $p < .001$ for paternal love; $t (83) = 4.01$, $p < .001$ for maternal rejection; $t (80) = 6.11$, $p < .001$ for father rejection; $t (78) = 6.06$, $p < .001$ for maternal neglect; and $t (78) = 7.99$, $p < .001$ for father neglect. Participants in the earned-secure group also were scored as significantly more coherent than were those in the insecure group, $t (131) = 20.99$, $p < .001$ for coherence of mind. It should be noted that participants with earned-secure status were rated as significantly less coherent than were those in the continuous-secure group, $t (104) = 2.64$, $p < .05$ for coherence of mind, a finding with precedent in prior studies in this literature (Phelps et al., 1998; Roisman et al., 2002, 2006).

## TABLE 6.1

### Means, Standard Deviations (in parentheses), and Ns of AAI Groups by Key AAI Inferred-Experience Scales and Coherence of Mind

| | Pearson Definition | | | | Main and Goldwyn Definition | | | | |
|---|---|---|---|---|---|---|---|---|---|
| | Non-F | E-S | C-S | U/F | Non-F | E-S | C-S | F-NQ | U/F |
| Maternal love | 3.39 (0.92) 338 | 4.24 (1.33) 74 | 5.25 (1.17) 434 | 4.31 (1.49) 8 | 3.39 (0.92) 338 | 2.78 (0.43) 18 | 6.92 (0.75) 46 | 5.00 (1.07) 444 | 4.31 (1.49) 8 |
| Paternal love | 2.80 (0.97) 316 | 2.78 (1.34) 74 | 4.54 (1.27) 424 | 3.63 (1.51) 8 | 2.80 (0.97) 316 | 2.42 (0.55) 18 | 6.63 (0.77) 45 | 4.11 (1.23) 435 | 3.63 (1.51) 8 |
| Maternal rejection | 2.25 (1.24) 340 | 2.41 (1.37) 74 | 1.75 (0.85) 434 | 2.69 (1.10) 8 | 2.25 (1.24) 340 | 2.67 (1.01) 18 | 1.40 (0.65) 46 | 1.86 (0.98) 444 | 2.69 (1.10) 8 |
| Paternal rejection | 2.55 (1.37) 318 | 3.31 (1.79) 74 | 2.01 (0.91) 424 | 2.34 (1.27) 8 | 2.55 (1.37) 318 | 2.64 (1.41) 18 | 1.64 (0.74) 45 | 2.24 (1.19) 435 | 2.34 (1.27) 8 |
| Maternal neglect | 1.93 (1.25) 340 | 2.30 (1.37) 74 | 1.31 (0.63) 434 | 1.75 (1.17) 8 | 1.93 (1.25) 340 | 2.67 (1.50) 18 | 1.19 (0.39) 46 | 1.43 (0.82) 444 | 1.75 (1.17) 8 |
| Paternal neglect | 2.73 (1.59) 320 | 3.83 (2.07) 74 | 1.88 (0.95) 424 | 2.00 (1.69) 8 | 2.73 (1.59) 320 | 3.67 (1.57) 18 | 1.33 (0.56) 45 | 2.19 (1.37) 435 | 2.00 (1.69) 8 |
| Coherence of mind | 3.59 (0.96) 341 | 5.72 (0.75) 74 | 5.97 (0.81) 434 | 5.00 (0.54) 8 | 3.59 (0.96) 341 | 5.50 (0.71) 18 | 6.91 (0.69) 46 | 5.85 (0.75) 444 | 5.00 (0.54) 8 |

*Note.* Non-F = insecure; E-S = earned-secure; C-S = continuous-secure; U/F = unresolved/secure; F-NQ = secure case that does not qualify for either earned- or continuous-secure group according to Main and Goldwyn scoring system. Scales range from 1 to 9.

In addition, the inferred-experience ratings of adults with earned-secure status, as expected, were in general comparable to or suggestive of more difficult experiences with caregivers compared with those in the insecure group (see Table 6.1): $t$ (89) $= 5.23$, $p < .001$ for maternal love; $t$ (92) $= 0.14$, $p = .89$ for paternal love; $t$ (101) $= 0.95$, $p = .34$ for maternal rejection; $t$ (94) $= 3.45$, $p < .01$ for paternal rejection; $t$ (101) $= 2.12$, $p < .05$ for maternal neglect; and $t$ (94) $= 4.32$, $p < .001$ for paternal neglect. In fact, all but one of the significant differences observed between these two groups revealed that those with earned-secure status actually indicated significantly *greater* maternal neglect and paternal rejection and neglect on average than did those in the insecure group (the paternal neglect finding has precedent in Paley et al., 1999; Roisman et al., 2002). Only one planned comparison suggested that participants who met criteria for earned-security had inferred-experience ratings that might not be comparable to or worse than participants in the insecure group: Echoing data presented in virtually every study of earned-security published (Phelps et al., 1998; Paley et al., 1999; Roisman et al., 2002, 2006), the earned-secure group had a higher mean on the mother loving scale than did the insecure group. (Note that the comparisons reported above do not assume equal variances across groups as Levene's test of homogeneity of variances was significant for these analyses. In all cases estimated degrees of freedom are rounded to the nearest whole number. Degrees of freedom vary in analyses regarding experience scales as in several cases individuals were assigned "cannot rate" codes and therefore dropped from analysis; see Table 6.1).

### Main and Goldwyn Groups

Earned-security also was operationalized using the more conservative criteria outlined by Main and Goldwyn in more recent editions of their unpublished AAI coding manual. More specifically, individuals with earned-secure status are defined by Main as participants who receive loving scores less than or equal to 2.5 for both caregivers. (As the Main and Goldwyn scoring system provides no guidance as to what kinds of experiences qualify for between-scale point ratings, AAI coders in the present study did not use half points in their ratings. As such, we adjusted this criterion to 3 in the current analysis). In contrast, by the Main and Goldwyn criteria the continuous-secure group has mother and father loving scores averaging 6.5 or greater. The resulting sample of individuals in the earned- and continuous-secure groups was 18 and 46 participants, respectively (the 8 participants with unresolved/secure status in our sample were excluded from either group as they could not be described unambiguously as appropriately placed in the secure or insecure group). Relevant to the utility of the Main and Goldwyn system is that the vast majority of participants who met criteria for security in our study (86%; $n = 444$) could not be classified into *either* the continuous- or earned-secure group by the Main and Goldwyn criteria (for purposes of comparison, 54% fell into this secure-not classifiable group in the Roisman et al., 2006, mood induction study, and 72% in the Roisman et al., 2002, investigation of the Minnesota sample).

By definition, participants in the earned-secure group received inferred-experience ratings indicating less maternal and paternal love than did those in the continuous-secure group. They also received scores suggesting significantly more maternal and paternal rejection and neglect than did continuous-secures (all $ps < .001$; contact first author for details).[10] Compared with those with insecure status, the earned-secure group also tended to be rated as reporting significantly lower levels of maternal love, $t (26) = 5.34$, $p < .001$, and less (albeit non-significantly) paternal love, $t (376) = 1.69$, $p = .09$, as well as significantly higher levels of paternal neglect, $t (19) = 2.47$, $p < .05$. Keeping in mind the limited statistical power of these analyses, similar effects were obtained for maternal rejection, $t (20) = 1.69$, $p = .11$, and maternal neglect, $t (18) = 2.06$, $p = .06$ (continuous-secure group > insecure group). The paternal rejection scores of those in the earned-secure and insecure groups, however, were not distinguishable, $t (19) = 0.27$, $p = .79$. Also of note, although the earned-secure group's coherence of mind ratings were significantly higher than those of the insecure group, $t (20) = 10.96$, $p < .001$, their coherence ratings were significantly ($t [31] = 7.23$, $p < .001$) and substantially ($d = 2.01$, $r = 0.71$) lower than those in the continuous-secure group. (All analyses above with the exception of paternal love do not assume homogeneity of variance; see Table 6.1 for $Ms$ and $SDs$).

### Participant Internalizing Symptomatology

Participant internalizing symptomatology from childhood to late adolescence was assessed using the internalizing scale of the Child Behavior Checklist obtained using the parent (CBCL) and teacher-report (TRF) versions (Achenbach, 1991a; Achenbach & Edelbrock, 1986; Achenbach, Edelbrock, & Howell, 1987). Participant self-reported internalizing symptomatology also was assessed in adolescence using the Youth Self Report (YSR) of the Child Behavior Checklist (Achenbach, 1991b). T-scores were used. In the current analyses, maternal reports on the CBCL were used from all assessment points at which mother-reported CBCL data were acquired: 24, 36, and 54 months; Kindergarten, Grades 1, 3, 4, 5, and 6; and ages 15 and 18. Teacher reports were used from the following assessment points: Kindergarten and Grades 1, 2, 3, 4, 5, and 6. Youth self-reports were obtained at ages 15 and 18. Scores within informant were averaged across time yielding a total internalizing score for each informant ($\alpha = .92$ for mothers, $\alpha = .64$ for teachers, and $\alpha = .69$ for self-report).

## Indicators of Family Stress

### Parental Depressive Symptomatology

For this chapter, self-reported maternal and paternal depressive symptom composites were created using every assessment point at which the CES-D (Radloff, 1977) was acquired: 1, 6, 15, 24, 36, 54 months; Grades 1, 3, 5, and 6; and ages 15 and 18 years for mothers and 54 months; Grades 1, 3, 5, and 6; and ages 15 and 18 years for fathers (see Chapter 5, this volume, for additional details regarding the CES-D). Scores were averaged across time yielding mean maternal ($\alpha = .90$) and paternal ($\alpha = .87$) depression scores.

### Family Income-to-Needs

Family financial resources were operationalized as income-to-needs (see Chapter 5), computed separately for every assessment point at which relevant data were acquired (1, 6, 15, 24, 36, 54 months; Grades 1, 3, 4, 5, 6; age 15) and averaged over time.

### Father Absence

The proportion of data-collection contacts for which the father was not living in the household was computed from 1 month of age to 15 years (1, 3, 6, 9, 12, 15, 24, 36, 42, 46, 50, 54, 60, and 66 months; Kindergarten-Fall [F], Kindergarten-Spring [S]; Grades 1F, 1S, 2F, 2S, 3, 4, 5, 6, 7; ages 14 and 15).

## Antecedent Early Mother–Child Attachment and Parental Sensitivity

### Antecedent Early Mother–Child Attachment Security

The proportion of times secure variable from Chapter 4 (this volume) was used in the current analysis.

### Antecedent Maternal and Paternal Sensitivity

Measures of maternal and paternal sensitivity were obtained from videotaped semi-structured play interactions from early childhood through adolescence (see Chapter 5). Maternal ($\alpha = .83$) and paternal ($\alpha = .70$) ratings were averaged over time to create total summary measures of antecedent maternal and paternal sensitivity. Maternal and paternal ratings also were averaged within early childhood (6–54 months for maternal ratings; 54 months only for paternal ratings), grade school (G1–G5), and adolescence (age 15) for maternal and paternal caregivers.[11]

## RESULTS

In this chapter we employed the analytic template of prior studies of retrospectively defined earned-security (e.g., Pearson et al., 1994; Roisman et al., 2002) in that the key analyses are planned comparisons of the Pearson (followed by Main and Goldwyn) earned-secure group with the continuous-secure and insecure groups. Although ANOVAs with post-hoc follow-ups are to be preferred in exploratory research, planned comparisons are ideal when focusing on a well-defined set of a priori contrasts of interest, as was the case here. Given that there were three key groups in each analysis (although we report means and *SD*s for all groups depicted in Table 6.1)—and because a maximum of *k*-1 comparisons can be completed per outcome variable using planned comparisons (where *k* is defined as the number of levels in the independent variable)—each set of analyses described below contrasts the earned-secure group with the other two security groups (e.g., earned-secure group vs. continuous-secure group, earned-secure group vs. insecure group). In addition to *t*-statistics and their associated *p*-values, standardized differences between means (Cohen's *d*; effect sizes) were calculated and are indicated for all contrasts. Note finally that *n*s vary across analyses to maximize data available from each assessment (Table 6.2) and that when (as indicated) Levene's test was significant, we report below estimated *df*s, *t*-, and *p*-values that do not assume homogeneity of variance across groups.

As we have already discussed, both the Pearson and the Main and Goldwyn earned-security groupings tend to result in earned- and continuous-secure groups that differ in mean levels of security (i.e., coherence of mind; see Table 6.1). Moreover, the Main and Goldwyn system results in a sizable proportion of participants with secure status being excluded from analysis, and we have demonstrated previously no evidence for a categorical distinction between earned- and continuous-security (Roisman et al., 2007; Chapter 3, this volume). As such, we conclude the Results section with an illustration (suggested in Roisman & Haydon, 2011; but also see Reiner & Spangler, 2010) of how questions related to the correlates of earned-security can be addressed using the four dimensions demonstrated to underlie individual differences in AAI narratives (see Chapters 2 and 3, this volume) in the context of a moderated regression framework.

## Mother-, Self-, and Teacher-Reports of Internalizing Symptomatology

### Pearson Groups

Analyses presented in Table 6.2 revealed, as expected, that participants in the earned-secure group showed higher levels of internalizing symptomatology relative to those in the continuous-secure group, as assessed both via mother- and self-report. Specifically, mother-reports on the CBCL of participants' internalizing distress averaged from 24 months through 18 years indicated that those with earned-secure status had higher levels of internalizing distress than did those in the continuous-secure group, $t$ (844) = 1.96, $p = .05$, $d = 0.25$, and they were not discriminable from the insecure group, $t$ (844) = 0.98, $p = .33$, $d = 0.13$. Similarly, participants

## TABLE 6.2

MEANS, STANDARD DEVIATIONS (IN PARENTHESES), AND Ns OF AAI GROUPS BY PARTICIPANT INTERNALIZING SYMPTOMS, FAMILY STRESS, AND ANTECEDENT PARENTAL CAREGIVING

| | Pearson Definition | | | | Main and Goldwyn Definition | | | | |
|---|---|---|---|---|---|---|---|---|---|
| | Non-F | E-S | CS | U/F | Non-F | E-S | CS | F-NQ | U/F |
| **Participant internalizing symptoms** | | | | | | | | | |
| Mother-report (CBCL) | 48.40 (7.20) 339 | 49.30 (6.95) 74 | 47.55 (7.04) 434 | 50.57 (7.78) 8 | 48.40 (7.20) 339 | 48.41 (5.58) 18 | 48.50 (8.85) 46 | 47.71 (6.90) 444 | 50.57 (7.78) 8 |
| Teacher-report (TRF) | 50.29 (5.68) 337 | 49.54 (5.83) 73 | 48.83 (5.25) 430 | 54.27 (6.89) 8 | 50.29 (5.68) 337 | 53.01 (5.65) 18 | 48.00 (3.97) 46 | 48.86 (5.39) 439 | 54.27 (6.89) 8 |
| Self-report (YSR) | 49.46 (9.94) 339 | 50.85 (10.88) 74 | 47.80 (9.07) 430 | 50.82 (11.50) 8 | 49.46 (9.94) 339 | 54.81 (10.24) 18 | 47.54 (9.16) 45 | 48.06 (9.32) 438 | 50.82 (11.50) 8 |
| **Indicators of family stress** | | | | | | | | | |
| Maternal depression (CES-D) | 9.45 (6.25) 341 | 10.59 (7.18) 74 | 8.61 (6.18) 434 | 12.54 (5.65) 8 | 9.45 (6.25) 341 | 13.26 (8.87) 18 | 8.47 (7.41) 46 | 8.76 (6.08) 444 | 12.54 (5.65) 8 |
| Paternal depression (CES-D) | 9.31 (6.44) 306 | 9.27 (6.86) 61 | 7.18 (5.46) 402 | 10.99 (6.94) 7 | 9.31 (6.44) 306 | 7.64 (5.79) 15 | 7.35 (6.80) 45 | 7.46 (5.58) 403 | 10.99 (6.94) 7 |
| Family income-to-needs | 3.65 (2.67) 341 | 3.79 (2.86) 74 | 4.60 (3.45) 433 | 2.06 (1.34) 8 | 3.65 (2.67) 341 | 3.02 (1.95) 18 | 6.00 (3.68) 46 | 4.39 (3.35) 443 | 2.06 (1.34) 8 |
| Proportion father absence | 31% 341 | 28% 74 | 15% 434 | 39% 8 | 31% 341 | 28% 18 | 5% 46 | 18% 444 | 39% 8 |
| **Early mother–child attachment** | | | | | | | | | |
| Proportion secure (15–36 months) | 56% 327 | 60% 70 | 63% 420 | 48% 8 | 56% 327 | 53% 18 | 58% 43 | 63% 429 | 48% 8 |
| **Antecedent maternal caregiving** | | | | | | | | | |
| Maternal sensitivity (Overall) | −0.33 (1.08) 341 | −0.01 (0.93) 74 | 0.28 (0.85) 434 | −0.69 (1.34) 8 | −0.33 (1.08) 341 | 0.01 (1.43) 18 | 0.65 (0.57) 46 | 0.20 (0.85) 444 | −0.69 (1.34) 8 |
| Maternal sensitivity (Early) | −0.29 (1.09) 339 | −0.05 (0.88) 74 | 0.24 (0.87) 433 | −0.45 (1.49) 8 | −0.29 (1.09) 339 | −0.16 (1.41) 18 | 0.56 (0.69) 46 | 0.18 (0.86) 443 | −0.45 (1.49) 8 |
| Maternal sensitivity (Grade) | −0.30 (1.08) 329 | −0.01 (1.01) 74 | 0.25 (0.85) 427 | −0.65 (1.18) 8 | −0.30 (1.08) 329 | 0.18 (1.21) 18 | 0.60 (0.69) 46 | 0.17 (0.87) 437 | −0.65 (1.18) 8 |
| Maternal sensitivity (Adol.) | −0.26 (1.07) 285 | 0.18 (0.98) 63 | 0.18 (0.90) 385 | −0.99 (1.06) 7 | −0.26 (1.07) 285 | 0.46 (0.83) 16 | 0.34 (0.83) 42 | 0.15 (0.90) 390 | −0.99 (1.06) 7 |
| **Antecedent paternal caregiving** | | | | | | | | | |
| Paternal sensitivity (Overall) | −0.21 (1.06) 289 | −0.06 (1.20) 60 | 0.16 (0.89) 390 | −0.04 (1.26) 6 | −0.21 (1.06) 289 | 0.36 (0.73) 13 | 0.49 (0.76) 44 | 0.09 (0.95) 393 | −0.04 (1.26) 6 |
| Paternal sensitivity (Early) | −0.18 (1.04) 206 | −0.09 (1.31) 40 | 0.12 (0.91) 319 | 0.44 (0.56) 4 | −0.18 (1.04) 206 | 0.30 (0.95) 12 | 0.26 (0.89) 37 | 0.07 (0.97) 310 | 0.44 (0.56) 4 |
| Paternal sensitivity (Grade) | −0.22 (1.09) 263 | −0.11 (1.12) 58 | 0.17 (0.87) 371 | −0.03 (1.41) 6 | −0.22 (1.09) 263 | 0.38 (0.64) 13 | 0.44 (0.77) 44 | 0.09 (0.93) 372 | −0.03 (1.41) 6 |
| Paternal sensitivity (Adol.) | −0.15 (1.01) 178 | 0.08 (1.05) 39 | 0.10 (0.98) 270 | −0.72 (0.99) 3 | −0.15 (1.01) 178 | 0.26 (0.75) 6 | 0.39 (0.79) 36 | 0.05 (1.01) 267 | −0.72 (0.99) 3 |

*Note.* Non-F = insecure; E-S = earned-secure; CS = continuous-secure; U/F = unresolved/secure; F-NQ = secure cases that did not qualify for either earned- or continuous-secure group according to Main and Goldwyn scoring system.

retrospectively defined into the earned-secure group rated themselves as more distressed than did those in the continuous-secure group in adolescence (mean of YSR scores at ages 15 and 18 years), $t(840) = 2.53$, $p < .05$, $d = 0.30$, and they could not be distinguished from those with insecure status, $t(840) = 1.13$, $p = .26$, $d = 0.13$. That said, group comparisons of teacher-reports of participants' internalizing symptomatology revealed no significant group differences (participants with retrospective earned-secure status were not statistically distinguishable from either the continuous-secure, $t[837] = 1.03$, $p = .30$, $d = 0.13$, or the insecure group, $t[837] = 1.06$, $p = .29$, $d = 0.13$, on teacher reports of participants' internalizing problems).

### Main and Goldwyn Groups

The general pattern of findings was similar when we turned to the earned-secure, continuous-secure, and insecure groups based on the Main and Goldwyn definition in the AAI coding manual. Specifically, although the mother reports of internalizing symptomatology failed to yield significant differences among the three groups (earned-secure group vs. continuous-secure group, $t[20] = 0.04$, $p = .97$, $d = 0.01$; earned-secure group vs. insecure group, $t[47] = 0.00$, $p = .99$, $d = 0.00$; statistics do not assume homogeneity of variances), the earned-secure group self-reported higher levels of internalizing problems than did both the continuous-secure group, $t(399) = 2.64$, $p < .05$, $d = 0.75$, and the insecure group, $t(399) = 2.24$, $p < .05$, $d = 0.53$; and had significantly higher levels of teacher-reported internalizing problems than did both the continuous-secure group, $t(398) = 3.27$, $p < .01$, $d = 1.03$, and the insecure group, $t(398) = 2.04$, $p < .05$, $d = 0.48$.

### Indicators of Family Stress: Parental Depression, Income-to-needs, and Paternal Absence

#### Pearson Groups

As already noted, Roisman et al. (2002) reported that the mothers of participants in the Pearson earned-secure group in the Minnesota Longitudinal Study of Risk and Adaptation reported elevated levels of depressive symptomatology. Analyses presented in Table 6.2 replicate this result in the SECCYD. Specifically, averaged over (participant age) 1 month through 18 years, maternal caregivers of participants in the retrospective earned-secure group reported significantly more depressive symptomatology than did mothers of participants in the continuous-secure group, $t(846) = 2.50$, $p < .05$, $d = 0.30$, and were not discriminable from the mothers of participants in the insecure group, $t(846) = 1.41$, $p = .16$, $d = 0.17$. An identical pattern emerged for paternal caregivers' reports of their own depressive symptomatology in that the paternal caregivers of participants in the earned-secure group reported higher levels of internalizing problems than did the paternal caregivers of participants in the continuous-secure group, $t(72) = 2.28$, $p < .05$, $d = 0.34$, but were not discriminable from the paternal caregivers of participants in the insecure group, $t(82) = 0.04$, $p = .97$, $d = 0.01$. The results obtained for family income-to-needs (1 month through 15 years) paralleled those for the depression findings above. Specifically, the earned-secure group had lower income-to-needs than did the continuous-secure group, $t(113) = 2.20$, $p < .05$, $d = 0.26$, but were not discriminable from the insecure group, $t(102) = 0.36$, $p = .72$, $d = 0.05$. Similarly, the earned-secure group was more likely to experience the absence of their fathers than was the continuous-secure group, $t(89) = 2.94$, $p < .01$, $d = 0.38$, and the earned-secure group was comparable to the insecure group in this regard, $t(107) = 0.61$, $p = .54$, $d = 0.08$. (Analyses do not assume equal variances).

### Main and Goldwyn Groups

Similarly, maternal reports of their own depressive symptomatology also were elevated among the earned-secure group by the Main and Goldwyn definition (see Table 6.2), both relative to the continuous-secure group, $t(402) = 2.64$, $p < .01$, $d = 0.59$, and the insecure group, $t(402) = 2.41$, $p < .05$, $d = 0.50$. However, a significant difference did not emerge between the earned- and continuous-secure group, $t(363) = 0.15$, $p = .88$, $d = 0.05$, or the earned-secure and insecure group, $t(363) = 0.98$, $p = .33$, $d = 0.27$, on paternal reports of their own depressive symptomatology. That said, the earned-secure group had considerably lower income-to-needs than did the continuous-secure group, $t(56) = 4.19$, $p < .001$, $d = 1.01$, but were not discriminable from the insecure group, $t(21) = 1.33$, $p = .20$, $d = 0.27$. Similarly, the earned-secure group was more likely to experience an absent father than was the continuous-secure group, $t(20) = 2.82$, $p = .01$, $d = 0.87$, and were comparable to the insecure group in this regard, $t(19) = 0.35$, $p = .73$, $d = 0.08$. (The income-to-needs and father absence analyses do not assume equal variances).

### Antecedent Early Mother-Child Attachment and Parental Sensitivity

#### Pearson Groups

As reported in Table 6.2, the earned-secure group was not discriminable from the continuous-secure group, $t(92) = 0.84$, $p = .40$, $d = 0.10$, or the insecure group, $t(106) = 0.93$, $p = .35$, $d = 0.13$, on early attachment security (i.e., proportion of times secure in early childhood; Note that these analyses do not assume homogeneity of variances). In terms of antecedent maternal sensitivity (assessed from 6 months through 15 years), the earned-secure group on average received maternal caregiving at the sample mean ($z$-score close to zero), of significantly higher quality than did the insecure group, $t(120) = 2.64$, $p < .01$, $d = 0.32$, and of significantly lower quality than did the continuous-secure group, $t$ (95) $= 2.49$, $p < .05$, $d = 0.33$, in this omnibus analysis in which homogeneity of variances was not assumed. A similar pattern emerged when maternal sensitivity was broken down by developmental period (early childhood, grade school, adolescence) in that the earned-secure group experienced levels of maternal sensitivity at approximately the same mean for maternal sensitivity in early childhood and grade school, although they experienced above average maternal sensitivity by the age 15 assessment). More specifically, in early childhood, the earned-secure group experienced significantly higher levels of maternal sensitivity than did the insecure group, $t$ (126) $= 2.02$, $p < .05$, $d = 0.24$, and significantly lower levels than did the continuous-secure group, $t$ (99) $= 2.59$, $p < .05$, $d = 0.33$; in grade school they experienced significantly higher levels of maternal sensitivity than did the insecure group, $t$ (114) $= 2.25$, $p < .05$, $d = 0.28$, and significantly lower levels than did the continuous-secure group, $t$ (92) $= 2.06$, $p < .05$, $d = 0.28$; and in adolescence they experienced significantly higher levels of maternal sensitivity than did the insecure group, $t$ (730) $= 3.29$, $p < .01$, $d = 0.43$, and levels of maternal sensitivity comparable to the continuous-secure group, $t$ (730) $= 0.03$, $p = .97$, $d = 0.00$. (All maternal sensitivity analyses broken down by developmental period except those focused on maternal sensitivity at age 15 years do not assume homogeneity of variances.)

With respect to paternal sensitivity, the earned-secure group once again was observed to have experienced average caregiving for the sample, although they were not discriminable from either the insecure group, $t$ (79) $= 0.89$, $p = .38$, $d = 0.13$, or the continuous-secure group, $t$ (69) $= 1.38$, $p = .17$, $d = 0.21$ (homogeneity of variances not assumed). A similar pattern emerged when paternal sensitivity was examined by developmental period (early childhood, grade school, adolescence) in that no significant differences emerged between the earned-secure and insecure groups on paternal sensitivity experienced in early childhood, $t$ (49) $= 0.43$, $p = .67$, $d = 0.08$, grade school, $t$ (82) $= 0.71$, $p = .48$, $d = 0.10$, or adolescence, $t$ (484) $= 1.31$, $p = .19$, $d = 0.22$, or between the earned- and continuous-secure groups in early childhood, $t$ (44) $= 0.99$, $p = .33$, $d = 0.19$, grade school, $t$ (68) $= 1.80$, $p = .08$, $d = 0.28$, or adolescence, $t$ (484) $= 0.11$, $p = .91$, $d = 0.02$. (Note that homogeneity of variances was not assumed except in the analysis of paternal sensitivity in adolescence.)

### Main and Goldwyn Groups

As with the Pearson groups, the Main and Goldwyn earned-secure group was no more or less likely than the continuous-secure group, $t$ (385) $= 0.58$, $p = .54$, $d = 0.18$, or the insecure group, $t$ (385) $= 0.39$, $p = .69$, $d = 0.10$, to have had secure attachments in infancy (proportion of times secure). Moreover, Main and Goldwyn's earned-secure group was observed to have experienced maternal sensitivity (assessed from 6 months through Age 15 years) at approximately the sample mean, although they were not discriminable from the insecure group on maternal sensitivity, $t(18) = 1.01$, $p = .33$, $d = 0.27$, and received marginally less sensitive caregiving than did the continuous-secure group, $t(19) = 1.84$, $p = .08$, $d = 0.59$. (Note that statistics reported do not assume homogeneity of variances.)

Looking more closely by developmental period revealed the only evidence from this study suggesting that the earned-secure group (by any retrospective definition) experienced below-average maternal caregiving that was comparable to the experiences of the insecure group, and this happened in the early-childhood period, $t(18) = 0.39$, $p = .70$, $d = 0.10$. (In this analysis, the earned-secure group experienced lower levels of maternal sensitivity than did the continuous-secure group, $t[20] = 2.06$, $p = .052$, $d = 0.65$.) In contrast, in grade school the earned-secure group experienced maternal sensitivity at levels not significantly distinguishable from the continuous-secure group, $t(21) = 1.39$, $p = .18$, $d = 0.43$, or the insecure group, $t(19) = 1.64$, $p = .12$, $d = 0.42$; in adolescence the earned-secure group experienced maternal sensitivity comparable to the continuous-secure group, $t(340) = 0.37$, $p = .71$, $d = 0.14$, but significantly higher than the insecure group, $t(340) = 2.67$, $p < .01$, $d = 0.75$. (Levene's test was significant for the early childhood and grade school analyses, but not the analysis of maternal sensitivity in adolescence.)

In contrast, the earned-secure group by the Main and Goldwyn definition experienced above average paternal sensitivity (as assessed from 54 months through adolescence), which was significantly higher than paternal sensitivity towards participants in the insecure group, $t(343) = 1.98$, $p < .05$, $d = 0.63$, and at levels comparable to the continuous-secure group, $t(343) = 0.40$, $p = .59$, $d = 0.17$. When paternal sensitivity was examined by developmental period (early childhood, grade school, adolescence), these differences were most apparent in the grade-school years. Specifically, in early childhood, the earned-secure group was comparable to the insecure group, $t(252) = 1.58$, $p = .11$, $d = 0.48$, and the continuous-secure group, $t(252) = 0.12$, $p = .90$, $d = 0.04$, in paternal sensitivity. In grade school, the earned-secure group experienced significantly higher levels of paternal sensitivity than did the insecure group, $t(317) = 2.04$, $p < .05$, $d = 0.67$, and levels comparable to the continuous-secure group, $t(317) = 0.19$, $p = .85$, $d = 0.08$. Lastly, in adolescence the earned-secure group experienced levels of paternal sensitivity not significantly different than the insecure group, $t(217) = 1.02$, $p = .31$, $d = 0.46$, or the continuous-secure group, $t(217) = 0.30$, $p = .77$, $d = 0.17$.

## A Moderated Regression Approach

As noted earlier in this chapter, several serious problems challenge the unambiguous interpretation of the correlates of earned-security using categories including, but not limited to the fact that the earned- and continuous-secure groups are not equilibrated on coherence (the earned-secure group is less secure than the continuous-secure group, particularly by Main and Goldwyn's definition). Moreover, as Chapters 2 and 3 of this volume demonstrate (see also Haydon et al., 2012; Roisman et al., 2007), the assumption that inferred experience is distributed categorically (as assumed by both Pearson and Main & Goldwyn) or is caregiver-general (implied by the Main & Goldwyn definition of earned-security) is not supported by the data.

A different, and we believe superior, analytic approach to examining the correlates of earned-security is to use the four AAI dimensions described in Chapter 2: dismissing and preoccupied states of mind (we use Kobak's [1993] prototype scores below in primary analyses) and maternal and paternal inferred experiences (from the Chapter 2 confirmatory factor analysis). If it is true that high levels of difficult maternal and/or paternal inferred experiences accurately and representatively portray the reality of early experiences for individuals who are prototypically secure (individuals who receive low scores on the dismissing and/or preoccupied state-of-mind scales), this focused prediction can be tested in a straightforward manner using moderated multiple regression analyses. Specifically, if individuals who can be retrospectively characterized as having earned-secure status are reporting representatively about their difficult early experiences, the predicted negative association between early maternal (paternal) sensitivity and dismissing/preoccupied states of mind should be significantly weaker (and indeed close to zero) for individuals whose maternal (paternal) experiences were rated to be of lower quality. In other words, we would expect a significant Dismissing/Preoccupied × Maternal (Paternal) Inferred Experience interaction to be retrodictive of observed antecedent maternal (paternal) sensitivity.

To test this prediction, we estimated two omnibus regression equations (see Table 6.3). In the first, observed *maternal* sensitivity (6 months through 15 years) was regressed on (i.e., retrodicted by) dismissing states of mind, preoccupied states of mind, and *maternal* inferred experience (step 1) and then (in step 2) these three variables and the Dismissing × Maternal Inferred Experience and the Preoccupied × Maternal Inferred Experience interaction terms (all variables were standardized prior to analysis). The full omnibus model retrodicting maternal sensitivity was significant $F(5, 851) = 28.11$, $p < .001$; $R^2 = 0.14$. As can be seen from Table 6.3, however, neither of the interaction terms was statistically significant, although dismissing and preoccupied states of mind were associated negatively with earlier maternal sensitivity (for additional discussion of the developmental origins of the four AAI dimensions see Chapter 7, this volume). Moreover, when maternal sensitivity was broken down by developmental period (early childhood, grade school, adolescence), a similar pattern of results was obtained.

## TABLE 6.3

Results of Regression Models Predicting Maternal and Paternal Sensitivity From the Combination of State-of-Mind Scales, Maternal and Paternal Inferred-Experience Scales, and Relevant Interactions

**Maternal Sensitivity**

| | B (SE) | β | p | $\Delta R^2$; p |
|---|---|---|---|---|
| **Overall (6 months–15 years)** | | | | |
| Step 1 | | | | .14; .00 |
| Dismissing | −.29 (.04) | −.29 | .00 | |
| Preoccupied | −.15 (.04) | −.15 | .00 | |
| Maternal Inferred Exp | −.07 (.04) | −.07 | .13 | |
| Step 2 | | | | .00; .41 |
| Dismissing | −.29 (.04) | −.29 | .00 | |
| Preoccupied | −.16 (.04) | −.16 | .00 | |
| Maternal Inferred Exp | −.07 (.04) | −.07 | .08 | |
| Dismissing × Maternal Exp | .02 (.04) | .02 | .59 | |
| Preoccupied × Maternal Exp | .04 (.03) | .04 | .24 | |
| **Early childhood (6–54 months)** | | | | |
| Step 1 | | | | .11; .00 |
| Dismissing | −.26 (.04) | −.26 | .00 | |
| Preoccupied | −.15 (.04) | −.15 | .00 | |
| Maternal Inferred Exp | −.04 (.04) | −.04 | .34 | |
| Step 2 | | | | .00; .21 |
| Dismissing | −.26 (.04) | −.26 | .00 | |
| Preoccupied | −.16 (.04) | −.16 | .00 | |
| Maternal Inferred Exp | −.05 (.04) | −.05 | .23 | |
| Dismissing × Maternal Exp | .05 (.04) | .05 | .17 | |
| Preoccupied × Maternal Exp | .03 (.03) | .04 | .30 | |
| **Grade School (G1–G5)** | | | | |
| Step 1 | | | | .11; .00 |
| Dismissing | −.22 (.04) | −.22 | .00 | |
| Preoccupied | −.11 (.04) | −.11 | .01 | |
| Maternal Inferred Exp | −.11 (.04) | −.11 | .01 | |

**Paternal Sensitivity**

| | B (SE) | β | p | $\Delta R^2$; p |
|---|---|---|---|---|
| **Overall (54 months–15 years)** | | | | |
| Step 1 | | | | .04; .00 |
| Dismissing | −.11 (.04) | −.11 | .01 | |
| Preoccupied | −.06 (.04) | −.06 | .14 | |
| Paternal Inferred Exp | −.10 (.04) | −.10 | .02 | |
| Step 2 | | | | .01; .07 |
| Dismissing | −.12 (.04) | −.12 | .00 | |
| Preoccupied | −.08 (.04) | −.08 | .05 | |
| Paternal Inferred Exp | −.09 (.04) | −.09 | .06 | |
| Dismissing × Paternal Exp | .08 (.04) | .07 | .06 | |
| Preoccupied × Paternal Exp | .05 (.04) | .05 | .21 | |
| **Early childhood (54 mo)** | | | | |
| Step 1 | | | | .02; .01 |
| Dismissing | −.08 (.05) | −.08 | .08 | |
| Preoccupied | −.05 (.05) | −.05 | .29 | |
| Paternal Inferred Exp | −.07 (.05) | −.07 | .20 | |
| Step 2 | | | | .00; .36 |
| Dismissing | −.09 (.05) | −.09 | .06 | |
| Preoccupied | −.07 (.05) | −.06 | .20 | |
| Paternal Inferred Exp | −.05 (.05) | −.05 | .36 | |
| Dismissing × Paternal Exp | .07 (.05) | .06 | .20 | |
| Preoccupied × Paternal Exp | .03 (.05) | .03 | .57 | |
| **Grade School (G1–G5)** | | | | |
| Step 1 | | | | .04; .00 |
| Dismissing | −.13 (.04) | −.13 | .00 | |
| Preoccupied | −.03 (.04) | −.03 | .54 | |
| Paternal Inferred Exp | −.09 (.05) | −.09 | .04 | |

(Continued)

TABLE 6.3. (Continued)

| | Maternal Sensitivity | | | | Paternal Sensitivity | | | |
|---|---|---|---|---|---|---|---|---|
| | B (SE) | β | p | ΔR²; p | B (SE) | β | p | ΔR²; p |
| Step 2 | | | | .00; .50 | | | | .01; .18 |
| Dismissing | −.22 (.04) | −.22 | .00 | | −.14 (.04) | −.14 | .00 | |
| Preoccupied | −.12 (.04) | −.12 | .00 | | −.05 (.04) | −.05 | .27 | |
| Maternal/Paternal Inferred Exp | −.12 (.04) | −.12 | .01 | | −.08 (.05) | −.08 | .10 | |
| Dismissing × Maternal/Paternal Exp | −.02 (.04) | −.02 | .54 | | .06 (.04) | .05 | .19 | |
| Preoccupied × Maternal/Paternal Exp | .03 (.03) | .04 | .30 | | .05 (.04) | .05 | .20 | |
| Adolescence (15 years) | | | | | | | | |
| Step 1 | | | | .06; .00 | | | | .03; .00 |
| Dismissing | −.24 (.04) | −.23 | .00 | | −.09 (.05) | −.09 | .08 | |
| Preoccupied | −.12 (.04) | −.12 | .01 | | −.13 (.06) | −.11 | .02 | |
| Maternal/Paternal Inferred Exp | .06 (.05) | .05 | .25 | | −.04 (.05) | −.04 | .48 | |
| Step 2 | | | | .00; .76 | | | | .02; .02 |
| Dismissing | −.23 (.04) | −.23 | .00 | | −.10 (.05) | −.10 | .05 | |
| Preoccupied | −.12 (.05) | −.11 | .01 | | −.14 (.06) | −.12 | .01 | |
| Maternal/Paternal Inferred Exp | .06 (.05) | .06 | .24 | | .00 (.06) | .00 | .96 | |
| Dismissing × Maternal/Paternal Exp | −.03 (.04) | −.03 | .46 | | .15 (.05) | .13 | .01 | |
| Preoccupied × Maternal/Paternal Exp | −.00 (.04) | −.00 | .96 | | −.01 (.05) | −.01 | .90 | |

Note. Dismissing and preoccupied state-of-mind scales are Kobak (1993) prototype scores discussed in Chapters 2 and 3. Maternal and paternal inferred-experience scales are drawn from confirmatory factor analysis of the AAI Q-sort in Chapter 2. Intercept values for each regression equation are available from the first author of this chapter upon request.

103

In the second omnibus regression (see Table 6.3), *paternal* sensitivity (54 months through 15 years) was similarly regressed on dismissing states of mind, preoccupied states of mind, and *paternal* inferred experience (step 1) and then (in step 2) these 3 variables and the Dismissing × Paternal Inferred Experience and the Preoccupied × Paternal Inferred Experience interaction terms. The full omnibus model predicting paternal sensitivity was again significant $F(5, 563) = 2.88$, $p < .015$; $R^2 = 0.16$. Further, in this case, the Dismissing (but not Preoccupied) × Paternal Inferred Experience interaction approached significance ($p = .06$).

When analyses were conducted by developmental period (paternal sensitivity in early childhood, grade school, and adolescence), the only significant interaction effect was Dismissing × Paternal Inferred Experience regressed on paternal sensitivity experienced in adolescence. Only in this single instance was the association between paternal sensitivity experienced in adolescence significantly weaker with dismissing (vs. secure) states of mind for individuals with more (as compared with less) problematic paternal inferred experiences as rated in the AAI. Moreover, simple slopes analysis suggested that the association between dismissing states of mind and observed paternal sensitivity in adolescence for those with relatively negative inferred paternal caregiving (i.e., +1 *SD*) was not significantly different than zero whereas the association for those with relatively positive inferred experiences with paternal caregivers (i.e., −1 *SD*) was significantly negative. That said, unlike the prototypical Model 1 depicted in Figure 6.1, these data (similar to the Figure depicted as 1b in our electronic supplement to this Monograph) suggested a clear *cross-over* interaction where those high on inferred negative experiences scored at around the sample mean of paternal sensitivity irrespective of whether they were coded as more or less dismissing. (Recall that high scores on the inferred-experience scales indicate more difficult caregiving experiences reported during the AAI.)

Note finally that we examined whether the interaction results reported above changed when we substituted the exploratory factor analysis-derived dismissing and preoccupied state-of-mind dimensions for the prototype-derived assessments. Consistent with results reported above, all interactions were non-significant except the Dismissing × Paternal experience effect in the retrodiction of paternal sensitivity during adolescence.

## DISCUSSION

This chapter largely replicated the key result of Roisman et al. (2002), providing scant evidence that individuals with earned-secure status based on retrospective criteria are either likely to have experienced insecure mother-child attachment in infancy or pervasively negative caregiving experiences.

We believe this finding is an important one because, despite the evidence to the contrary (e.g., Roisman et al., 2002, 2006), investigations of earned-security continue to be interpreted under the assumption that retrospective approaches to defining positive attachment-related change (i.e., toward security) are valid. For example, Reiner and Spangler (2010) found that participants who could be characterized as having earned-secure status based on retrospective criteria were disproportionately likely to be carriers of the 7-repeat Dopamine Receptor D4 variable number tandem repeat polymorphism, speculating that "individuals with the DRD4 7-repeat might carry certain temperamental characteristics which facilitate the development of a secure attachment in spite of unloving caregiving experiences" (p. 222). Similarly, on the basis of evidence that those in the earned-secure group described support in their AAI narratives from alternative caregivers and therapists, Saunders et al. (2011) suggested that these experiences might account for why those with earned-secure status overcome earlier adversities. Although both findings are intriguing, it seems unwise to interpret them on the basis of the assumption that such individuals actually overcame pervasively difficult early caregiving experiences in light of prospective data on the observed early histories of individuals with earned-secure status now available on the high-risk Minnesota Longitudinal Study of Risk and Adaptation (Roisman et al. 2002) and the more normative-risk SECCYD.

It should be emphasized, nonetheless, that one finding reported in this chapter was consistent with the possibility that those with earned-secure status experience below-average caregiving comparable to participants in the insecure group. Specifically, in the early years (6–54 months), the earned-secure group (by Main and Goldwyn's definition only) was observed to have experienced below-average sensitivity from maternal caregivers. However, a number of important caveats attach to the interpretation of this result. First, as we have already noted, categorical analysis of the earned-security question is fraught with problems, not the least of which is the fact that the earned-secure group (especially by the Main and Goldwyn definition) was less secure than the continuous-secure group. Second, we did not find that the Main and Goldwyn earned-secure group was at significantly enhanced risk for *insecurity* in early childhood with their mothers and, at roughly the same time that the maternal sensitivity findings emerged, the Main and Goldwyn earned-secure group received *paternal* caregiving above the sample mean (and were indistinguishable from the continuous-secure group in this regard). This last finding strikes us as remarkable given that Main and Goldwyn's criteria specifically attempt to conservatively establish which adults with secure status on the AAI had *pervasively* negative childhood experiences with maternal and paternal caregivers. Also of note is the fact that the Main and Goldwyn earned-secure group was observed to have experienced average or better maternal caregiving post-early childhood, during the very years covered by the AAI protocol.[12]

105

One novel result from this analysis is the finding that the earned-secure group (whether defined using the Pearson or Main and Goldwyn criteria) experienced relatively low family income relative to their needs and more father absence, comparable in this regard to the insecure group, and significantly worse than that experienced by the continuous-secure group. These findings—when juxtaposed with the earned-secure group's parents reporting relatively high levels of depressive symptoms but relatively sensitive observed caregiving—suggest that retrospective systems for assessing early parental adversity may be ironically short-changing caregivers who, in fact, appear to be notably effective in their role as parents in light of their stressful life circumstances. Alternatively, such findings could reflect some evidence that those in the earned-secure group experienced adversity in their early lives —however, it would not seem accurate to characterize such adversity as specific to the quality of caregiving during childhood, a fundamental assumption that frames retrospective assessments of earned-security.

The current findings provide new clarification on many fronts by leveraging prospectively assessed developmental histories of individuals who coherently describe (as adults) negative caregiving experiences during childhood. Specifically, these results begin to close the book on the long-held assumption that these individuals' lower inferred-experience scores are valid reflections of significantly poorer-quality maternal and paternal caregiving. Nonetheless, the question remains as to why these individuals have significantly lower scores on inferred-experience scales than do those in the continuous secure group. We see at least three, non-mutually exclusive possibilities that might account for this difference in terms of biased encoding and/or retrieval of memories about early caregiving (consistent with Roisman et al.'s 2006 experimental work).

One source of such bias may be internalizing symptoms that are transmitted intergenerationally, a possibility bolstered by evidence of links between inferred experience and child psychopathology reported in Chapter 7 (this volume). Another potential source of bias is contextual stress affecting the child (a possibility suggested by evidence that the earned-secure group experienced lower family income and more paternal absence than did the continuous secure group). A third potential source of bias resides in the AAI coding process itself rather than participants' encoding and retrieval processes. That is, it is possible that accounts of caregiving in the context of financial strain or other forms of adversity receive elevated negative experience scores from coders compared with accounts of caregiving in families not facing these challenges.

In sum, the current analysis extended findings regarding the origins of earned-security based on the Minnesota Longitudinal Study of Risk and Adaptation (Roisman et al., 2002) by examining multiple definitions of earned-security and with a focus on direct observations of both maternal and paternal caregiving in the SECCYD, a large, normative-risk cohort. In the main, this study replicated the key finding from Roisman et al. (2002) that individuals who produce coherent discourse during the AAI are more likely to have experienced average or better care—irrespective of whether such individuals describe their experiences as supportive or more difficult in nature.

## NOTES

9. A blended model was suggested by Kobak and Zajac (2011) that retrospective earned-secures' negative evaluations of their (in reality, average or above-average) childhood experiences with primary caregivers result from the biasing filter of more recent difficulties with primary caregivers—an intriguing prediction because it suggests that earned-secures might actually have *increasingly* problematic experiences with parents over time.

10. The primary reason we elected not to report these data is because, in a number of cases (mother and father love), the distribution of scores is non-overlapping by definition.

11. $\alpha = .76$ for maternal sensitivity 6–54 months, $\alpha = .70$ for maternal sensitivity G1–G5 months, and $\alpha = .60$ for paternal sensitivity G1–G5 months (other indicators are based on a single assessment) in the AAI sub-sample of the SECCYD.

12. Similarly, little evidence emerged for Kobak and Zajac's (2011; see footnote 9) suggestion that the earned-secure group experienced increasingly problematic caregiving (i.e., under the assumption that their security derives from earlier sensitive caregiving but their inferred-experiences ratings derive instead from more recent experiences with caregivers).

# VII. SHARED AND DISTINCTIVE ANTECEDENTS OF ADULT ATTACHMENT INTERVIEW STATE-OF-MIND AND INFERRED-EXPERIENCE DIMENSIONS

*Katherine C. Haydon, Glenn I. Roisman, Margaret T. Owen, Cathryn Booth-LaForce, and Martha J. Cox*

Accumulating evidence demonstrates that the primary coding systems for the AAI (Main & Goldwyn, 1984–1998; Main et al., 2003–2008; Kobak, 1993) capture variation on four relatively independent dimensions. Two of these capture adults' *states of mind regarding attachment*, with the first reflecting the degree to which adults freely evaluate or defensively discuss their attachment histories (i.e., dismissing states of mind) and the second capturing the extent to which adults become emotionally overwhelmed while discussing their early attachment experiences (i.e., preoccupied states of mind). Two additional dimensions capture caregiver-specific variation in how adults describe their early experiences (inferred negative experiences with maternal and paternal caregivers, respectively). This factor structure has been observed in a number of independent samples, using both exploratory (Bernier et al., 2004; Haydon et al., 2012; Kobak & Zajac, 2011; Larose et al., 2005; Roisman et al., 2007) and confirmatory techniques (Chapter 2, this volume). Taken together, these findings support an updated conceptualization of the key axes of variation in adult attachment as captured by the AAI and pave the way for more statistically powerful and empirically informed approaches to assessing the correlates and antecedents of adult attachment.

Previous work has validated this approach by documenting the distinctive predictive significance of the dimensions described above in key attachment-related domains: interpersonal functioning, psychopathology, and attachment-related cognitions. Perhaps most notably, dismissing states of mind have been associated uniquely with the provision of maternal insensitivity, whereas preoccupied states of mind have been associated uniquely with caregiving marked by higher levels of maternal intrusiveness (Whipple et al., 2011).

Corresponding author: Katherine C. Haydon, Department of Psychology & Education, Mount Holyoke College, South Hadley, MA 01075, email: kchaydon@mtholyoke.edu

Dismissing states of mind have also been associated uniquely with observed suppression of positive and negative affect during romantic conflict interactions, whereas preoccupied states of mind have been associated uniquely with affective activation in the same context (Haydon et al., 2012). These findings were also accompanied by evidence of divergent associations between dismissing versus preoccupied states of mind and electrodermal reactivity assessed during romantic conflict interactions (Haydon et al., 2012), suggesting effortful inhibition of attachment-related stress was positively associated with dismissing but negatively associated with preoccupied states of mind.

Similarly, in the domain of attachment-related cognition, dismissing states of mind have been associated uniquely with faster reaction time during the attachment Stroop task (possibly indicative of suppression of attachment-related content), whereas preoccupied states of mind were associated uniquely with activation of negative views of self (Haydon et al., 2011). Finally, and consistent with prior evidence, dismissing states of mind have been associated with lower self-reported symptoms of psychopathology (Haydon et al., 2012).

Variation in how adults discuss their early experiences with caregivers, as captured by the AAI inferred-experience dimensions, also appears to have some predictive significance over and above state-of-mind dimensions, particularly in relation to adult psychopathology. For example, we have reported previously that preoccupied states of mind were associated positively with internalizing distress, but this effect was attenuated to non-significance once variation in inferred negative experiences with caregivers was taken into account (Haydon et al., 2012).

Distinctive correlates of dismissing versus preoccupied states of mind observed in each of these attachment-relevant domains support theoretical claims about the divergent emotional, behavioral, and cognitive profiles associated with dismissing versus preoccupied states of mind. In this chapter we examined whether, in addition to distinctive correlates in adult attachment-related functioning, these dimensions have shared or distinctive *developmental origins*. Specifically, we built on the regression-based approach from Chapter 6 to examine shared and distinctive antecedents of AAI state-of-mind and inferred-experience dimensions, including core antecedents proposed by attachment theory (i.e., caregiver sensitivity and availability) as well as other developmental liabilities and assets (i.e., psychopathology and general cognitive ability). We also tested whether links between AAI dimensions and these antecedents were robust to the inclusion of key covariates commonly used in the social sciences (i.e., gender, ethnicity, maternal education, and family income-to-needs) and the other attachment dimensions.

These hierarchical regression models were designed to examine the *robustness* of key effects in the context of increasingly rigorous conditions,

109

including (1) other potentially developmentally relevant antecedents, (2) covariates, and (3) the other three attachment dimensions. This approach also allowed us to systematically examine the *uniqueness* of predictors of dismissing versus preoccupied states of mind when shared variance between dismissing and preoccupied states of mind was taken into account. Our goal in using this approach was to leverage the entire SECCYD dataset by aggregating assessments across early childhood, middle childhood, and adolescence; nevertheless, we briefly discuss specificity of key effects within these developmental periods in the Discussion section.

## CAREGIVER SENSITIVITY AND AVAILABILITY

Attachment theory distinguishes two kinds of relevant earlier experiences that promote attachment security between infants and their caregivers: caregiver sensitivity and availability.

The attachment literature has documented associations between caregiver sensitivity and infant security (Braungart-Rieker, Garwood, Powers, & Wang, 2001; Pederson, Gleason, Moran, & Bento, 1998; for a meta-analysis, see De Wolff & Van IJzendoorn, 1997) as well as adult secure/autonomous AAI classifications (Beckwith, Cohen, & Hamilton, 1999; Beijersbergen et al., 2012; Grossmann et al., 2002). Consistent with this literature, and in light of recent evidence that security in the context of the AAI may actually reflect low levels of dismissing states of mind (Haydon et al., 2012), we expected that the experience of maternal and paternal sensitivity across infancy, childhood, and adolescence would negatively predict later dismissing states of mind.

The developmental origins of preoccupied states of mind are less clear conceptually; in addition, studies of antecedents of attachment states of mind have often combined participants classified as dismissing and preoccupied into one insecure group for analysis, precluding examination of distinctive antecedents of each (e.g., Crowell, Treboux, & Brockmeyer, 2009; Weinfield et al., 2004). Nevertheless, both the infant and adult attachment literatures offer some guidance in developing predictions about antecedents of preoccupied states of mind. Inconsistent caregiving is a known antecedent of anxious-resistant attachment in infancy (Ainsworth et al., 1978; Isabella & Belsky, 1991). For example, changes in paternal presence have been associated with instability of attachment in infancy (Egeland & Farber, 1984). Divorce in the family of origin, which is often accompanied by changes in caregiver presence, has also been associated with preoccupied—but not dismissing—AAI classifications in adults (Beckwith et al., 1999; Riggs & Jacobvitz, 2002). Using these findings as a point of departure, we expected that caregiver absence earlier in development would predict preoccupied

110

states of mind in adulthood. Given that mothers in this sample were likely to be present continuously, we chose to focus on variation in *paternal* availability.

### Other Developmental Assets and Liabilities

In addition to these theoretically core antecedents, we also considered the roles of two compelling alternative antecedents: general cognitive ability and childhood psychopathology. Greater cognitive ability may be a developmental asset associated with the capacity to produce a more coherent narrative about childhood experiences. Although the attachment literature suggests relatively weak links between IQ scores and AAI classifications (Bakermans-Kranenburg & Van IJzendoorn, 1993; Crowell et al., 1996; Hesse, 1999), we nonetheless thought it important to examine links between key antecedents and AAI dimensions while controlling for variation in cognitive ability.

Whereas cognitive ability may serve as an asset in the production of a coherent narrative, childhood psychopathology may function as a developmental liability that could potentially affect later attachment states of mind and color how adults talk about their experiences with caregivers. Specifically, dismissing states of mind have been concurrently associated with externalizing symptomatology whereas preoccupied states of mind have been concurrently associated with internalizing symptomatology (Bakermans-Kranenburg & Van IJzendoorn, 2009; Dozier, Stovall-McClough, & Albus, 2008; Rosenstein & Horowitz, 1996). Given that the attachment system and psychopathology may develop concomitantly, we thought it prudent to control for earlier psychopathology as a potential antecedent of adult attachment states of mind. Prior evidence also suggests that elevated levels of internalizing distress in particular occur among those who describe negative early experiences with caregivers (Chapter 6, this volume; Pearson et al., 1994). Thus, we included both mother- and teacher-reported psychopathology as potential antecedents of the AAI dimensions.

## INFERRED NEGATIVE EXPERIENCE WITH CAREGIVERS

We also examined the antecedents of AAI *inferred-experience dimensions* in light of remaining questions about their developmental origins. Evidence presented in Chapter 6 supports the conclusion that inferred-experience dimensions are not entirely valid indicators of earlier caregiver sensitivity for relatively secure adults and casts some doubt on the possibility that they reflect negative trajectories of caregiver sensitivity across childhood and adolescence. Nevertheless, we examined here whether inferred-experience dimensions were associated with earlier caregiver sensitivity, net of variation in state of mind, and whether inferred-experience dimensions accounted for links between state of mind and antecedent measures. In other words, we examined the incremental retrodictive validity of the inferred-experience dimensions over state-of-mind dimensions.

## COVARIATES AND CONTROLS

In testing these hypotheses, we sought to take into account standard covariates used in psychology and the social sciences more broadly: child gender and ethnicity, maternal education, and family income-to-needs ratio. Surprisingly, many models in attachment research have not controlled for or examined the role of these factors, despite mixed evidence regarding their links to attachment-relevant functioning. For example, prior work proposes an evolutionary basis for gender differences in attachment that emerge in middle childhood and persist into adulthood (Del Guidice & Belsky, 2010), whereas a meta-analysis of the AAI literature did not find evidence of gender differences in AAI classifications (Bakermans-Kranenburg & Van IJzendoorn, 2009). As a final test to address the uniqueness of antecedent predictors, we examined whether links between AAI dimensions and antecedent measures were robust when other attachment dimensions were taken into account. In other words, we tested whether effects were specific to one state-of-mind dimension when its shared variance with the other state-of-mind and inferred experience dimensions was statistically controlled.

## METHOD

Missing data, particularly for paternal sensitivity assessments, resulted in a total of 734 participants being included in the current analyses. Regression analyses rerun with the paternal sensitivity variable excluded resulted in a total of 845 participants in the analysis. The pattern of results was essentially identical to those we report below.

### Adult Attachment Interview Dimensions and Classifications

#### AAI Q-Sort Dimensions
The AAI Q-Sort (Kobak, 1993) prototype dismissing and preoccupied state-of-mind dimensions and the empirically derived inferred maternal and paternal experience dimensions used throughout this volume were used in the current analysis.

#### AAI Classifications
Two binary outcome variables were created for use in parallel analyses: dismissing versus not dismissing and preoccupied versus not preoccupied

based on the AAI three-way classification system (Main & Goldwyn, 1998). Descriptive and inter-rater reliability statistics are presented in Chapter 1.

### Caregiver Sensitivity and Availability

#### Maternal and Paternal Sensitivity

The maternal sensitivity (6 months–age 15) and paternal sensitivity (54 months–age 15) composite variables detailed in Chapter 6 (this volume) were used in the current analysis.

#### Father Absence

The proportion of father absence variable from Chapter 6 (this volume) was used in the current analysis (1 month through age 15). Higher scores indicate greater proportion of assessments at which fathers were absent.

### Developmental Assets and Liabilities

#### Cognitive Ability

Cognitive ability was assessed with the Woodcock–Johnson Psycho-Educational Battery–Revised (WJ–R; Woodcock, 1990; Woodcock & Johnson, 1989) yielding scores at 54 months; Grades 1, 3, and 5; and age 15 as an objective measure of academic skills. Note that for the WJ–R, a slightly different sub-set of scales was used at each assessment point. For purposes of this analysis, we averaged the $W$ (standard) scores for all available subscales at each time point (within-time alphas ranged from .81 to .91; $M = .87$; alpha across the five assessment points for the composite was .93; see Fraley, Roisman, & Haltigan, 2013, for details).

#### Child Psychopathology

Child psychopathology symptoms were assessed using *total problems* scales reported by mothers on the CBCL (Achenbach, 1991) and by teachers on the Teacher Report Form (TRF; Achenbach & Edelbrock, 1986). *T*-scores within informant were averaged over assessments ($\alpha = .93$ for mothers and $\alpha = .96$ for teachers). Although age-18 mother-reported CBCL data were collected and reported in Chapter 6, we excluded parallel total problems data at age 18 from the total problems CBCL composite in the current chapter so as to keep the focus exclusively on data collected prior to the AAI assessment.

#### Covariates

To indicate child gender, males were coded 1 and females were coded 2. The child ethnicity, maternal education, and the family income-to-needs measures described in Chapter 6 (this volume) were used in the current analyses.

113

# RESULTS

## Analytic Plan

We conducted a series of hierarchical regression analyses for each AAI Q-Sort prototype dimension in which conceptually related groups of variables were entered in successive blocks. The first block tested the core antecedents anticipated by attachment theory: maternal sensitivity, paternal sensitivity, and paternal absence. The second block tested the value added of alternative antecedents: maternal and teacher reports of child psychopathology and assessments of academic skills. The third block controlled for key covariates commonly used in psychological research: child gender and ethnicity, maternal education, and family income-to-needs. The fourth block tested whether effects were robust to the inclusion of the other three AAI dimensions. Descriptive statistics and zero-order correlations appear in Table 7.1. (Note that results pertaining to the state-of-mind dimensions are based on the AAI Q-sort prototype scores. We also examined whether results diverged when exploratory factor analysis-derived dismissing and preoccupied state-of-mind dimensions described in Chapter 2 were substituted for the prototype dimensions. Focal results did not differ from those reported here).

Finally, we examined whether analyses using categorical measures of dismissing and preoccupied status yielded the same pattern of effects observed in analyses using dimensional measures of dismissing and preoccupied states of mind. Specifically, we conducted two hierarchical logistic regressions in which dummy-coded categorical measures of dismissing versus not (i.e., those classified as dismissing vs. those classified as either secure/autonomous or preoccupied) and preoccupied versus not (i.e., those classified as preoccupied vs. those classified as dismissing or secure) were regressed on the same blocked sets of antecedent measures and covariates described above.

## Dismissing States of Mind

We first tested our hypothesis that dismissing states of mind should be associated uniquely with lower caregiver sensitivity whereas preoccupied states of mind should be associated uniquely with paternal absence (see Table 7.2). As expected, in Block 1 of the model in which the dismissing dimension was regressed on this set of antecedent measures, dismissing states of mind were negatively associated with maternal sensitivity but were not significantly related to paternal sensitivity. Contrary to expectations, dismissing states of mind were positively associated with paternal absence. In Block 2, the pattern of effects observed in Block 1 did not change and dismissing states of mind were negatively associated with cognitive ability and

TABLE 7.1

DESCRIPTIVE STATISTICS AND PAIRWISE BIVARIATE CORRELATIONS

| | 1 | 2 | 3 | 4 | 5 | 6 | 7 | 8 | 9 | 10 | 11 | 12 | 13 | 14 |
|---|---|---|---|---|---|---|---|---|---|---|---|---|---|---|
| 1 Dismissing | — | | | | | | | | | | | | | |
| 2 Preoccupied | .07* | — | | | | | | | | | | | | |
| 3 M inf. exp. | .48*** | .49*** | — | | | | | | | | | | | |
| 4 P inf. exp. | .43*** | .41*** | .28*** | — | | | | | | | | | | |
| 5 M sensitivity | -.33*** | -.20*** | -.27*** | -.23*** | — | | | | | | | | | |
| 6 P sensitivity | -.16*** | -.11** | -.10** | -.18*** | .40*** | — | | | | | | | | |
| 7 F absence | .23*** | .20*** | .20*** | .26*** | -.42*** | -.10* | — | | | | | | | |
| 8 CBCL | .11** | .17*** | .13*** | .18*** | -.27*** | -.16*** | .20*** | — | | | | | | |
| 9 TRF | .25*** | .26*** | .27*** | .26*** | -.43*** | -.23*** | .34*** | .39*** | — | | | | | |
| 10 WJR | -.24*** | -.13*** | -.14*** | -.15*** | .43*** | .22*** | -.22*** | -.15*** | -.33*** | — | | | | |
| 11 Gender | -.25*** | .10** | -.05 | -.08* | .08* | .07† | -.01 | .02 | -.01 | -.07† | — | | | |
| 12 Ethnicity | -.14** | -.14*** | -.16*** | -.18*** | .40*** | .13** | -.33*** | -.04 | -.21*** | .24*** | .04 | — | | |
| 13 M education | -.23*** | -.12** | -.16*** | -.19*** | .51*** | .24*** | -.34*** | -.21*** | -.33*** | .41*** | .05 | .25*** | — | |
| 14 Fam. income | -.16*** | -.14*** | -.13*** | -.18*** | .42*** | .21*** | -.32*** | -.23*** | -.29*** | .36*** | .03 | .23*** | .55*** | — |
| Mean | -.02 | -.23 | 4.05 | 4.87 | 0.00 | 0.00 | 22.7% | 47.76 | 49.49 | 488.81 | 50.1% | 78.2% | 14.56 | 4.13 |
| SD | .40 | .22 | 1.36 | 1.35 | 1.00 | 1.00 | | 8.13 | 6.94 | 12.01 | | | 2.44 | 3.13 |

Note. M, maternal; P, paternal; F, father; Inf. Exp, inferred experience; CBCL, composite of mother-reported total problems $T$-scores; TRF, composite of teacher-reported total problems $T$-scores; WJR, composite of Woodcock Johnson-R academic skills scores; Fam. income, composite of family income-to-needs; $N = 857$ for all correlations except those including paternal sensitivity ($N = 745$), CBCL ($N = 855$), TRF ($N = 848$), and income ($N = 848$). For correlations between paternal sensitivity and CBCL, $N = 743$; paternal sensitivity and TRF, $N = 737$; paternal sensitivity and income, $N = 744$; CBCL and TRF, $N = 846$; CBCL and income, $N = 854$. TRF and income, $N = 847$. SD, standard deviation. Descriptive statistics for gender and ethnicity are expressed as proportions of participants who are female and of White ethnicity, respectively. The mean for father absence reflects the proportion of assessments at which fathers were absent.

$†p < .10.$
$*p < .05.$
$**p < .01.$
$***p < .001.$

115

TABLE 7.2

HIERARCHICAL REGRESSION MODELS PREDICTING AAI DIMENSIONS

| | Dismissing | | | Preoccupied | | | M Inf. Exp. | | | P Inf. Exp. | | |
|---|---|---|---|---|---|---|---|---|---|---|---|---|
| | $\beta$ | $p$ | $R^2$ | $\beta$ | $p$ | $R^2$ | $\beta$ | $p$ | $R^2$ | $\beta$ | $p$ | $R^2$ |
| 1. M sensitivity | −.25 | .00 | .12 | −.11 | .01 | .06 | −.24 | .00 | .09 | −.11 | .01 | .08 |
| P sensitivity | −.05 | .15 | | −.06 | .14 | | .01 | .83 | | −.13 | .00 | |
| F absence | .13 | .00 | | .17 | .00 | | .12 | .00 | | .16 | .00 | |
| 2. M sensitivity | −.19 | .00 | .13 | −.04 | .39 | .09 | −.19 | .00 | .11 | −.05 | .27 | .10 |
| P sensitivity | −.04 | .29 | | −.04 | .32 | | .02 | .56 | | −.11 | .01 | |
| F absence | .11 | .00 | | .13 | .00 | | .09 | .02 | | .13 | .00 | |
| CBCL | −.04 | .28 | | .04 | .28 | | −.01 | .83 | | .06 | .15 | |
| TRF | .10 | .01 | | .16 | .00 | | .17 | .00 | | .12 | .01 | |
| WJR | −.10 | .01 | | −.02 | .56 | | .01 | .71 | | −.04 | .34 | |
| 3. M sensitivity | −.16 | .00 | .20 | −.03 | .52 | .11 | −.17 | .00 | .12 | −.01 | .82 | .11 |
| P sensitivity | −.03 | .42 | | −.05 | .25 | | .02 | .54 | | −.11 | .01 | |
| F absence | .12 | .00 | | .13 | .00 | | .09 | .02 | | .12 | .00 | |
| CBCL | −.03 | .40 | | .05 | .23 | | .00 | .99 | | .06 | .11 | |
| TRF | .11 | .01 | | .16 | .00 | | .17 | .00 | | .12 | .01 | |
| WJR | −.12 | .00 | | −.01 | .77 | | .01 | .78 | | −.03 | .42 | |
| Gender | −.24 | .00 | | .12 | .00 | | −.04 | .21 | | −.05 | .16 | |
| Ethnicity | .02 | .64 | | −.10 | .01 | | −.06 | .10 | | −.07 | .06 | |
| M education | −.04 | .38 | | .03 | .55 | | .00 | .99 | | −.02 | .61 | |
| Fam. income | .05 | .20 | | −.02 | .67 | | .02 | .71 | | −.01 | .84 | |
| 4. M sensitivity | −.09 | .02 | .48 | −.00 | .95 | .43 | −.07 | .05 | .47 | .05 | .23 | .36 |
| P sensitivity | −.02 | .58 | | −.03 | .34 | | .05 | .13 | | −.07 | .04 | |
| F absence | .07 | .02 | | .09 | .01 | | −.02 | .62 | | .03 | .35 | |
| CBCL | −.04 | .19 | | .01 | .70 | | .00 | .97 | | .06 | .08 | |
| TRF | .03 | .31 | | .06 | .07 | | .06 | .08 | | .03 | .43 | |
| WJR | −.12 | .00 | | −.05 | .14 | | .07 | .03 | | .03 | .40 | |
| Child gender | −.17 | .00 | | .07 | .02 | | .01 | .67 | | .01 | .79 | |
| Child ethnicity | .04 | .16 | | −.03 | .30 | | −.03 | .27 | | −.05 | .13 | |
| M education | −.02 | .56 | | .02 | .55 | | .00 | .94 | | −.02 | .66 | |
| Fam. income | .04 | .20 | | −.01 | .89 | | −.00 | .95 | | −.02 | .53 | |
| Dismissing | — | — | | −.36 | .00 | | .49 | .00 | | .46 | .00 | |
| Preoccupied | −.33 | .00 | | — | — | | .49 | .00 | | .41 | .00 | |
| M inf. exp. | .48 | .00 | | .52 | .00 | | — | — | | −.16 | .00 | |
| P inf. exp. | .37 | .00 | | .37 | .00 | | −.13 | .00 | | — | — | |

*Note.* $n = 734$. M, maternal; P, paternal; F, father; Inf. exp, inferred experience; CBCL, composite of maternally reported total problems *T*-scores; TRF, composite of teacher-reported total problems *T*-scores; WJR, composite of Woodcock Johnson-R academic skills scores; Fam. income, composite of family income-to-needs. All models were significant at $p < .001$ at each step. $R^2$ values increase significantly at $p < .01$ in each block except for Block 3 in the models predicting maternal inferred experience ($p = .35$) and paternal inferred experience ($p = .19$).

positively associated with teacher (but not maternal) reports of psychopathology. In Block 3, effects for key antecedents remained unchanged; dismissing states of mind were positively associated with being male but were not significantly related to other covariates. All effects were robust to the inclusion of the other three AAI dimensions in Block 4 (with the exception of teacher-reported psychopathology, which was no longer significant), suggesting that these effects were specific to dismissing states of mind rather than to shared variance with the other attachment dimensions. The full model was significant ($F[13,720] = 51.33$, $p < .001$) and each step of the model resulted in a significant increase in $R^2$ (Block 1 $R^2 = .12$, Block 2 $R^2 = .13$, Block 3 $R^2 = .20$, Block 4 $R^2 = .48$; all $ps < .01$).

### Preoccupied States of Mind

Preoccupied states of mind, as expected, were associated with father absence. In Block 1 of the model in which the preoccupied dimension was regressed on the first set of antecedent measures, preoccupied states of mind were negatively associated with maternal sensitivity and positively associated with father absence but were not significantly associated with paternal sensitivity. In Block 2, preoccupied states of mind remained significantly associated with paternal absence and were positively associated with teacher-reported psychopathology symptoms but were not significantly related to maternal reports of psychopathology or cognitive ability and were no longer significantly associated with maternal sensitivity.[13] In Block 3, preoccupied states of mind remained significantly associated with father absence and were positively associated with being female and of non-White ethnicity but were not significantly related to maternal education or income-to-needs. When the other three AAI dimensions were entered in Block 4 the effect of paternal absence remained significant (i.e., specific to preoccupied states of mind rather than stemming from shared variance with dismissing states of mind or the inferred-experience dimensions) but the effects of teacher-reported psychopathology and ethnicity were no longer significant. The full model was significant ($F[13,720] = 41.52$, $p < .001$) and each step of the model resulted in a significant increase in $R^2$ (Block 1 $R^2 = .06$, Block 2 $R^2 = .09$, Block 3 $R^2 = .11$, Block 4 $R^2 = .43$ all $ps < .01$).

### Categorical Measures of Dismissing and Preoccupied Status

Next, we tested whether the same pattern of results obtained using categorical rather than dimensional measures of dismissing and preoccupied states of mind. The first model regressed participants' status as either dismissing (coded 1) or secure/autonomous and preoccupied (both coded 0) on the blocked sets of antecedents and covariates. The results were nearly identical to the pattern of effects observed in the models using dimensional measures of attachment states of mind (Table 7.3). In Block 1, dismissing status was negatively associated with maternal sensitivity and positively associated with paternal absence but was not significantly related to paternal

TABLE 7.3

LOGISTIC REGRESSION PREDICTING DISMISSING VERSUS NOT DISMISSING STATUS

| | $B$ | $SE$ | $Wald\ X^2$ | $p$ | Odds |
|---|---|---|---|---|---|
| 1. M sensitivity | −0.42 | 0.10 | 18.00 | 0.00 | 0.66 |
| P sensitivity | −0.14 | 0.09 | 2.69 | 0.10 | 0.87 |
| F absence | 0.96 | 0.28 | 11.67 | 0.00 | 2.62 |
| 2. M sensitivity | −0.32 | 0.11 | 9.04 | 0.00 | 0.73 |
| P sensitivity | −0.12 | 0.09 | 1.86 | 0.17 | 0.89 |
| F absence | 0.91 | 0.29 | 9.85 | 0.00 | 2.48 |
| CBCL | −0.01 | 0.01 | 1.46 | 0.23 | 0.99 |
| TRF | 0.02 | 0.01 | 2.24 | 0.13 | 1.02 |
| WJR | −0.02 | 0.01 | 6.05 | 0.01 | 0.98 |
| 3. M sensitivity | −0.31 | 0.12 | 6.72 | 0.01 | 0.74 |
| P sensitivity | −0.11 | 0.09 | 1.52 | 0.22 | 0.90 |
| F absence | 1.00 | 0.30 | 11.17 | 0.00 | 2.73 |
| CBCL | −0.01 | 0.01 | 1.14 | 0.29 | 0.98 |
| TRF | 0.02 | 0.01 | 2.45 | 0.12 | 1.02 |
| WJR | −0.02 | 0.01 | 8.16 | 0.00 | 0.98 |
| Gender | −0.73 | 0.17 | 18.89 | 0.00 | 0.48 |
| Ethnicity | 0.12 | 0.22 | 0.30 | 0.59 | 1.13 |
| M education | −0.00 | 0.05 | 0.01 | 0.94 | 1.00 |
| Fam. income | 0.03 | 0.03 | 0.67 | 0.41 | 1.03 |
| 4. M sensitivity | −0.28 | 0.14 | 4.13 | 0.04 | 0.75 |
| P sensitivity | −0.13 | 0.10 | 1.64 | 0.20 | 0.88 |
| F absence | 0.77 | 0.36 | 4.62 | 0.03 | 2.17 |
| CBCL | −0.02 | 0.01 | 2.51 | 0.11 | 0.98 |
| TRF | −0.00 | 0.02 | 0.03 | 0.87 | 1.00 |
| WJR | −0.03 | 0.01 | 8.97 | 0.00 | 0.97 |
| Child gender | −0.74 | 0.20 | 14.09 | 0.00 | 0.48 |
| Child ethnicity | 0.41 | 0.27 | 2.40 | 0.12 | 1.51 |
| M education | 0.02 | 0.05 | 0.21 | 0.65 | 1.02 |
| Fam. income | 0.03 | 0.04 | 0.58 | 0.45 | 1.03 |
| Preoccupied vs. not | −22.88 | 7215.33 | 0.00 | 1.00 | 0.00 |
| M inf. exp. | 0.71 | 0.08 | 76.89 | 0.00 | 2.04 |
| P inf. exp. | 0.59 | 0.08 | 52.83 | 0.00 | 1.80 |

Note. $n = 734$. M, maternal; P, paternal; F, father; Inf. exp, inferred experience; CBCL, composite of maternally reported total problems $T$-scores; TRF, composite of teacher-reported total problems $T$-scores; WJR, composite of Woodcock Johnson-R academic skills scores; Fam. income, composite of family income-to-needs. Omnibus chi-squares were significant at $p < .001$ at each step. Step-level chi square values were significant at $p < .05$ in each block.

sensitivity. In Block 2, effects from Block 1 were unchanged and dismissing status was negatively associated with cognitive ability but was not significantly associated with teacher or maternal reports of psychopathology. In Block 3, effects from Block 2 were unchanged and dismissing status was positively associated with being male but was not significantly related to other covariates. All effects were robust to inclusion of the categorical measure of preoccupied status and inferred-experience dimensions in Block 4. The full model was significant ($X^2[13,720] = 292.58$, $p < .001$) and each step of the model resulted in a significant $X^2$ (Block 1 $X^2 = 61.82$, Block 2 $X^2 = 10.55$, Block 3 $X^2 = 20.14$, Block 4 $X^2 = 200.08$; all $ps < .05$).

In contrast, the model predicting preoccupied (coded 1) versus dismissing or secure status (both coded 0) failed to replicate effects observed in the model using dimensional measures of attachment states of mind (Table 7.4). In Block 1, preoccupied status was not significantly associated

TABLE 7.4

LOGISTIC REGRESSION PREDICTING PREOCCUPIED VERSUS NOT PREOCCUPIED STATUS

| | B | SE | $X^2$ | p | Odds |
|---|---|---|---|---|---|
| 1. M sensitivity | −0.29 | 0.22 | 1.76 | .19 | 0.75 |
| P sensitivity | −0.17 | 0.20 | 0.73 | .39 | 0.85 |
| F absence | 0.49 | 0.64 | 0.58 | .45 | 1.63 |
| 2. M sensitivity | −0.22 | 0.25 | 0.78 | .38 | 0.81 |
| P sensitivity | −0.15 | 0.20 | 0.55 | .46 | 0.86 |
| F absence | 0.31 | 0.66 | 0.22 | .64 | 1.37 |
| CBCL | 0.00 | 0.03 | 0.01 | .92 | 1.00 |
| TRF | 0.05 | 0.03 | 2.57 | .11 | 1.06 |
| WJR | 0.02 | 0.01 | 0.68 | .41 | 1.02 |
| 3. M sensitivity | −0.31 | 0.27 | 1.28 | .26 | 0.74 |
| P sensitivity | −0.17 | 0.20 | 0.78 | .37 | 0.84 |
| F absence | 0.50 | 0.68 | 0.54 | .46 | 1.64 |
| CBCL | 0.01 | 0.03 | 0.08 | .78 | 1.01 |
| TRF | 0.06 | 0.03 | 3.22 | .07 | 1.06 |
| WJR | 0.02 | 0.02 | 0.58 | .45 | 1.02 |
| Gender | 0.69 | 0.44 | 2.51 | .11 | 2.00 |
| Ethnicity | −0.64 | 0.50 | 1.63 | .20 | 0.53 |
| M education | 0.21 | 0.11 | 3.85 | .05 | 1.24 |
| Fam. income | −0.02 | 0.09 | 0.06 | .80 | 0.98 |
| 4. M sensitivity | −0.60 | 0.39 | 2.34 | .13 | 0.55 |
| P sensitivity | −0.19 | 0.28 | 0.44 | .51 | 0.83 |
| F absence | 0.25 | 0.89 | 0.08 | .78 | 1.29 |
| CBCL | −0.05 | 0.04 | 1.46 | .23 | 0.96 |
| TRF | 0.03 | 0.04 | 0.52 | .47 | 1.03 |
| WJR | −0.02 | 0.03 | 0.32 | .57 | 0.98 |
| Child gender | 0.51 | 0.56 | 0.82 | .37 | 1.66 |
| Child ethnicity | −0.35 | 0.65 | 0.29 | .59 | 0.71 |
| M education | 0.28 | 0.13 | 4.30 | .04 | 1.32 |
| Fam. income | 0.05 | 0.11 | 0.20 | .66 | 1.05 |
| Dismissing vs. not | −20.48 | 2126.73 | 0.00 | .99 | 0.00 |
| M inf. exp. | 1.11 | 0.23 | 23.77 | .00 | 3.02 |
| P inf. exp. | 1.02 | 0.23 | 19.43 | .00 | 2.80 |

*Note.* $N = 734$. M, maternal; P, paternal; F, father; Inf. exp, inferred experience; CBCL, composite of maternally reported total problems *T*-scores; TRF, composite of teacher-reported total problems *T*-scores; WJR, composite of Woodcock Johnson-R academic skills scores; Fam. income, composite of family income-to-needs. Omnibus and step-level chi-squares were not significant until Block 4, in which step-level and omnibus values were significant at $p < .001$.

with maternal sensitivity, paternal sensitivity, or paternal absence. In Block 2, effects from Block 1 were unchanged and preoccupied status was not significantly associated with cognitive ability, teacher reports of psychopathology, or maternal reports of psychopathology. In Block 3, effects from Block 2 were unchanged and preoccupied status was negatively associated with maternal education but was not significantly associated with other covariates. Inclusion of the categorical measure of dismissing status and inferred-experience dimensions in Block 4 did not change this pattern of effects. The full model was reached significance only in Block 4 ($X^2[13,720] = 107.10$, $p < .001$) and only Block 4 resulted in a significant step-level chi square (Block 1 $X^2 = 5.77$, $p = .12$; Block 2 $X^2 = 3.22$, $p = .36$; Block 3 $X^2 = 8.25$, $p = .08$; Block 4 $X^2 = 89.87$, $p < .001$).

### Inferred Negative Experiences With Maternal Caregivers

We next examined the retrodictive validity of the two dimensions assessing inferred negative experiences with caregivers net of the effects of the state-of-mind dimensions (i.e., we tested whether these dimensions were negatively associated with maternal and paternal sensitivity, respectively, while controlling for shared variation with both dismissing and preoccupied states of mind), shown in Table 7.2. As expected, In Block 1 of the model in which the inferred maternal experience dimension was regressed on the first set of antecedent measures, inferred negative maternal experience was negatively associated with maternal sensitivity and positively associated with paternal absence but was not significantly associated with paternal sensitivity. In Block 2, effects from Block 1 remained unchanged and inferred maternal experience was positively associated with teacher-reported psychopathology symptoms, but was not significantly related to maternal reports of psychopathology and cognitive ability. In Block 3, effects from Block 2 were unchanged and inferred maternal experience was not significantly associated with any of the standard covariates. When the other three AAI dimensions were entered in Block 4 the effects of maternal sensitivity and teacher-reported psychopathology became marginally significant predictors. The full model was significant ($F[13,720] = 48.30$, $p < .001$) and each step of the model resulted in a significant increase in $R^2$ with the exception of Block 3 (Block 1 $R^2 = .09$, Block 2 $R^2 = .11$, Block 3 $R^2 = .12$, Block 4 $R^2 = .47$; all $ps < .01$).

### Inferred Negative Experiences With Paternal Caregivers

In Block 1 of the model in which the inferred negative paternal experience dimension was regressed on the first set of antecedent measures, inferred negative paternal experience was negatively associated with maternal

120

and paternal sensitivity and positively associated with paternal absence. In Block 2, the maternal sensitivity effect was no longer significant, but the effects of paternal sensitivity and paternal absence remained significant. Inferred negative paternal experience was positively associated with teacher-reported psychopathology symptoms, but was not significantly related to maternal reports of psychopathology or cognitive ability. In Block 3, the paternal sensitivity and paternal absence effects remained significant, and inferred negative paternal experience was not significantly associated with any of the covariates. In Block 4, only the paternal sensitivity effect remained significant when the other three dimensions were taken into account. The full model was significant ($F[13,720] = 30.48$, $p < .001$) and each step of the model resulted in a significant increase in $R^2$ with the exception of Block 3 (Block 1 $R^2 = .08$, Block 2 $R^2 = .10$, Block 3 $R^2 = .11$, Block 4 $R^2 = .36$; $ps < .01$).

## DISCUSSION

Building on evidence of divergent emotional, cognitive, and behavioral profiles of dismissing and preoccupied states of mind in multiple attachment-related domains (Haydon et al., 2011, 2012; Whipple et al., 2011), the current findings represent the first comprehensive examination of shared and distinctive developmental antecedents of adult attachment states of mind using the four AAI dimensions described in Haydon et al. (2011, 2012) and Chapter 2 of this volume. As we hypothesized, dismissing and preoccupied states of mind had theory-consistent developmental antecedents (averaged across all available time periods from 1 month through 15 years of age) in the SECCYD. In addition, our findings shed some light on the retrodictive validity of the AAI inferred-experience dimensions that have been the focus of some debate within the literature on earned-security (see Chapter 6, this volume).

### Shared and Distinctive Antecedents of Dismissing and Preoccupied States of Mind

Consistent with our expectations, dismissing and preoccupied states of mind had shared and distinctive antecedents in two kinds of relevant earlier experiences with caregivers: sensitivity and availability. At the bivariate level, dismissing and preoccupied states of mind were associated with each other and with both sensitivity and paternal absence. However, as we systematically introduced more rigorous controls into the regression models (i.e., blocked sets of alternative antecedents, covariates, and the other attachment dimensions), we observed that a developmental history of father absence was uniquely associated with both dismissing and preoccupied states of mind, whereas a developmental history of lower maternal sensitivity was associated distinctively with dismissing states of mind but was unrelated to preoccupied states of mind when appropriate controls were included in the model. The current results highlight the distinctiveness of maternal sensitivity as a predictor of dismissing but not preoccupied states of mind when appropriate controls are in place, as well as the uniqueness (i.e., independent of shared variance with other attachment dimensions) of links between father absence and both dismissing and preoccupied states of mind. These theory-consistent findings complement the distinctive correlates of dismissing and preoccupied states of mind in adulthood observed in previous work (Haydon et al., 2011, 2012; Whipple et al., 2011). One possibility that may warrant further exploration is whether *inconsistent* (and possibly unpredictable) access to paternal figures distinctively promotes preoccupation whereas a *consistent* pattern of paternal absence distinctively promotes dismissing states of mind.

Of note, the predictive associations described above were robust to the inclusion of two compelling alternative antecedents and several covariates. Although cognitive ability was negatively associated with dismissing states of mind (i.e., producing a less coherent narrative about early attachment experiences), maternal sensitivity remained a unique predictor of dismissing states of mind even when cognitive ability was taken into account. Teacher- (but not mother-) reported childhood psychopathology was also positively associated with both dismissing and preoccupied states of mind, but these effects were no longer significant once variation in how adults discussed earlier experiences with maternal and paternal caregivers were taken into account. Similarly, although we observed evidence of gender differences in dismissing versus preoccupied states of mind such that males were more likely to be dismissing than were females and females were more likely to be preoccupied than were males, these effects did not account for the predictive associations of sensitivity and paternal absence for dismissing and preoccupied states of mind, respectively.

We should emphasize that the uniqueness of these predictors appears to depend upon which effects are modeled at any given time, as evidenced by the changing pattern of effects across blocks of the regression models (Table 7.2). Our goal was to take into account not only key theoretically anticipated antecedents (i.e., from the caregiving domain) but also other important developmental resources, risks, and covariates. In the initial steps of each model, both dismissing and preoccupied states of mind were related to father absence and maternal insensitivity, a finding consistent with the view that insecurity, broadly construed, is associated with low caregiver sensitivity. However, we identified that preoccupied states of mind were no longer uniquely associated with caregiver insensitivity when appropriate controls were in place (i.e., by controlling for dismissing state of mind and other sources of shared variance). In our view, this underscores the conceptual and empirical value of using the dismissing and preoccupied dimensions to identify unique antecedents and correlates.

Although our goal was to leverage the entire dataset to examine aggregate effects across infancy, childhood, and adolescence, a question of interest to attachment researchers is whether these effects are restricted to specific developmental periods. We examined the relevant bivariate correlations within each of these developmental periods and found that effects were similar across time. For example, correlations between dismissing states of mind and maternal sensitivity were consistent across assessment period ($r= -.29$ in early childhood, $-.28$ in grade school, and $-.22$ in adolescence; $ps < .001$). Similarly, correlations between preoccupied states of mind and paternal absence also were comparable irrespective of when absence was measured ($r= .15$ in early childhood [prior to kindergarten], .21 in grade school [(kindergarten through Grade 6] and .17 in adolescence [Grade 7 through age 15]; $ps < .001$).

The current study also addressed a fundamental methodological question about dimensional versus categorical measurement of dismissing and preoccupied states of mind. Evidence suggests that the decision to use categorical versus continuous measures of attachment states of mind may warrant careful consideration. Separate analyses using dimensional versus categorical measures of dismissing states of mind resulted in identical patterns of key effects; however, analysis of categorically assessed preoccupied status failed to replicate key effects observed in the models using dimensional measures of preoccupied states of mind. One reason for this disparity may have to do with how the classification system handles low to moderate levels of preoccupation.

In the SECCYD sample, like many others, preoccupied status is a relatively low base-rate phenomenon, particularly when assessed categorically. In this sample, only 4% were classified as preoccupied, whereas a somewhat larger proportion of the sample had low to moderate scores on the AAI scales most closely associated with preoccupied status (i.e., passivity, and maternal and paternal anger scales). Specifically, 7.4% had maternal anger scores $\geq 2$ and $\leq 5$, 7.9% had paternal anger scores $\geq 2$ and $\leq 5$, and 82% scored $\geq 2$ and $\leq 5$ on passivity. In a categorical framework, individuals who manifest "sub-threshold" preoccupation may be placed in the dismissing or secure/autonomous group, resulting in unparsable noise within categories and a truncated range of preoccupied states of mind available for analysis. A dimensional measurement framework more accurately represents the full spectrum of preoccupied states of mind, including low levels of preoccupation manifested in individuals who would otherwise be classified as dismissing or secure/autonomous, which enables more power to detect theoretically anticipated effects. This is especially relevant for empirically documenting antecedents and concurrent correlates of preoccupied states of mind, which so far have proven rather elusive (Haydon et al., 2012).

*Inferred Negative Experiences With Caregivers*

The current findings extend efforts to establish the construct validity of the inferred-experience dimensions presented in prior reports (Haydon et al., 2011, 2012) by examining their retrodictive validity. Specifically, we examined whether inferred experiences were associated with caregiver-specific sensitivity, net of the effects of state-of-mind dimensions. Negative associations between maternal sensitivity and inferred negative maternal experiences, and between paternal sensitivity and inferred negative paternal experiences, were accounted for in part by the state-of-mind dimensions, although weak though significant associations were documented between inferred maternal experiences with observed maternal sensitivity and inferred paternal experiences with observed paternal sensitivity even with the state-of-mind dimensions in place as covariates. That said, the current analyses provide more confidence that variation in state of mind, rather than in how people talk about their caregiver relationships, provides a somewhat more robust window on early caregiving experiences.

## Limitations and Conclusion

In the current report, we have tested what we believe to be the core antecedents of adult attachment states of mind as anticipated by attachment theory. Nonetheless, the current findings by no means represent a comprehensive causal model of variation in adult attachment as assessed by the AAI. Many sources of potential variation have yet to be investigated within this framework. In light of evidence from Chapter 2 (this volume) suggesting that drawing a sharp distinction between unresolved and preoccupied states of mind is inconsistent with the latent structure of the AAI, loss and abuse history during childhood and adolescence might account for additional variation in preoccupied states of mind. Another potential source of variation in adult attachment states of mind that may warrant consideration in future research is input from compensatory relationships in childhood and adolescence.

We believe the current approach to examining the shared and distinctive antecedents of attachment states of mind may serve as a useful conceptual and methodological template for future work in this area. In particular, we see value in using an empirically derived and, as the current results help establish, well-validated approach to assessing variation in individual differences in adult attachment as assessed by the AAI. By scaling adults on relatively independent dismissing versus preoccupied dimensions, we have documented theory-consistent, distinctive antecedents and concurrent correlates of adult attachment states of mind. We believe this approach will continue to yield new insights in a number of additional areas of interest to attachment researchers.

# NOTE

13. The bivariate association between preoccupied states of mind and maternal sensitivity was no longer significant in Step 2, suggesting that this might be due to mediation of sensitivity on preoccupied states of mind by teacher-reported child psychopathology. However, in unreported analyses we re-ran this regression analysis dropping Step 2 (i.e., omitting general cognitive ability and teacher/maternal reports of child psychopathology) and found that the association between early maternal sensitivity and preoccupation was accounted for by the demographic covariates alone. For this reason, we conclude that the association between preoccupation and maternal sensitivity is not particularly robust.

# VIII. GENERAL DISCUSSION

*Glenn I. Roisman and Cathryn Booth-LaForce*

The introduction of the Adult Attachment Interview (AAI) and corresponding "Move to the Level of Representation" that Main, Kaplan, and Cassidy (1985) ushered in to attachment research has obviously had a generative impact on developmental science (Bakermans-Kranenburg & Van IJzendoorn, 2009), perhaps most notably by making it possible to address some of the life-span questions that have motivated sustained interest in attachment relationships for decades (Hesse, 1999, 2008). In that historical context, our goal for this Monograph was for it to serve as a means of taking stock of important developments in our evolving understanding of the psychometric properties and developmental antecedents of individual differences in adult attachment as assessed by the AAI in a manner informed by the largest relevant investigation conducted to date, the NICHD Study of Early Child Care and Youth Development (SECCYD). Toward that end, this General Discussion was developed to summarize and synthesize the major findings of this volume. After discussing Parts 1 (*Psychometrics*) and 2 (*Stability, Change, and Developmental Origins*) of the Monograph, we conclude by discussing some of the limitations of the current work as well as the opportunities they present for future research based on the AAI.

## PART 1: PSYCHOMETRICS

As has been discussed in detail elsewhere (Haydon et al., 2012), the literature on the AAI relies on a conceptualization of attachment-related individual differences that is built on two distinct but easily conflated sets of assumptions. The first of these concerns the *taxonomic* (i.e., distributional) properties of individual differences in adults' narratives about their early experiences and, more specifically, the expectation that attachment-related

Corresponding author: Glenn I. Roisman, Institute of Child Development, University of Minnesota, Minneapolis, MN 5545, email: roism001@umn.edu

individual differences represent true categories (i.e., secure, dismissing, preoccupied, and unresolved; see Fraley & Spieker, 2003a; Fraley & Waller, 1998; Roisman et al., 2007). Importantly, however, the question of whether AAI individual differences are continuously or categorically distributed is easily confused with a second, arguably more crucial set of assumptions related to how AAI narratives vary with respect to one another—that is, the *factor structure* of these individual differences. As one of the two primary goals of this Monograph was to inform both of these core psychometric issues concerning the AAI, we discuss each of them in turn below in light of results of Part 1 (Chapters 2 and 3) of this volume. We conclude this section with some practical suggestions for future research on the AAI informed by the results of these psychometric analyses.

As noted in Chapter 3, a better understanding of whether attachment-related individual differences are distributed along continua or categorically is important because when groups are created on the basis of artificial cut-points, statistical power can be severely compromised (Cohen, 1983; Fraley & Spieker, 2003a).[14] It is for this reason that the taxometric results of Chapter 3 of this volume are important in emphasizing that the primary distinction made by AAI coders between secure and dismissing states of mind is more consistent with an underlying dimensional rather than taxonic model. Although Fraley and Roisman's taxometric analyses of indicators of preoccupation were indeterminate in Chapter 3 (as was also the case in Roisman et al., 2007), we believe that the statistical power advantages associated with assessing AAI-related variation as continua argue in favor of routinely doing so.

As is likely obvious from this Monograph, however, there are myriad ways to assess variation in AAI narratives continuously—irrespective of whether an investigator uses the Main and Goldwyn coding system or Kobak's AAI Q-sort for coding (see Chapter 4, this volume). For example, it is common for investigators to use the coherence-of-mind dimension rated by AAI coders as an omnibus assessment of "security" in analyses (see, e.g., Roisman et al., 2001). Similarly, at least over the first ten years of its use, Kobak's AAI Q-sort was largely used to scale participants on two focal dimensions: (a) security versus insecurity and (b) hyperactivation versus deactivation (Kobak et al., 1993).[15] As emphasized in Chapter 2 of this volume, however, implicit in the dimensional approaches outlined immediately above are two testable assumptions regarding the factor structure of individual differences in attachment as assessed by the AAI. The first of these is that our current approaches to measuring variation in adult attachment really do suggest that adults vary naturally on a unitary dimension of security versus insecurity (i.e., autonomous versus non-autonomous discourse; Haydon et al., 2012). The second and closely related assumption is that preoccupied and dismissing states of mind are largely incompatible (and hence the reason that, in Main

127

and Goldwyn's coding system, insecure adults are assigned either to the dismissing or the preoccupied group for analysis, but not both).

In some contrast to this standard view of the factor structure of the AAI, results of the confirmatory factor analyses of the SECCYD AAI data presented in Chapter 2 of this volume indicate that trained and reliable AAI coders instead scale participants on two *weakly correlated* state-of-mind dimensions— dismissing and preoccupied, along with two relatively independent inferred-experience dimensions that are caregiver-specific (i.e., maternal and paternal). This now well-replicated factor structure (Bernier et al., 2004; Haltigan et al., 2014; Haydon et al., 2012; Kobak & Zajac, 2011; Larose et al., 2005; Roisman et al., 2007) has non-trivial implications for research on the AAI. Perhaps most obvious, of course, is that researchers in this area will need to seriously engage with the fact that autonomous versus non-autonomous discourse does not emerge as a distinct axis of adult attachment-related variation. Instead, what has been historically referred to as secure-autonomous states of mind reflects the *co-occurrence* of low levels of dismissing and preoccupied states of mind.

Four important caveats are nonetheless in order. First, secure states of mind are not accurately understood within this empirically informed approach to AAI assessment as simply the *absence of evidence* for both dismissing and preoccupied discourse. Rather, for the dismissing dimension in particular, it should be appreciated that low levels are actually char-acterized by *positive evidence* that an adult can freely evaluate his or her early attachment experiences.

Second, as was emphasized in Chapter 2, the various approaches that have been used to measure variation in secure and insecure discourse using the AAI show high levels of empirical convergence. Said another way, demonstrating that the approach we advocate has incremental utility over other approaches (e.g., two-, three-, and four-way attachment group comparisons) is not productively conceptualized in terms of examining the predictive significance of the dismissing and preoccupied state-of-mind dimensions once controlling statistically for categorical distinctions. Instead, the "value added" of the approach we emphasize is going to depend on both the research questions that are being asked and the design of the study that an investigator has at his or her disposal to address those questions.

For example, as simulation evidence has made clear (Fraley & Spieker, 2003a; see Footnote 14), the use of AAI dimensions over categories per se is likely to be valuable primarily when sample sizes are moderate (rather than either small or large). This is one reason why we did not anticipate, nor did Groh et al. find, more statistically significant evidence for stability in security from infancy to adulthood in Chapter 4 of this volume using dimensional versus categorical approaches to assessment.[16] In contrast, using a coding system that allows individuals to vary freely on both dismissing and preoccupied states of mind is likely to be most useful when the explicit goal of an investigation is to understand the distinctive correlates of these weakly correlated axes on which AAI narratives vary (e.g., see Chapter 7 of this volume).

Third, we wish to state clearly that it might well be appropriate for pragmatic reasons to scale participants on a broadband security-insecurity dimension in some instances, as we have done in some of our other work and in Chapters 4 and 5 of this volume. Nonetheless, we urge caution moving forward with this approach as a default because it carries a number of risks, including reifying a distinction not reflected in the data and making it extremely easy to overlook the potentially differential correlates of empirically distinctive elements of autonomous discourse (i.e., dismissing and preoccupied states of mind).

Fourth and finally, as Haydon et al. (2012) previously emphasized, factor analysis does not literally "carve nature at its joints." Rather, when based on relatively large datasets such as the SECCYD, such analyses provide increased confidence about the latent structure of data derived from a given measure as informed by coding systems applied to it. As evidence from multiple independent studies has consistently converged on the conceptualization of individual differences in adult attachment confirmed in this large-scale analysis of the SECCYD (e.g., Bernier et al., 2004; Haltigan et al., 2014; Haydon et al., 2012; Roisman et al., 2007), we believe that there is considerable reason to be confident that the AAI—as well as other diverse attachment-related individual differences measures administered across the life course (Fraley & Spieker, 2003a, 2003b; Fraley, & Waller, 1998)—scale individuals on two key axes of attachment-related variation, which at the highest level of abstraction can be conceptualized as reflecting attachment-related anxiety and avoidance (Roisman, 2009).

*Practical considerations.* As is no doubt clear from the foregoing discussion, we conclude that the taxometric and factor analyses presented in Chapters 2 and 3 of this volume, along with other published findings (Bernier et al., 2004; Haltigan et al., 2013; Haydon et al., 2012; Kobak & Zajac, 2011; Larose et al., 2005; Roisman et al., 2007) provide ample evidence that the AAI captures two modestly correlated state-of-mind dimensions—one that reflects the degree to which individuals either freely evaluate or defensively discuss their early experiences (i.e., dismissing states of mind) and the other reflecting attachment-related preoccupation (i.e., preoccupied states of mind)—along with empirically distinctive variation in participants' recalled experiences of support or difficulty with maternal and paternal caregivers. For those interested in leveraging this measurement approach in their own work, we conclude this section by offering some practical recommendations for doing so.

We begin by emphasizing that there are in fact a number of defensible strategies for operationally defining the two state-of-mind and two inferred-experience dimensions that are in our view so central to what the AAI measures. As detailed in Chapter 2, it is possible to scale participants on all four of these dimensions using *either* the Main and Goldwyn or the AAI Q-sort coding systems for the AAI. Moreover, as Table 2.5 of this volume revealed, we observed large correlations among the various means of operationalizing these 4 dimensions in the SECCYD (e.g., mean $r = .88$ for dismissing, mean $r = .73$ for preoccupied).[17]

That said, where applicable throughout this Monograph, authors consistently used a combination of the AAI Q-sort *prototype* scores to scale participants on dismissing and preoccupied states of mind, along with factor analytically derived maternal and paternal inferred-experience scales (i.e., unit-weighted composites of Q-sort items identified as strong indicators of these factors in prior large sample exploratory factor analyses; see Chapter 2). We recognize that most researchers who have administered the AAI will have coded participants' narratives using the Main and Goldwyn coding system and we encourage such investigators to consider using indicators of dismissing and preoccupied drawn from that coding system to scale participants on the two state-of-mind dimensions (see Chapter 2 for details; for examples see Haltigan et al., 2014; Whipple et al., 2011). However, this approach does have some limitations including that: (a) there is no "gold standard" criterion in place to ensure that coders are reliably using the Main and Goldwyn inferred-experience and state-of-mind scales used to scale participants on the four dimensions of interest, (b) the few indicators in the Main and Goldwyn system specific to preoccupation and unresolved discourse have less than ideal psychometric properties (e.g., extreme skew due to low base rates; see Chapter 1), and (c) as detailed in Chapter 2, the Main and Goldwyn system intentionally confounds state of mind and inferred experiences among adults with insecure states of mind.

For these reasons, we see an incremental advantage to making greater use of Kobak's Q-Sort system by scaling participants using the dismissing and preoccupied prototype scores which, while a part of Kobak's system for some time, nonetheless remain underutilized (but see, e.g., Spangler & Zimmermann, 1999). To be clear, it is certainly possible to use item-level data from the AAI Q-sort to scale participants on state-of-mind dimensions, for example using the results of large-sample factor analyses as a guide to the selection of items (see Chapter 2 for details). However, we prefer the use of the "standard" prototype scores (i.e., dismissing and preoccupied) because this approach has the advantage of participants being scaled *identically* on these crucial dimensions across laboratories. The main negative consequence of using the prototype scores, however, is that they will almost certainly be more highly correlated with exploratory factor analysis-derived inferred-experience scales (for which no prototype scores exist) than dismissing and preoccupied scales also derived from exploratory factor analysis (exploratory factor analysis more optimally orthogonalizes the variation of interest). It is for this reason that, throughout this volume, we requested that authors of affected chapters swap in the exploratory factor analysis-derived dismissing and preoccupied state-of-mind dimensions based on the AAI Q-sort for the prototype dimensions in secondary analyses to check the robustness of results based on the prototype state-of-mind scores. In no case did the results of any analysis change with this substitution (for details, see Chapters 4, 6, and 7).

## PART 2: STABILITY, CHANGE, AND DEVELOPMENTAL ORIGINS

Part 2 of this volume began with two chapters designed to build directly on the extant literature on attachment stability and change from infancy to late adolescence (Grossmann et al., 2005; see also Roisman & Haydon, 2011). More specifically, Chapter 4 focused on stability in security from early childhood through age 18 years and Chapter 5 examined predictors (e.g., maternal sensitivity) of within-person stability and change in security over time, research questions that are empirically and conceptually distinct (Rogosa, 1995). In some contrast, Chapters 6 (Earned-Security) and 7 (Antecedents of AAI Dimensions) addressed questions about the origins of adult attachment in a manner that more clearly highlights the promise of leveraging some of the psychometric insights gleaned from Part 1 of this volume. Below we discuss the main results of these chapters, and provide additional context for future work building on these findings.

As noted in Chapter 4, prior evidence based on smaller sample studies suggested that attachment security is significantly more stable in lower- versus higher-risk samples (Fraley, 2002). It was for this reason that the normative-risk SECCYD sample represented a theoretically attractive context within which to study rank-order stability in attachment-related individual differences from infancy through age 18 years. Interestingly, the modest degree of stability estimated in the SECCYD ($r = .12$) was all but identical to the magnitude of continuity documented in the higher-risk Minnesota Longitudinal Study of Risk and Adaptation—prior to the SECCYD, the largest investigation of attachment security from infancy to adulthood (Sroufe et al., 2005). This convergence across the largest datasets in this area is important because it is inconsistent with the consensus that the high-risk nature of the Minnesota Longitudinal Study of Risk and Adaptation was suppressing higher rank-order attachment-related stability in that dataset in comparison with small sample studies of more normative-risk cohorts (e.g., Main et al., 2005; Waters, Merrick, et al., 2000). It also is a good reminder of the general value of anchoring empirical expectations in relation to the largest datasets available to the field at any given time.

In Chapter 4 we reported weak but significant stability from the early-childhood proportion-of-times-secure measure to the AAI dismissing and preoccupied state-of-mind scales ($r = .12$), but we did not find stability when we used the "gold-standard" categories from the Strange Situation procedure in infancy and the AAI in late adolescence. These results highlight the psychometric limitations of the approach generally taken in the field for addressing to what degree early attachment security is stable over relatively expansive developmental periods.

To be sure, it was entirely reasonable for the first wave of research in this area to focus on bivariate associations between security, as assessed behaviorally via the Strange Situation procedure, with the AAI—a representational assessment of the coherence of participants' discourse about their childhood experiences—upwards of two decades later (for a review, see Grossmann et al., 2005). However, this approach—particularly in the face of modest stability—leaves behind several interpretative ambiguities. Perhaps most obvious, unlike the Strange Situation procedure, the AAI was not designed as an assessment of security in relation to any particular relationship—it instead reflects states of mind regarding childhood attachment experiences more broadly construed. Even more important in our view, the Strange Situation offers a tenuous basis for assessing early attachment experiences writ large. The Strange Situation is doubtless an ingenious and invaluable methodological tool in developmental science. However, in studies examining stability over decades, it seems unlikely on psychometric grounds alone for a measure coded in relation to several minutes of behavior in infancy to produce evidence of a high degree of stability in attachment over time. Hence, we chose the strategy of combining several measures of attachment in early childhood to yield a more robust indicator of individual differences in attachment security.

Nonetheless, we acknowledge that some scholars who read this Monograph will assume that studies such as the SECCYD and Minnesota Longitudinal Study of Risk and Adaptation have significantly underestimated the stability in security over the first two decades of life. For such researchers, we encourage renewed attention to improving the assessment of security in the early life course in a manner that is both scalable to large sample investigations and allows for the aggregation of data on security over time. The SECCYD relied on the three well-validated attachment assessments then available— the Strange Situation procedure at 15 months, the Attachment Q-sort at 24 months, and the modified Strange Situation procedure at 36 months. As was reported in Chapter 4, however, the intercorrelations among these measures of security, while significant, were quite weak. It is for this reason that it is possible that we might have observed more stability in security from early childhood to late adolescence had the SECCYD instead, for example, administered the Attachment Q-sort multiple times in early childhood (assuming that these assessments showed enough stability within this period to aggregate into a reliable composite assessment of security). Data aggregation of this sort has the potential to create more valid and reliable assessments of early security, yet studies in this area have focused on brief, often one-off assessments (for reviews, see Fraley, 2002; Roisman & Haydon, 2011).

We also aggregated the early attachment data when we examined caregiving and contextual sources of continuity and change in attachment security from early childhood to late adolescence in Chapter 5, a topic that has long been of interest to attachment scholars. In line with the expectation that changes in security over time are "lawful," we found that individuals changing from early security to later insecurity, compared with those who were stably secure, experienced lower levels and a greater decline in maternal sensitivity, were less likely to be living with their fathers, and their mothers reported a larger increase in negative life events over time. Those who changed from early insecurity to later security, compared with those who were stably insecure, experienced a higher level of maternal sensitivity in the intervening years. Thus, our results supported one of the basic tenets of attachment theory. Of particular note is that in our analyses we chose to use a categorical designation of secure/insecure status at both the early-childhood and the late-adolescent attachment assessments rather than using dimensional scores, in part, for ease of comparison with the extant literature and, in part, due to analytic considerations and ease of interpretability. As we noted earlier, our recommendations about how AAI data should be parsed are not intended to be dogmatic but should be considered in the context of the specific questions being addressed.

Chapter 6 of this volume marks something of a departure from the first two chapters in Part 2. Rooted in prior research on retrospectively defined earned-security from Pearson et al. (1994) forward, this chapter makes two distinct contributions. First, Roisman, Haltigan, Haydon, and Booth-LaForce replicated an important, previously published finding based on the Minnesota Longitudinal Study of Risk and Adaptation demonstrating that retrospectively defined earned-secures paradoxically experienced average or better parental caregiving (Roisman et al., 2002). For this reason, we believe that the cumulative evidence firmly advocates against accepting the initially reasonable assumption that earned-security can be assessed retrospectively in a valid and reliable manner. Second, Chapter 6 introduced a regression-based approach to studying questions that remain about earned-security within a dimensional framework. Importantly, this approach ameliorates the rather basic concern that, when categorically operationalized, retrospectively-defined earned- and continuous secures are not equilibrated on security, which creates the kinds of interpretative ambiguities described by Roisman, Haltigan, Haydon, and Booth-LaForce (Chapter 6).

Chapter 7 concludes Part 2 of this volume with a model for future research on the AAI using the state-of-mind and inferred-experience dimensions highlighted throughout this Monograph. Building on prior publications (Fortuna et al., 2011; Haydon et al., 2011, 2012; Whipple et al., 2011) Haydon and her colleagues highlighted how AAI dimensions can be profitably leveraged to study distinctive correlates of dismissing and preoccupied states of mind, in this case for the first time in relation to their developmental origins. More specifically, Chapter 7 reports that, at the bivariate level, dismissing and preoccupied states of mind were both associated with both sensitivity and paternal absence. However, as Haydon et al. introduced more rigorous controls into their regression models (i.e., blocked sets of alternative antecedents, covariates, and the other attachment dimensions), they observed that a developmental history of paternal absence was uniquely associated with both dismissing and preoccupied states of mind, whereas a developmental history of lower maternal sensitivity was associated uniquely with dismissing but not preoccupied states of mind.

All of this said, Chapter 7 clearly raises more questions than it can definitively address. First, only between 10% and 20% of the variance was accounted for in each of the AAI dimensions, leaving much variation yet to be accounted for in AAI states of mind and inferred experiences. Second, and relatedly, limitations associated with the normative-risk nature of the SECCYD sample (discussed next) will likely provide many future opportunities to examine distinctive antecedents of dismissing and preoccupied states of mind more comprehensively than was possible in SECCYD. Third, Chapter 7 largely treats variation in maternal and paternal inferred-experience as potential "nuisance covariance" in relation to the state-of-mind scales. As has been detailed elsewhere (Haydon & Roisman, 2011; Kobak & Zajac, 2011), there is much yet to understand about the inferred-experience scales of the AAI in their own right, including questions as to how individuals come to vary in their reports about the nature of their early experiences with primary caregivers in ways that are not always veridical with the quality of those relationships observed prospectively (see Chapter 6).

## LIMITATIONS AND FUTURE DIRECTIONS

We hope that the foregoing summary of the major findings of this Monograph has made clear that this set of chapters cumulatively represents a significant contribution to attachment scholarship, particularly in relation to the AAI's core psychometric properties, stability and change in attachment over time, and developmental antecedents of attachment in late adolescence. Nonetheless, we believe it is important to conclude by considering some of the limitations of this work above and beyond those explored in detail in other

134

chapters in this volume (e.g., the absence of father-child attachment data in infancy in the SECCYD). We anticipate that, in highlighting the kinds of issues we discuss below, it should be possible to help set the stage for productive research in this area in the decades to come.

*The SECCYD is a normative-risk sample.* As aforementioned, the normative-risk nature of the SECCYD provided a theoretically attractive context within which to study attachment-related stability and change. However, in part due to the more normative-risk nature of this cohort, lower base rate phenomena that have been of great interest to attachment researchers—including preoccupied and unresolved AAI classifications—were not especially well represented in the SECCYD. Even more crucially, the kinds of relatively low-base-rate *experiences* hypothesized to generate preoccupation or serve as diatheses for unresolved discourse could not, or simply were not measured in the early lives of those participating in the SECCYD. As such, we believe there is much work yet to be done to better understand the kinds of developmental experiences likely to uniquely predispose adults to states of mind character-ized by psychological confusion and anger. For example, we speculate that studies focused on different forms of childhood maltreatment might be especially valuable in better understanding the origins of dismissing versus preoccupied discourse.

A related issue is that, although our evaluation of the relevant factor analytic evidence is that indicators of unresolved discourse and preoccupa-tion tend to load on a single factor (e.g., Chapter 2, this volume; Haltigan et al., 2014; Roisman et al., 2007), the normative risk nature of the SECCYD does not provide an optimal test of the distinctiveness of unresolved versus preoccupied discourse. It is for this reason that factor analytic work focused on higher risk cohorts has the potential to be especially informative in this regard. To be clear, our view is that there is not a strong empirical basis for the assumption that preoccupied and unresolved discourse represent empirically distinct phenomena. Nonetheless, much of the factor analytic evidence now available on the AAI is based on either lower risk samples or AAIs that were coded using Kobak's Q-sort, which has too few items pertinent to unresolved states of mind to examine its distinctiveness vis-à-vis preoccupation.

*The AAI was administered to the SECCYD cohort at age 18 years.* As with almost all other studies examining stability and change in attachment-related variation from infancy to the years of maturity (Roisman & Haydon, 2011), the AAI was administered to the SECCYD cohort on the cusp of adulthood. On the one hand, a major advantage of having done so is that the analyses presented in this Monograph can be directly compared with prior studies of attachment-related stability and change (see Grossmann et al., 2005). On the other hand, a consequence of our choice to administer the AAI before participants had fully transitioned to adulthood is that all of our findings are necessarily specific to individuals' attachment states of mind in late adolescence, before many had left their families of origin. For this reason, there may be value in re-administering AAIs to the SECCYD cohort, particularly because participants will increasingly encounter the kinds of "qualifying" experiences with attachment-related trauma and loss that are likely to increase the rates of unresolved (and we would hypothesize preoccupied) discourse, even in a normative risk cohort.

*There is a pressing need for genetically informed research on the AAI.* Chapter 7 of this volume demonstrates that we were able to explain non-trivial proportions of the variance in adults' AAI states of mind and inferred experiences based on a set of "usual suspect" developmental resources and liabilities. Nonetheless, Haydon et al. (Chapter 7) are forthcoming that much work remains in order to account more fully for individual differences in attachment states of mind and inferred experiences. One class of individual differences that in our view deserves more attention in future research in this area is that of genetic variation (see Supplement to this Monograph authored by Roisman & Booth-LaForce for analyses of the molecular-genetic correlates of the AAI dimensions). To be sure, behavior-genetic studies of infant attachment have so far suggested little evidence for a strong role of genetic variation in individual differences in security in the early life course (e.g., Fearon et al., 2006; Roisman & Fraley, 2008) and emerging molecular-genetic studies focused on infant attachment have fared little better (Luijk et al., 2011; Roisman et al., 2013). Nonetheless, we believe that a pressing need remains for large-sample behavior-genetic studies (i.e., adoption and twin comparisons) focused on the AAI both to examine aggregate genetic influences on adults' AAI narratives and to improve causal inference in this area of research (Beijersbergen et al., 2012; Dozier, Stovall, Albus, & Bates, 2001; Veríssimo, & Salvaterra, 2006).[18]

## CONCLUSION

We expect that the future of research on the AAI will be bright indeed by building on the psychometric and theoretical insights that form the foundation of research in this area, while embracing the best new research design-related and statistical innovations developmental science has to offer. Our hope is that this Monograph will serve as an empirically rooted, secure base from which to explore exciting developments related to the AAI.

## NOTES

14. Two important caveats attach here as regards the conditions under which statistical power is impaired by treating continuous variation as categorically distributed. First, the latent

variation must actually be continuously distributed, of course—hence the importance of "structure uncovering" analyses such as the taxometric procedures implemented in Chapter 3. Second, as demonstrated by Fraley and Spieker (2003a) in their simulation analyses, the statistical power increments associated with measuring continuously distributed variation on a continuum rather than categorically in general apply when the sample size of the investigation is neither small nor large and the true effect size of interest is moderate in magnitude. Small samples and small effects will tend to return non-significant results irrespective of whether a latent continuum is operationally defined continuously or categorically. Likewise, in a large sample study such as the SECCYD, there is little reason to expect incremental advantage of continuous (vs. categorical) assessment of latent continua per se. However, the situation in most studies in this area—which rely on more modest sample sizes—is quite different (see, e.g., Whipple et al., 2011).

15. Similarly, Waters et al. (2013) have demonstrated that the Main and Goldwyn scales can be used to scale participants on (a) secure versus insecure and (b) deactivation versus hyperactivation dimensions using weights derived from discriminant function analysis. Moreover, unlike the identically named Kobak AAI Q-sort prototype dimensions (which are highly correlated and in general should not be entered into analyses simultaneously; see Chapter 2), the Waters et al. dimensions are (as would be expected) weakly associated in the SECCYD (contact the first author of this chapter for details).

16. One possible exception, whereby the use of continuous (over categorical) assessment of AAI individual differences might prove incrementally useful even in the large $N$ context, is in relation to low base rate, highly skewed variables such as preoccupation (see Chapter 7 for details). However, even in the case highlighted in Chapter 7, it remains unclear whether the continuous assessment of preoccupation performed better than the categorical one due to continuous versus categorical measurement per se or the fact that, in the continuous case, highly dismissing individuals were not forced to be low on preoccupation (as was the case in the categorical comparison presented there).

17. Importantly, there are also some empirical questions actually *better* addressed using the Main and Goldwyn coding system. For example, as described in greater detail later in this chapter, the Main and Goldwyn system is better positioned than the AAI Q-sort to examine the empirical distinctiveness of indicators of preoccupation (e.g., anger, passivity) and unresolved status (e.g., unresolved loss and abuse). Similarly, for reasons described in Chapter 3, taxometric analyses of the AAI are only possible using the Main and Goldwyn indicators.

18. Note that, although as of the writing of this Monograph the field awaits a large sample behavior-genetic decomposition of the AAI, two small-sample, genetically informed studies of the interview have been published (Caspers et al., 2007; Torgersen, Grova, & Sommerstad, 2007).

Achenbach, T. M. (1991a). *Manual for the Child Behavior Checklist/4–18 and 1991 Profile.* Burlington, VT: University of Vermont Department of Psychiatry.

Achenbach, T. M. (1991b). *Manual for the Youth Self-Report and 1991 profile.* Burlington, VT: University of Vermont, Department of Psychiatry.

Achenbach, T. M., & Edelbrock, C. (1986). *Manual for the Teacher's Report Form and Teacher Version of the Child Behavior Profile.* Burlington, VT: University of Vermont Department of Psychiatry.

Achenbach, T. M., Edelbrock, C., & Howell, C. (1987). Empirically-based assessment of the behavioral/emotional problems of 2–3 year old children. *Journal of Abnormal Child Psychology, 15,* 629–650.

Ainsworth, M. D. S., Blehar, M. C., Waters, E., & Wall, S. (1978). *Patterns of attachment: A psychological study of the strange situation.* New York, NY: Lawrence Erlbaum.

Bahadur, M. A. (1998). *The continuity and discontinuity of attachment: A longitudinal study from infancy to adulthood* (Unpublished doctoral dissertation). New York University, New York, NY.

Bakermans-Kranenburg, M. J., & Van IJzendoorn, M. H. (1993). A psychometric study of the Adult Attachment Interview: Reliability and discriminant validity. *Developmental Psychology, 29,* 870–879.

Bakermans-Kranenburg, M. J., & Van IJzendoorn, M. H. (2009). The first 10,000 Adult Attachment Interviews: Distributions of adult attachment representations in clinical and non-clinical groups. *Attachment & Human Development, 11,* 223–263.

Beckwith, L., Cohen, S. E., & Hamilton, C. E. (1999). Maternal sensitivity during infancy and subsequent life events relate to attachment representation at early adulthood. *Developmental Psychology, 35,* 693–700.

Beijersbergen, M. D., Juffer, F., Bakermans-Kranenburg, M. J., & Van IJzendoorn, M. H. (2012). Remaining or becoming secure: Parental sensitive support predicts attachment continuity from infancy to adolescence in a longitudinal adoption study. *Developmental Psychology, 48,* 1277–1282.

Belsky, J., Steinberg, L., & Draper, P. (1991). Childhood experience, interpersonal development, and reproductive strategy: An evolutionary theory of socialization. *Child Development, 62,* 647–670.

Belsky, J., Vandell, D. L., Burchinal, M., Clarke-Stewart, K. A., McCartney, K., Owen, M. T., & the NICHD Early Child Care Research Network. (2007). Are there long-term effects of early child care? *Child Development, 78,* 681–701.

Bernier, A., Larose, S., Boivin, M., & Soucy, N. (2004). Attachment state of mind: Implications for adjustment to college. *Journal of Adolescent Research, 19,* 783–806.

Bowlby, J (1969 /1982). *Attachment and loss: Vol. 1. Attachment* (2nd ed.). New York, NY: Basic Books.

Braungart-Rieker, J. M., Garwood, M. M., Powers, B. P., & Wang, X. (2001). Parental sensitivity, infant affect, and affect regulation: Predictors of later attachment. *Child Development*, **72**, 252–270.

Bretherton, I. (2005). In pursuit of the internal working model construct and its relevance to attachment relationships. In K. E. Grossmann, K. Grossmann, & E. Waters (Eds.), *Attachment from infancy to adulthood: The major longitudinal studies* (pp. 13–47). New York, NY: Guilford Press.

Brown, T. A. (2006). *Confirmatory factor analysis for applied research*. New York, NY: Guilford Press.

Caspers, K., Yucuis, R., Troutman, B., Arndt, S., & Langbehn, D. (2007). A sibling adoption study of adult attachment: The influence of shared environment on attachment states of mind. *Attachment & Human Development*, **9**, 375–391.

Cassidy, J., Marvin, R. S., & the MacArthur Working Group on Attachment. (1992). *Attachment organization in preschool children: Coding guidelines* (4th ed.). Unpublished manuscript, University of Virginia, Charlottesville, VA.

Cassidy, J., & Shaver, P. R. (Eds.). (2008). *Handbook of attachment: Theory, research, and clinical applications*. New York, NY: Guilford Press.

Cohen, J. (1983). The cost of dichotomization. *Applied Psychological Measurement*, **7**, 249–253.

Cohen, J. (1988). *Statistical power analysis for the behavioral sciences* (2nd ed.). Hillsdale, NJ: Lawrence Erlbaum.

Crowell, J. A., Treboux, D., & Brockmeyer, S. (2009). Parental divorce and adult children's attachment representations and marital status. *Attachment & Human Development*, **11**, 87–101.

Crowell, J. A., Waters, E., Treboux, D., O'Connor, E. O., Colon-Downs, C., Feider, O., et al. (1996). Discriminant validity of the Adult Attachment Interview. *Child Development*, **67**, 2584–2599.

Del Guidice, M., & Belsky, J. (2010). Sex differences in attachment emerge in middle childhood: An evolutionary hypothesis. *Child Development Perspectives*, **4**, 97–105.

De Wolff, M. S., & Van IJzendoorn, M. H. (1997). Sensitivity and attachment: A meta-analysis of parental antecedents of infant attachment. *Child Development*, **68**, 571–591.

Dozier, M., Stovall-McClough, C., & Albus, K. E. (2008). Attachment and psychopathology in adulthood. In J. Cassidy & P. R. Shaver (Eds.), *Handbook of attachment: Theory, research, and clinical applications* (2nd ed., pp. 718–744). New York, NY: Guilford Press.

Dozier, M., Stovall, K. C., Albus, K. E., & Bates, B. (2001). Attachment for infants in foster care: The role of caregiver state of mind. *Child Development*, **72**, 1467–1477.

Egeland, B., & Farber, A. E. (1984). Infant-mother attachment: Factors related to its development and changes over time. *Child Development*, **55**, 753–771.

Fearon, R. M. P., Van IJzendoorn, M. H., Fonagy, P., Bakermans-Kranenburg, M. J., Schuengel, C., & Bokhorst, C. L. (2006). In search of shared and nonshared environmental factors in security of attachment: A behavior-genetic study of the association between sensitivity and attachment security. *Developmental Psychology*, **42**, 1026–1040.

Floyd, F. J., & Widaman, K. F. (1995). Factor analysis in the development and refinement of clinical assessment instruments. *Psychological Assessment*, **7**, 286–299.

Fortuna, K., Roisman, G. I., Haydon, K. C., Groh, A. M., & Holland, A. S. (2011). Attachment states of mind and the quality of young adults' sibling relationships. *Developmental Psychology*, **47**, 1366–1373.

Fraley, R. C. (2002). Attachment stability from infancy to adulthood: Meta-analysis and dynamic modeling of developmental mechanisms. *Personality and Social Psychology Review*, **6**, 123–151.

Fraley, R. C., Roisman, G. I., & Haltigan, J. D. (2013). The legacy of early experiences in development: Formalizing alternative models of how early experiences are carried forward over time. *Developmental Psychology*, **49**, 109–126.

Fraley, R. C., Roisman, G. I., Holland, A. S., Booth-LaForce, C., & Owen, M. T. (2013). Interpersonal and genetic origins of adult attachment styles: A longitudinal study from infancy to early adulthood. *Journal of Personality and Social Psychology*, **104**, 817–838.

Fraley, R. C., & Spieker, S. J. (2003a). Are infant attachment patterns continuously or categorically distributed? A taxometric analysis of Strange Situation behavior. *Developmental Psychology*, **39**, 387–404.

Fraley, R. C., & Spieker, S. J. (2003b). What are the differences between dimensional and categorical models of individual differences in attachment? Reply to Cassidy (2003), Cummings (2003), Sroufe (2003), and Waters and Beauchaine (2003). *Developmental Psychology*, **39**, 423–429.

Fraley, R. C., & Waller, N. G. (1998). Adult attachment patterns: A test of the typological model. In J. A. Simpson & W. S. Rholes (Eds.), *Attachment theory and close relationships* (pp. 77–114). New York, NY: Guilford Press.

Frodi, A., Grolnick, W., & Bridges, L. (1985). Maternal correlates of stability and change in infant–mother attachment. *Infant Mental Health Journal*, **6**, 60–67.

Furman, W., & Simon, V. A. (2004). Concordance in attachment states of mind and styles with respect to fathers and mothers. *Developmental Psychology*, **40**, 1239–1247.

Furman, W., & Wehner, E. A. (1999). The Behavioral Systems Questionnaire—Revised. Unpublished measure, University of Denver, Denver, CO.

George, C., Kaplan, N., & Main, M. (1984–1996). Adult Attachment Interview protocol. Unpublished manuscript, University of California, Berkeley, CA.

Grice, H. P. (1975). Logic and conversation. In P. Cole & J. L. Moran (Eds.), *Syntax and semantics III: Speech acts* (pp. 41–58). New York, NY: Academic Press.

Grossmann, K., Grossmann, K. E., Fremmer-Bombik, E., Kindler, H., & Scheuerer-Englisch, H. (2002). The uniqueness of the child–father attachment relationship: Fathers' sensitive and challenging play as a pivotal variable in a 16-year longitudinal study. *Social Development*, **11**, 301–337.

Grossmann, K. E., Grossmann, K., & Kindler, H. (2005). Early care and the roots of attachment and partnership representations: The Bielefeld and Regensburg longitudinal studies. In K. E. Grossmann, K. Grossmann, & E. Waters (Eds.), *Attachment from infancy to adulthood: The major longitudinal studies* (pp. 98–136). New York, NY: Guilford Press.

Grossmann, K. E., Grossmann, K., & Waters, E. (Eds.). (2005). *Attachment from infancy to adulthood: The major longitudinal studies.* New York, NY: Guilford Press.

Haltigan, J. D., Leerkes, E. M., Wong, M. S., Fortuna, K., Roisman, G. I., Supple, A. J., et al. (2014). Adult attachment states of mind: Measurement invariance across ethnicity and associations with maternal sensitivity. *Child Development*, **85**, 1019–1035.

Hamilton, C. (2000). Continuity and discontinuity of attachment from infancy through adolescence. *Child Development*, **71**, 690–694.

Hankin, B. L., Fraley, R. C., Lahey, B. B., & Waldman, I. D. (2005). Is depression best viewed as a continuum or discrete category? A taxometric analysis of childhood and adolescent depression in a population-based sample. *Journal of Abnormal Psychology*, **114**, 96–110.

Haslam, N. (2011). The latent structure of personality and psychopathology: A review of trends in taxometric research. *Scientific Review of Mental Health Practice*, **8**, 17–29.

Haslam, N., Holland, E., & Kuppens, P. (2012). Categories versus dimensions in personality and psychopathology: A quantitative review of taxometric research. *Psychological Medicine*, **42**, 903–920.

Haydon, K. C., Roisman, G. I., & Burt, K. (2012). In search of security: The latent structure of the Adult Attachment Interview revisited. *Development and Psychopathology*, **24**, 589–606.

Haydon, K. C., Roisman, G. I., Marks, M. J., & Fraley, R. C. (2011). An empirically derived approach to the latent structure of the Adult Attachment Interview: Additional convergent and discriminant validity evidence. *Attachment and Human Development*, **13**, 503–524.

Hesse, E. (1999). The Adult Attachment Interview: Historical and current perspectives. In J. Cassidy & P. R. Shaver (Eds.), *Handbook of attachment: Theory, research, and clinical applications* (pp. 395–433). New York, NY: Guilford Press.

Hesse, E. (2008). The Adult Attachment Interview: Protocol, method of analysis, and empirical studies. In J. Cassidy & P. R. Shaver (Eds.), *Handbook of attachment: Theory, research, and clinical applications* (2nd ed., pp. 552–598). New York, NY: Guilford Press.

Hu, L., & Bentler, P. M. (1999). Cutoff criteria for fit indexes in covariance structure analysis: Conventional criteria versus new alternatives. *Structural Equation Modeling*, **6**, 1–55.

Isabella, R. A., & Belsky, J. (1991). Interactional synchrony and the origins of infant-mother attachment. *Child Development*, **62**, 373–384.

Jöreskog, K. G. (1969). A general approach to confirmatory maximum likelihood factor analysis. *Psychometrika*, **34**, 183–202.

Kerns, K. A., Klepac, L., & Cole, A. (1996). Peer relationships and preadolescents' perceptions of security in the child-mother relationship. *Developmental Psychology*, **32**, 457–466.

Kobak, R. R. (1993). The Adult Attachment Interview Q-set. Unpublished document, University of Delaware, Newark, DE.

Kobak, R. R., Cole, H. E., Ferenz-Gillies, R., Fleming, W. S., & Gamble, W. (1993). Attachment and emotion regulation during mother–teen problem solving: A control theory analysis. *Child Development*, **64**, 231–245.

Kobak, R. R., & Zajac, K. (2011). Rethinking adolescent states of mind: A relationship/lifespan view of attachment and psychopathology. In D. Cicchetti & G. I. Roisman (Eds.), *The origins and organization of adaptation and maladaptation: Minnesota Symposia on Child Psychology* (Vol. 36). New York, NY: Wiley.

Larose, S., Bernier, A., & Soucy, N. (2005). Attachment as a moderator of the effect of security in mentoring on subsequent perceptions of mentoring and relationship quality with college teachers. *Journal of Social and Personal Relationships*, **22**, 399–415.

Lewis, M., Feiring, C., & Rosenthal, S. (2000). Attachment over time. *Child Development*, **71**, 707–720.

Luijk, M. P. C. M., Roisman, G. I., Haltigan, J. D., Tiemeier, H., Booth-LaForce, C., Van IJzendoorn, M. H., et al. (2011). Dopaminergic, serotonergic, and oxytonergic candidate genes associated with infant attachment security and disorganization? In search of main and interaction effects. *Journal of Child Psychology and Psychiatry*, **52**, 1295–1307.

Main, M. (2000). The Adult Attachment Interview as related to the Ainsworth Strange Situation. *Journal of the American Psychoanalytic Association*, **48**, 1055–1096.

Main, M. (2001). *Attachment to mother and father in infancy as related to the Adult Attachment Interview and to a self-visualization task at age 19*. Poster session presented at the biennial meeting of the Society for Research in Child Development, Minneapolis, MN.

Main, M., & Goldwyn, R. (1984–1998). *Adult attachment scoring and classification system*. Unpublished manuscript, University of California at Berkeley, Berkeley, CA.

Main, M., Goldwyn, R., & Hesse, E. (2003–2008). *Adult attachment scoring and classification system*. Unpublished manuscript, University of California at Berkeley, Berkeley, CA.

Main, M., Hesse, E., & Kaplan, N. (2005). Predictability of attachment behavior and representational processes at 1, 6, and 19 years of age: The Berkeley Longitudinal Study. In K. E. Grossmann, K. Grossmann, & E. Waters (Eds.), *Attachment from infancy to adulthood: The major longitudinal studies* (pp. 245–304). New York, NY: Guilford Press.

Main, M., Kaplan, N., & Cassidy, J. (1985). Security in infancy, childhood, and adulthood: A move to the level of representation. In I. Bretherton & E. Waters (Eds.), *Growing points in attachment theory and research. Monographs of the Society for Research in Child Development*, **50**, 66–106.

Main, M., & Solomon, J. (1990). Procedures for identifying infants as disorganized/disoriented during the Ainsworth Strange Situation. In M. T. Greenberg, D. Cicchetti, & E. M. Cummings (Eds.), *Attachment in the preschool years* (pp. 121–160). Chicago: University of Chicago Press.

MacCallum, R. C., Zhang, S., Preacher, K. J., & Rucker, D. D. (2002). On the practice of dichotomization of quantitative variables. *Psychological Methods*, **7**, 19–40.

McCartney, K., Owen, M. T., Booth, C. L., Clarke-Stewart, A., & Vandell, D. L. (2004). Testing a maternal attachment model of behavior problems in childhood. *Journal of Child Psychology and Psychiatry*, **45**, 765–778.

Meehl, P. E. (1973). MAXCOV-HITMAX: A taxonomic search method for loose genetic syndromes. In P. E. Meehl (Ed.)., *Psychodiagnosis: Selected papers* (pp. 200–224). Minneapolis: University of Minnesota Press.

Meehl, P. E. (1995). Bootstraps taxometrics: Solving the classification problem in psychopathology. *American Psychologist*, **50**, 266–275.

Meehl, P. E., & Yonce, L. J. (1994). Taxometric analysis: I. Detecting taxonicity with two quantitative indicators using means above and below a sliding cut (MAMBAC procedure). *Psychological Reports*, **74**, 1059–1274.

Meehl, P. E., & Yonce, L. J. (1996). Taxometric analysis: II. Detecting taxonicity using covariance of two quantitative indicators in successive intervals of a third indicator (MAXCOV procedure). *Psychological Reports*, **78**, 1091–1227.

National Research Council and Institute of Medicine. (2009). *Depression in parents, parenting, and children: Opportunities to improve identification, treatment, and prevention*. Washington, DC: National Academies Press.

NICHD Early Child Care Research Network. (1997). The effects of infant child care on infant–mother attachment security: Results of the NICHD Study of Early Child Care. *Child Development*, **68**, 860–879.

NICHD Early Child Care Research Network. (2001). Child-care and family predictors of preschool attachment and stability from infancy. *Developmental Psychology*, **37**, 847–862.

NICHD Early Child Care Research Network. (2004). Father's and mother's parenting behavior and beliefs as predictors of child social adjustment in the transition to school. *Journal of Family Psychology*, **18**, 628–638.

142

NICHD Early Child Care Research Network. (Eds.). (2005). *Child care and child development*. New York, NY: Guilford Press.

NICHD Early Child Care Research Network. (2006). Infant–mother attachment classification: Risk and protection in relation to changing maternal quality. *Developmental Psychology*, **42**, 38–58.

NICHD Early Child Care Research Network. (2008). Mothers' and fathers' support for child autonomy and early school achievement. *Developmental Psychology*, **44**, 895–907.

Paley, B., Cox, M. J., Burchinal, M. R., & Payne, C. C. (1999). Attachment and marital functioning: Comparison of spouses with continuous-secure, earned-secure, dismissing, and preoccupied attachment stances. *Journal of Family Psychology*, **13**, 580–597.

Pearson, J. L., Cohn, D. A., Cowan, P. A., & Cowan, C. P. (1994). Earned- and continuous-security in adult attachment: Relation to depressive symptomatology and parenting style. *Development and Psychopathology*, **6**, 359–373.

Pederson, D. R., Gleason, K. E., Moran, G., & Bento, S. (1998). Maternal attachment representations, maternal sensitivity, and the infant–mother attachment relationship. *Developmental Psychology*, **34**, 925–933.

Phelps, J. L., Belsky, J., & Crnic, K. (1998). Earned security, daily stress, and parenting: A comparison of five alternative models. *Development and Psychopathology*, **10**, 21–38.

Radloff, L. S. (1977). The CES-D Scale: A self-report depression scale for research in the general population. *Applied Psychological Measurement*, **1**, 385–401.

Richters, J. E., Waters, E., & Vaughn, B. E. (1988). Empirical classification of infant–mother relationships from interactive behavior and crying during reunion. *Child Development*, **59**, 512–522.

Reiner, I., & Spangler, G. (2010). Adult attachment and gene polymorphisms of the dopamine D4 receptor and serotonin transporter (5-HTT). *Attachment & Human Development*, **12**, 209–229.

Riggs, S. A., & Jacobvitz, D. (2002). Expectant parents' representations of early attachment relationships: Associations with mental health and family history. *Journal of Consulting and Clinical Psychology*, **70**, 195–204.

Rogosa, D. (1995). Myths and methods: "Myths about longitudinal research" plus supplemental questions. In J. M. Gottman (Ed.), *The analysis of change* (pp. 3–66) Mahwah, NJ: Lawrence Erlbaum.

Roisman, G. I. (2009). Adult attachment: Toward a rapprochement of methodological cultures. *Current Directions in Psychological Science*, **18**, 122–126.

Roisman, G. I., Booth-LaForce, C., Belsky, J., Burt, K. B., & Groh, A. M. (2013). Molecular-genetic correlates of infant attachment: A cautionary tale. *Attachment & Human Development*, **15**, 384–406.

Roisman, G. I., Fortuna, K., & Holland, A. S. (2006). An experimental manipulation of retrospectively defined earned and continuous attachment security. *Child Development*, **77**, 59–71.

Roisman, G. I., & Fraley, R. C. (2008). A behavior-genetic study of parenting quality, infant attachment security, and their covariation in a nationally representative sample. *Developmental Psychology*, **44**, 831–839.

Roisman, G. I., Fraley, R. C., & Belsky, J. (2007). A taxometric study of the Adult Attachment Interview. *Developmental Psychology*, **43**, 675–686.

Roisman, G. I., & Haydon, K. C. (2011). Earned security in retrospect: Emerging insights from longitudinal, experimental, and taxometric investigations. In D. Cicchetti & G. I. Roisman (Eds.), *The Origins and Organization of Adaptation and Maladaptation* (pp. 109–154). Hoboken, NJ: Wiley.

Roisman, G. I., Madsen, S. D., Hennighausen, K. H., Sroufe, L. A., & Collins, W. A. (2001). The coherence of dyadic behavior across parent–child and romantic relationships as mediated by the internalized representation of experience. *Attachment & Human Development, 3,* 156–172.

Roisman, G. I., Padrón, E., Sroufe, L. A., & Egeland, B. (2002). Earned-secure attachment status in retrospect and prospect. *Child Development, 73,* 1204–1219.

Rosenstein, D. S., & Horowitz, H. A. (1996). Adolescent attachment and psychopathology. *Journal of Consulting and Clinical Psychology, 64,* 244–253.

Ruscio, J., Haslam, N., & Ruscio, A. M. (2006). *Introduction to the taxometric method: A practical guide.* Mahwah, NJ: Lawrence Erlbaum.

Ruscio, J., Ruscio, A. M., & Keane, T. M. (2004). Using taxometric analysis to distinguish a small latent taxon from a latent dimension with positively skewed indicators: The case of involuntary defeat syndrome. *Journal of Abnormal Psychology, 113,* 145–154.

Ruscio, J., Ruscio, A. M., & Meron, M. (2007). Applying the bootstrap to taxometric analysis: Generating empirical sampling distributions to help interpret results. *Multivariate Behavioral Research, 42,* 349–386.

Ruscio, J., Walters, G. D., Marcus, D. K., & Kaczetow, W. (2010). Comparing the relative fit of categorical and dimensional latent variable models using consistency tests. *Psychological Assessment, 22,* 5–21.

Sarason, I., Johnson, J., & Siegel, L. (1978). Assessing the impact of life changes: Development of the Life Experiences Survey. *Journal of Consulting and Clinical Psychology, 46,* 932–946.

Saunders, R., Jacobvitz, D., Zaccagnino, M., Beverung, L. M., & Hazen, N. (2011). Pathways to earned-security: The role of alternate support figures. *Attachment and Human Development, 13,* 403–420.

Spangler, G., & Zimmermann, P. (1999). Attachment representation and emotion regulation in adolescence: A psycho-biological perspective on internal working models. *Attachment and Human Development, 1,* 270–290.

Sroufe, L. A. (1983). Infant-caregiver attachment and patterns of adaptation in preschool: The roots of maladaptation and competence. In M. Perlmutter (Ed.), *Development and policy concerning children with special needs: The Minnesota Symposia on Child Psychology* (Vol. 16, pp. 41–83). Hillsdale, NJ: Lawrence Erlbaum.

Sroufe, L. A., Egeland, B., Carlson, E. A., & Collins, W. A. (2005). *The development of the person: The Minnesota Study of Risk and Adaptation from birth to adulthood.* New York, NY: Guilford Press.

Sroufe, L. A., Egeland, B., & Kreutzer, T. (1990). The fate of early experience following developmental change: Longitudinal approaches to individual adaptation in childhood. *Child Development, 61,* 1363–1373.

Steele, H., & Steele, M. (2005). Understanding and resolving emotional conflict: The London Parent–Child Project. In K. E. Grossmann, K. Grossmann, & E. Waters (Eds.), *Attachment from infancy to adulthood: The major longitudinal studies* (pp. 137–164). New York, NY: Guilford Press.

Thompson, R. A. (1999). Early attachment and later development. In J. Cassidy & P. R. Shaver (Eds.), *Handbook of attachment: Theory, research, and clinical applications* (pp. 265–286). New York, NY: Guilford Press.

Thurstone, L. L. (1947). *Multiple factor analysis.* Chicago: University of Chicago Press.

Torgersen, A. M., Grova, B. K., & Sommerstad, R. (2007). A pilot study of attachment patterns in adult twins. *Attachment & Human Development, 9,* 127–138.

Treboux, D., Crowell, J., & Waters, E. (2004). When "new" meets "old": Configurations of adult attachment representations and their implications for marital functioning. *Developmental Psychology, 40,* 295–314.

Van IJzendoorn, M. H. (1995). Adult attachment representations, parental responsiveness, and infant attachment: A meta-analysis on the predictive validity of the Adult Attachment Interview. *Psychological Bulletin, 117,* 387–403.

Van IJzendoorn, M. H., & Kroonenberg, P. M. (1990). Cross-cultural consistency of coding the Strange Situation. *Infant Behavior and Development, 13,* 469–485.

Van Ryzin, M. J., Carlson, E. A., & Sroufe, L. A. (2011). Attachment discontinuity in a high-risk sample. *Attachment & Human Development, 13,* 381–401.

Veríssimo, M., & Salvaterra, F. (2006). Maternal secure-base scripts and children's attachment security in an adopted sample. *Attachment & Human Development, 8,* 261–273.

Waller, N. G., & Meehl, P. E. (1998). *Multivariate taxometric procedures: Distinguishing types from continua.* Newbury Park, CA: SAGE.

Waller, N. G., Putnam, F. W., & Carlson, E. B. (1996). Types of dissociation and dissociative types: A taxometric analysis of dissociative experiences. *Psychological Methods, 1,* 300–321.

Waters, E. (2003). Assessing secure base behavior and attachment security using the q-sort method. Retrieved from http://www.psychology.sunysb.edu/attachment/measures/content/aqs_method.html

Waters, E., & Beauchaine, T. P. (2003). Are there really patterns of attachment? Comment on Fraley and Spieker (2003). *Developmental Psychology, 39,* 417–422.

Waters, E., & Deane, K. E. (1985). Defining and assessing individual differences in attachment relationships: Q-methodology and the organization of behavior in infancy and early childhood. *Monographs of the Society for Research in Child Development, 50,* 41–65.

Waters, E., Hamilton, C. E., & Weinfield, N. S. (2000). The stability of attachment security from infancy to adolescence and early adulthood: General introduction. *Child Development, 71,* 678–683.

Waters, E., Merrick, S., Treboux, D., Crowell, J., & Albersheim, L. (2000). Attachment security in infancy and early adulthood: A twenty-year longitudinal study. *Child Development, 71,* 684–689.

Waters, E., Weinfield, N. S., & Hamilton, C. E. (2000). The stability of attachment security from infancy to adolescence and early adulthood: General discussion. *Child Development, 71,* 703–706.

Weinfield, N. S., Sroufe, L. A., & Egeland, B. (2000). Attachment from infancy to adulthood in a high-risk sample: Continuity, discontinuity, and their correlates. *Child Development, 71,* 695–702.

Weinfield, N. S., Whaley, G. J. L., & Egeland, B. (2004). Continuity, discontinuity, and coherence in attachment from infancy to late adolescence: Sequelae of organization and disorganization. *Attachment and Human Development, 6,* 73–97.

Whipple, N., Bernier, A., & Mageau, G. A. (2011). A dimensional approach to maternal attachment state of mind: Relations to maternal sensitivity and maternal autonomy support. *Developmental Psychology, 47*, 396–403.

Woodcock, R. W., & Johnson, M. B. (1989). *WJ-R Tests of Cognitive Ability.* Itasca, IL: Riverside Publishing.

Woodcock, R. W. (1990). Theoretical foundations of the WJ-R measures of cognitive ability. *Journal of Psychoeducational Assessment, 8*, 231–258.

Zimmerman, P., Fremmer-Bombik, E., Spangler, G., & Grossmann, K. E. (1997). Attachment in adolescence: A longitudinal perspective. In W. Koops, J. B. Hoeksma, & D. C. van den Boom (Eds.), *Development of interaction and attachment: Traditional and non-traditional approaches* (pp. 281–292). North-Holland, Amsterdam: Koninklijke Nederlandse Akademie van Wetenschappen Verhandelingen, Afd.

# INVITED COMMENTARY

CATEGORIES OR DIMENSIONS: LESSONS LEARNED FROM A
TAXOMETRIC ANALYSIS OF ADULT ATTACHMENT INTERVIEW DATA

*John Ruscio*

**ABSTRACT** Booth-LaForce and Roisman's monograph on the Adult Attachment Interview (AAI) featured a taxometric analysis to determine whether variation along two components, dismissing and preoccupied states of mind, was categorical or dimensional. Empirically evaluating the latent structure of these constructs helps to avoid spurious categories or dimensions. This benefits researchers working with measures of adult attachment to maintain as much predictive validity and statistical power as possible, and it benefits researchers who build or test theories of adult attachment by steering the search for causal factors in fruitful directions. Fraley and Roisman (Chapter 3, this volume) performed their taxometric performed their taxometric analyses in an exemplary fashion, adhering carefully to empirically supported, practical guidelines. They adopted an appropriate inferential framework for their taxometric results that pits two competing structural models against one another. They were willing to accept that the taxometric results for preoccupied states of mind were ambiguous and they tentatively advocated a dimensional measure on the grounds that, even if this was not the best representation, using a spurious dimension might do less harm than using spurious categories. Rather than embracing a general preference for categories or for dimensions, researchers should evaluate the pros and cons of each potential structure-measurement mismatch on a case-by-case basis.

Together with the many collaborators who contributed to one or more of the chapters in their monograph, Booth-LaForce and Roisman presented a broad range of analyses of a large sample of data ($N = 857$) from the Adult

Corresponding author: Dr. John Ruscio, Psychology Department, The College of New Jersey, 2000 Pennington Road, Ewing, NJ 08628, email: ruscio@tcnj.edu

Attachment Interview (AAI). Part 1 included two chapters that examined fundamental psychometric issues. First, Haltigan, Roisman, and Haydon (Chapter 2) addressed the question of whether adult attachment is best represented as a unitary construct, with individuals classified into one of three mutually exclusive categories (secure-autonomous, dismissing, or preoccupied), or whether it is best represented using two components, with individuals varying relatively independently along these components (dismissing and preoccupied states of mind). They performed factor analyses of AAI data and obtained evidence favoring the latter model. Second, Fraley and Roisman (Chapter 3) pursued the follow-up question of whether variation along these components is categorical or dimensional in nature. They employed Meehl's (1995) taxometric method and obtained evidence suggesting that both components are best represented dimensionally.

In this comment, I focus on Fraley and Roisman's (Chapter 3) exemplary application of taxometric analysis, which helped pave the way for the many subsequent explorations of the stability, change, and developmental origins of adult attachment in Part 2 of the monograph. The fact that Fraley and Roisman were willing and able to perform taxometric analyses to tease apart categorical and dimensional structural models, the effectiveness with which they applied taxometric methodology, and the reasonableness of the conclusions that they drew from the taxometric results are all laudable aspects of their investigation. In what follows, I review these three areas of strength and expand on some of the points that the authors raised along the way.

## ADDRESSING LATENT STRUCTURE EMPIRICALLY

Incorporating a taxometric analysis into the program of research on the AAI is a model to follow. The taxometric method is neither the beginning nor the end of a research endeavor. Rather, it complements other data-analytic tools in a program of research on the latent structure of a target construct (Ruscio & Ruscio, 2004), which in turn lays the groundwork for subsequent theoretical and empirical research. Fraley and Roisman (Chapter 3) astutely noted that the factor-analytic findings of Haltigan et al. (Chapter 2) were ambiguous with regard to the categorical versus dimensional nature of variation along the two components of dismissing and preoccupied states of mind. The taxometric method was a well-chosen follow-up technique to help determine whether individuals differ in categorical or dimensional ways. More investigators would be wise to examine this issue empirically rather than take for granted that their preferred conceptualization, whether categorical or dimensional, is appropriate. An inappropriate presumption can carry substantial costs.

As Fraley and Roisman argue, using categorical measures of dimensional constructs can reduce predictive validity, underestimate stability, and weaken statistical power. Their arguments draw from and extend the earlier cases made by Fraley and Waller (1998) and Fraley and Spieker (2003). Both of these sources spoke specifically to issues in the domain of infant and adult attachment research, though the important points they make are more broadly applicable. It's worth adding that the mistake of using a categorical measure of a dimensional construct might also reify a spurious classification, lead to improperly specified theoretical models, or prompt searches for the wrong kinds of causal factors (Meehl, 1992; Ruscio, Haslam, & Ruscio, 2006). For example, adopting a categorical framework for adult attachment patterns despite their apparently dimensional variation might mislead readers into assuming that these categories exist in some theoretically meaningful sense, rather than merely serving as shorthand for endpoints along one or more latent dimensions. Likewise, investigators might undertake a search for the causes of bifurcation into categories when no such causes exist because individuals do not in fact divide themselves into categories. The types of causal models most consistent with dimensional structure tend to involve the sum of many small influences (e.g., additive genetic or environmental factors).

On the other hand, Fraley and Roisman also noted that for categorical constructs, the taxometric method can help to estimate base rates (i.e., relative group sizes) and improve assessment. Here, too, it's worth adding that there may be implications of a structural mismatch for building and testing theoretical models. Using a dimensional measure of a categorical construct may throw investigators off the trail of causes of bifurcation into categories. The types of causal models most consistent with categorical structure tend to involve dichotomous causal factors (e.g., a single gene or environmental influence necessary and sufficient to produce category membership), cumulative or interactive effects (e.g., neither a genetic predisposition nor an environmental influence is necessary to produce category membership, but they are jointly sufficient to do so), or threshold effects (e.g., an environmental factor has little influence up to a point, but beyond this level it bumps individuals into a new category).

Because either type of mismatch can have serious consequences for theory, research, or practice, investigators would be well-advised to evaluate the latent structure of target constructs empirically (Ruscio & Ruscio, 2002). Though there are many data-analytic procedures that relate observable, measured variables to unobservable, latent constructs, relatively few of these are useful as tests of whether a construct is best represented categorically or dimensionally. As Fraley and Roisman state, there is an important difference between structure-imposing techniques and structure-uncovering techniques. For example, cluster-analytic algorithms will always identify categories because the methodology presumes categorical variation. Though this can be useful for any number of other research purposes, cluster analysis does not afford very useful tests between categorical and dimensional structural models. This is an obvious case of a structure-imposing technique.

On the other hand, some techniques are misunderstood as imposing structure when in fact they do no such thing. Factor analysis, as Fraley and Roisman correctly note, can be used to determine the number of latent factors along which individuals differ, but it is a mistake to equate these factors with dimensions. Rather, variation along any specific factor can be categorical or dimensional in nature (Waller & Meehl, 1998).

Paul Meehl developed his taxometric method expressly to make the distinction between categories and dimensions (Meehl, 1995), and a wealth of research supports its utility under a wide range of data conditions (for an overview, see Ruscio, Ruscio, & Carney, 2011). McGrath and Walters (2012) described Meehl's taxometric method as a general-purpose tool for differentiating between categorical and dimensional structural models. Though there are other latent variable modeling techniques designed to achieve the same goal (e.g., factor mixture models), it is presently unknown whether any of these methods performs as well or better under comparable data conditions. Likewise, it is unknown whether other methods might perform well under data conditions unsuitable for taxometric analysis. Thus, it would be premature to conclude that Meehl's taxometric method is the only reasonable data-analytic choice one could make when attempting to tease apart categorical and dimensional structural models. It can, however, be considered a strong contender, backed by substantial theoretical and empirical support when its data requirements are satisfied (Ruscio et al., 2011).

Given the strong track record of taxometric analyses in simulation studies, it remains disappointing to observe how few important constructs in the social and behavioral sciences have been studied using this method. Nick Haslam and his colleagues have reviewed taxometric studies a number of times (e.g., Haslam, 2003, 2007, 2011; Haslam & Kim, 2002), including a quantitative review which showed that how the taxometric method is implemented can affect the conclusions researchers draw from the results (Haslam, Holland, & Kuppens, 2012), a subject that will be revisited shortly. Each of these reviews of taxometric research sheds light on the constructs that have been studied, the methods that have been used to do so, and trends in the conclusions that researchers have reached. Perhaps most striking of all is what is missing from these reviews: the large number of constructs that have not (yet) been studied taxometrically.

Even with the understanding that taxometric analysis is by no means the only way to differentiate between categorical and dimensional structures, theory and research in many, perhaps most, realms of social and behavioral science appears to operate on the presumption that important constructs are structured one way or the other without subjecting these presumptions to rigorous tests. Thus, an unusual and salient strength of the Booth-LaForce and Roisman monograph is that they included a taxometric analysis in the psychometric stage of the research. Providing empirical support for the dimensional structure of measures constructed using AAI data places all the subsequent chapters, and their data analyses in particular, on a more solid psychometric foundation.

## APPLICATION OF TAXOMETRIC METHODOLOGY

Just as the AAI monograph deserves credit for including a chapter on taxometric analysis, that analysis itself was performed in an exemplary manner by Fraley and Roisman. They described their methodology clearly and concisely, perhaps so much so that readers unfamiliar with taxometric analysis might fail to appreciate that it confronts researchers with many potentially important decision points. Ruscio et al. (2011) spelled these out and summarized the available research that can help researchers make smart choices. Though Fraley and Roisman did not cite this particular source, the fact that they carefully followed empirically supported, practical guidelines for implementing the taxometric method demonstrates their attention to the relevant literature.

Fraley and Roisman performed three taxometric procedures: MAXCOV (MAXimum COVariance; Meehl & Yonce, 1996), MAMBAC (Mean Above Minus Below A Cut; Meehl & Yonce, 1994), and L-Mode (Latent Mode; Waller & Meehl, 1998). These are well chosen as complements to one another because they analyze the data in distinct ways. By doing so, they provide nonredundant checks on the consistency of results. This constitutes a cornerstone of the taxometric method, Meehl's (1995) emphasis on "consistency tests" rather than tests of statistical significance. Fraley and Roisman not only performed three distinct procedures to examine the consistency of the results, they implemented each one in ways supported by the results of simulation studies. For example, whereas earlier taxometric studies often performed the MAXCOV procedure by dividing the sample of cases into ordered subsamples that did not overlap with one another (intervals), research suggests that MAXCOV yields more informative results when cases are divided into ordered subsamples that do in fact overlap substantially with one another (sliding windows). Waller and Meehl (1998) introduced this innovation along with the MAXEIG (MAXimum EIGenvalue) procedure, which is a multivariate generalization of MAXCOV. Sliding windows can be used just as profitably with the MAXCOV procedure (Walters & Ruscio, 2010), and Fraley and Roisman took advantage of this technique.

Perhaps the most important implementation decision that Fraley and Roisman made was to incorporate parallel analyses of categorical and dimensional comparison data. These data are generated in ways that reproduce the observed distributions and correlations of the research data, but starting from two different structural models (categorical and dimensional). Parallel analyses of these comparison data provide a baseline for interpreting the results for the research data that is tailored to these unique data conditions (Ruscio, Ruscio, & Meron, 2007). For example, positively skewed dimensional data can yield taxometric results that are easily misinterpreted as evidence of categorical structure (Ruscio & Marcus, 2007). Because skewed data are common (Micceri, 1989), so are potentially misleading taxometric results. The parallel analysis of comparably skewed comparison data can help to determine whether the results for the research data actually correspond more closely to those for the categorical or the dimensional comparison data (Ruscio & Marcus, 2007).

When parallel analyses of comparison data are performed, this also allows the calculation of the Comparison Curve Fit Index (CCFI; Ruscio et al., 2007). The CCFI quantifies how closely the results for the research data map onto those for the categorical and the dimensional comparison data. CCFI values can range from 0, representing the strongest support for dimensional structure, to 1, representing the strongest support for categorical structure. Values close to .5 are ambiguous. Haslam et al. (2012, p. 911) described "the analysis of simulated comparison data and the use of the CCFI" as "the most important historical development in taxometric practice." They noted that across 177 taxometric studies with 311 distinct structural findings, use of the CCFI is strongly correlated with other indices of methodological quality and reduces the likelihood of reaching categorical conclusions. This is consistent with speculation that, absent the more appropriate interpretational baseline provided by parallel analyses of comparison data, skewed data can easily lead to mistaken inferences of categorical structure.

Fraley and Roisman incorporated comparison data into all taxometric analyses and calculated the CCFI for each taxometric procedure (MAXCOV, MAMBAC, and L-Mode) as an objective decision aid to supplement their visual inspection of the taxometric curves. Each of their figures shows the taxometric results for one set of indicators, with the results for each procedure plotted in a way that affords an easy visual inspection against the baseline results for the comparison data. The CCFI values are presented in the text and summarized in a table. In this way, Fraley and Roisman examined the consistency of results in an open, comprehensive, and rigorous manner.

Before closing this section, one very minor criticism of Fraley and Roisman's taxometric analysis should be noted: They provided estimates of the taxon base rate, or the size of the higher-scoring of the two putative groups in a categorical model. These estimates would have been informative if the authors had concluded that one or more of the AAI factors was in fact categorical. These estimates do not correspond to any parameters in a dimensional structural model, though, so it's not clear why they were presented. There has been considerable speculation in the taxometric literature that taxon base rate estimates might be helpful as a kind of consistency test (e.g., Meehl, 1995). The idea is that these estimates should cohere around a single value if in fact a taxon exists, but not otherwise (i.e., not if the structure is dimensional rather than categorical). Plausible as this may seem, simulation studies have not supported the utility of such a base-rate consistency test (Ruscio, 2007; Ruscio et al., 2006). No particular threshold has been supported for differentiating the degree of consistency of taxon base rate estimates one would expect for categorical as opposed to dimensional data. The fundamental problem is that under many data conditions, taxon base rate estimates can be extremely consistent even for dimensional data. Providing taxon base rate estimates for constructs judged to be dimensional, though not a serious flaw in any event, is arguably the most questionable choice that Fraley and Roisman made when implementing the taxometric method and reporting the results.

## DRAWING CONCLUSIONS FROM TAXOMETRIC RESULTS

The inferential framework for taxometric analysis has been a subject of some dispute in the literature. Ruscio (2007) considered three inferential frameworks that had been advanced—detection of categorical structure, dimensional structure as a null hypothesis, and two competing structural hypotheses—and reviewed the advantages and disadvantages of each. The recommended approach, that of two competing structural hypotheses, is consistent with Meehl's (2004) conceptualization of his taxometric method as providing one of three kinds of evidence: support for categorical structure, support for dimensional structure, or ambiguous results. Fraley and Roisman implicitly adopted this inferential framework by being willing to withhold judgment when the CCFI fell within an ambiguous range of intermediate values. Specifically, their results for preoccupied state of mind indicators yielded a mean CCFI value of .46, which they characterized as ambiguous because it fell between the dual thresholds of .45 and .55 that Ruscio, Walters, Marcus, and Kaczetow (2010) recommended as defining the ambiguous range of mean CCFIs. Whereas the mean CCFI for every other series of analyses fell outside this range—in each case, it was below .45, supporting dimensional structure—this exception was cautiously interpreted as uninformative. It is arguably a feature, and not a bug, that the taxometric method is capable of identifying ambiguous results to prevent potential misinterpretations. Particularly in light of the temptation to draw some affirmative conclusion from every data-analytic result, it is significant that Fraley and Roisman were willing to exercise restraint and acknowledge that the results from one series of analyses were inconclusive.

Having chosen not to reach a conclusion of categorical or dimensional structure with respect to the preoccupied states of mind indicators, Fraley and Roisman explained why they tentatively preferred to use a dimensional measure of this construct. They contrasted the costs of both kinds of structure-measurement mismatches that were possible, a dimensional measure of a categorical construct or a categorical measure of a dimensional construct, and argued that the former mistake would be less harmful than the latter. Fraley and Roisman emphasized the assessment implications, noting that if later evidence lent support to categorical structure, one could always use the dimensional measure to reassign cases to categories, whereas if later evidence lent support to dimensional structure, it would not be possible to use a categorical measure to relocate cases along a dimension.

In this instance, Fraley and Roisman's argument is reasonable, but a reader should not leave with the impression that this same argument would necessarily be as persuasive in other contexts. It is conceivable that a consideration of the two types of structure-measurement mismatches might tip the other way in a different context. For example, if a practical decision needs to be made (e.g., determination of legal status such as competency to stand trial), a compelling case might be made that a categorical measure might be helpful even if the categorical distinction is spurious with respect to the latent structure of the target construct. A dimensional measure may be less helpful to real-world decision makers, perhaps leading to more arbitrary, subjective, or inconsistent judgments as different people interpret scores along a dimension in different ways by implicitly or explicitly applying their own thresholds. A categorical measure is less prone to this particular form of idiosyncratic interpretation.

This is not to suggest that spurious categories are, in general, more or less acceptable than spurious dimensions. The point is that the costs and benefits of each type of mismatch, or even each type of match, should be considered on a case-by-case basis. Researchers may have the luxury of focusing on the $R^2$ values in their statistical models, in which case even spurious dimensions can compete favorably with categories, be they real or spurious (Grove, 1991). But in the high-stakes realm of real-world decision making, other considerations can be more important, and the clarity and consistency afforded by categories may become compelling virtues. This is by no means a criticism of Fraley and Roisman's argument in favor of a tentative acceptance of a dimensional model for preoccupied states of mind. Rather, it is simply a reminder that there should be no general preference for categories or dimensions, that their relative merits depend on the context and should be carefully considered in each new application.

154

## REFERENCES

Fraley, R. C., & Spieker, S. J. (2003). Are infant attachment patterns continuously or categorically distributed? A taxometric analysis of strange situation behavior. *Developmental Psychology*, **39**, 387–404.

Fraley, R. C., & Waller, N. G. (1998). Adult attachment patterns: A test of the typological model. In J. A. Simpson & W. S. Rholes (Eds.), *Attachment theory and close relationships* (pp. 77–114). New York, NY: Guilford Press.

Grove, W. M. (1991). When is a diagnosis worth making? A statistical comparison of two prediction strategies. *Psychological Reports*, **68**, 3–17.

Haslam, N. (2003). The dimensional view of personality disorders: A review of the taxometric evidence. *Clinical Psychology Review*, **23**, 75–93.

Haslam, N. (2007). The latent structure of mental disorders: A taxometric update on the categorical vs. dimensional debate. *Current Psychiatry Reviews*, **3**, 172–177.

Haslam, N. (2011). The latent structure of personality and psychopathology: A review of trends in taxometric research. *Scientific Review of Mental Health Practice*, **8**, 17–29.

Haslam, N., Holland, E., & Kuppens, P. (2012). Categories versus dimensions in personality and psychopathology: A quantitative review of taxometric research. *Psychological Medicine*, **42**, 903–920.

Haslam, N., & Kim, H. (2002). Categories and continua: A review of taxometric research. *Genetic, Social, and General Psychology Monographs*, **128**, 271–320.

McGrath, R. E., & Walters, G. D. (2012). Taxometric analysis as a general strategy for distinguishing categorical from dimensional latent structure. *Psychological Methods*, **17**, 284–293.

Meehl, P. E. (1992). Factors and taxa, traits and types, differences of degree and differences in kind. *Journal of Personality*, **60**, 117–174.

Meehl, P. E. (1995). Bootstraps taxometrics: Solving the classification problem in psychopathology. *American Psychologist*, **50**, 266–274.

Meehl, P. E. (2004). What's in a taxon? *Journal of Abnormal Psychology*, **113**, 39–43.

Meehl, P. E., & Yonce, L. J. (1994). Taxometric analysis: I. Detecting taxonicity with two quantitative indicators using means above and below a sliding cut (MAMBAC procedure). *Psychological Reports*, **74**, 1059–1274.

Meehl, P. E., & Yonce, L. J. (1996). Taxometric analysis: II. Detecting taxonicity using covariance of two quantitative indicators in successive intervals of a third indicator (MAXCOV procedure). *Psychological Reports*, **78**, 1091–1227.

Micceri, T. (1989). The unicorn, the normal curve, and other improbable creatures. *Psychological Bulletin*, **105**, 156–166.

Ruscio, J. (2007). Taxometric analysis: An empirically-grounded approach to implementing the method. *Criminal Justice and Behavior*, **34**, 1588–1622.

Ruscio, J., Haslam, N., & Ruscio, A. M. (2006). *Introduction to the taxometric method: A practical guide*. Mahwah, NJ: Lawrence Erlbaum Associates.

Ruscio, J., & Marcus, D. K. (2007). Detecting small taxa using simulated comparison data: A reanalysis of Beach, Amir, and Bau's (2005) data. *Psychological Assessment*, **19**, 241–246.

Ruscio, J., & Ruscio, A. M. (2002). A structure-based approach to psychological assessment: Matching measurement models to latent structure. *Assessment*, **9**, 4–16.

Ruscio, J., & Ruscio, A. M. (2004). Clarifying boundary issues in psychopathology: The role of taxometrics in a comprehensive program of structural research. *Journal of Abnormal Psychology*, **113**, 24–38.

Ruscio, J., Ruscio, A. M., & Carney, L. M. (2011). Performing taxometric analysis to distinguish categorical and dimensional variables. *Journal of Experimental Psychopathology*, **2**, 170–196.

Ruscio, J., Ruscio, A. M., & Meron, M. (2007). Applying the bootstrap to taxometric analysis: Generating empirical sampling distributions to help interpret results. *Multivariate Behavioral Research*, **42**, 349–386.

Ruscio, J., Walters, G. D., Marcus, D. K., & Kaczetow, W. (2010). Comparing the relative fit of categorical and dimensional latent variable models using consistency tests. *Psychological Assessment*, **22**, 5–21.

Waller, N. G., & Meehl, P. E. (1998). *Multivariate taxometric procedures: Distinguishing types from continua.* Thousand Oaks, CA: SAGE.

Walters, G. D., & Ruscio, J. (2010). Where do we draw the line? Assigning cases to subsamples for MAMBAC, MAXCOV, and MAXEIG taxometric analyses. *Assessment*, **17**, 321–333.

# INVITED COMMENTARY

CONFINED QUEST FOR CONTINUITY: THE CATEGORICAL VERSUS
CONTINUOUS NATURE OF ATTACHMENT

*Marinus H. van IJzendoorn and Marian J. Bakermans-Kranenburg*

**ABSTRACT** The use of the Adult Attachment Interview (AAI) in the NICHD
Study of Early Child Care and Youth Development (NICHD SECCYD) is a
major contribution to the field. The core of the current monograph pertains
to psychometrics (dimensional vs. categorical assessment) of the AAI and
continuity of attachment over time. We argue that the generalizability of the
conclusions with regard to the AAI is limited to similar groups, because of the
low-risk adolescence nature of the sample, with concomitant underrepresen-
tation of the preoccupied and unresolved classifications in the current sample
(each only 3%). Baron von Münchhausen's paradox emerges in the use of the
same source of coded data for categorical classifications and continuous scales
of the AAI scoring procedure. At the same time, the monograph convincingly
demonstrates that earned security cannot be assessed retrospectively in a valid
and reliable manner, and the study highlights the power of scientific
collaboration as realized in the NICHD SECCYD.

LANDMARK STUDY

Cathryn Booth-LaForce, Glenn Roisman, and the other authors should
be congratulated on their largest study of adult attachment to date. The
authors make great use of the rich longitudinal dataset of the NICHD Study
of Early Child Care and Youth Development (NICHD SECCYD), and address
several key issues in the field of attachment research. Special emphasis is
on the psychometrics of the Adult Attachment Interview (AAI) that was

Corresponding author: Marinus H. van IJzendoorn, Centre for Child and Family Studies,
Leiden University, P.O. Box 9555, Leiden 2300 RB, the Netherlands, email: vanijzen@fsw.
leidenuniv.nl

introduced almost 30 years ago by Main, Kaplan, and Cassidy (1985) in another monograph of the SRCD, according to Google Scholar cited more than 4,000 times.

The set of empirical papers in the new monograph is part of the more than 250 scientific products of NICHD SECCYD that resulted from an investment of millions of dollars and tons of work in collecting and coding data. NICHD SECCYD is an unprecedented showcase of the power of scientific collaboration in a thoroughly fragmented developmental science, and the current monograph is solid evidence in favor of "big science" complementary to discovery-oriented small-is-beautiful studies.

The core of the monograph pertains to attachment continuity interpreted in two ways: measurement continuity (versus categorical assessment) and temporal continuity. The papers constitute a highly coherent narrative, and they read as a collectively authored monograph in the literal sense of the word. It is wonderful to see a fourth generation of attachment researchers emerging with major contributions to the ever-evolving theoretical framework of attachment theory. The large longitudinal NICHD SECCYD dataset, the eclectic use of measures at multiple levels of human functioning, and the application of advanced statistical tools make this monograph a truly outstanding achievement.

## EARNED SECURITY

Impressive is the work on earned security, and the monograph settles this uncomfortable issue definitely. Earned security has been defined as a coherent and secure adult attachment representation despite untoward attachment experiences in childhood—as retrospectively reported by the participant in the context of the AAI (Pearson, Cohn, Cowan, & Cowan, 1994). Roisman, Haltigan, Haydon, and Booth-LaForce (Chapter 6) replicate and extend the finding of the much smaller Minnesota Longitudinal Study of Risk and Adaptation (Sroufe, Egeland, Carlson, & Collins, 2005) that, on the contrary, earned-secures experienced average or better parental caregiving (Roisman, Padrón, Sroufe, & Egeland, 2002). This finding nicely converges with the brilliant experimental falsification of earned security as a sub-category that Roisman and colleagues presented some years ago (Roisman, Fortuna, & Holland, 2006). The conclusion must be that earned security cannot be assessed retrospectively in a valid and reliable manner.

This conclusion is strong support for the original and revolutionary shift that Mary Main and colleagues proposed in constructing the AAI as a measure of *current* cognitive representations of past attachment events and relationships. This shift roots the AAI firmly in cognitive theories of autobiographical memory and sets it squarely apart from all its predecessors and competitors

158

that cherish the hidden or explicit ambition to get a veridical account of childhood experiences (e.g., the Parental Bonding Instrument, Parker, Tupling, & Brown, 1979) which is impossible because of the permanently reconstructive nature of autobiographical memory (Hesse, 2008). Earned security and the concomitant reification of the inferred experiences scales of the AAI coding system (Main, Goldwyn, & Hesse, 2003–2008) were distressing digressions from this radical shift. The monograph convincingly exposes the idea of earned security as a dead-end, at least insofar the earned nature of attachment security is derived from the AAI.

## A LOW-RISK, LATE-ADOLESCENCE SAMPLE

The monograph also struggles with some limitations, and one of the most pervasive limitations is the low-risk, late-adolescence sample, an inevitable result of nonresponse, with a bias toward an overrepresentation of White and higher educated families in the remaining sample. Participants who completed the AAI were 857 adolescents with a mean age of 17.8 years. The authors compared demographic characteristics of the AAI sample with the nonrespondents ($n = 507$, 37%) and found the AAI respondents to be significantly more likely to be White non-Hispanic and female. Their parents had had more years of education. The AAI sample also had a higher family income-to-needs ratio. Of course, this type of attrition can be expected in a large-scale longitudinal study across an impressive time-span of 18 years, and in fact the nonresponse is remarkably low compared to similar cohort studies. Nevertheless, the current participants were not a random selection, and the selective nature of the response might have had some nasty consequences for sampling-sensitive measures. Although the largest long-term longitudinal study of attachment to date, and indeed the largest study including the labor-intensive AAI, the sample is not normative, but biased toward low-risk participants.

The distribution of AAI classifications is a case in point. Using the four-way AAI classification in which those classified as unresolved are placed in a separate category, 59% of the respondents were secure, 35% dismissing, 3% preoccupied, and 3% unresolved. From previous studies on nonclinical adolescents, we know that the overall four-way distribution of attachment representations across adolescent studies ($N = 503$; 44% secure, 34% dismissing, 11% preoccupied, and 11% unresolved) shows a significant overrepresentation of dismissing attachments as well, and at the same time fewer unresolved attachments compared to normative adult samples (Bakermans-Kranenburg & Van IJzendoorn, 2009). The NICHD adolescent distribution is however significantly different from the normative distribution of adolescent AAIs, $X^2$ (3, $N = 857$) $= 142.53$, $p < .001$, with lower percentages of preoccupied and unresolved AAI classifications, and a higher percentage of secure attachments in the NICHD SECCYD study. In fact, the NICHD SECCYD sample can be characterized by the abundant presence of secure or dismissing AAIs, and an almost complete absence of preoccupied and unresolved AAIs. The difference in distributions of the meta-analytic and NICHD SECCYD samples may not only be caused by selective nonresponse but also by difference in age (the NICHD SECCYD subjects being late adolescents) and by the way in which AAI data were collected. In 21% ($n = 178$) of the cases AAIs were completed by phone. The authors found that compared to in-person interviews phone interviews yielded fewer preoccupied attachments, maybe because participants might have felt less licensed to dwell on their (negative) childhood experiences on the phone.

## THREE CORE ASSUMPTIONS

In general, nonresponse is not a major problem for developmental studies. In fact, the large majority of developmental samples are absolutely not representative of any population, and convenience sampling is the rule rather than the exception. For proofs of principle, for tests of theoretical hypotheses, or evaluation of carefully designed interventions internal validity is more important than external validity because the first is a necessary condition for the latter. Only when we want to generalize to a larger population sampling limitations are crucial. In the current monograph, for the tests of substantive hypotheses such as those on earned security the selective attrition constitutes a minor problem, as long as the authors do mention that their findings might not hold in non-White or clinical populations. But empirical answers to other research questions may be seriously compromised by biased sampling leading to strong underrepresentations of specific AAI classifications. Attrition is part and parcel of any longitudinal study, and it is to be expected that participants with the less favorable circumstances or life histories are lost. The current study is not unique in that respect, and the authors are not to blame for it. But a consequence is that the results are generalizable to similar low-risk, late adolescents groups, and not generic to AAI studies with other populations.

What about the psychometric or taxometric study of the AAI? The authors' aim is to examine what they consider to be the core assumptions of the AAI coding system. The "categorical assumption" refers to the expectation that attachment-related individual differences represent true or natural categories (i.e., secure, dismissing, preoccupied, and unresolved). The "dimensionality assumption" pertains to the kind of dimensional structure implied by the AAI. Conventional coding would assume that adults vary on a "unitary" dimension of security versus insecurity (coherent vs. incoherent discourse), and that preoccupied and dismissing states of mind are largely incompatible. The authors also address a third assumption of the AAI, namely the "unresolved loss assumption," that is the idea that discourse on childhood experiences of loss and other potentially traumatic events would uncover lack of resolution of loss or trauma as a separate AAI classification (Hesse, 2008).

Here, we argue that the very low rates of preoccupied and unresolved classifications (each only 3%) in the NICHD SECCYD sample jeopardize rigorous examination of the three assumptions.

## CATEGORICAL OR CONTINUOUS?

The issue of whether a developmental phenotype is categorical in nature or should be considered an intersection of continuous dimensions is difficult to establish. Confronted with a lack of firm theoretical or empirical reasons for one or the other option one might choose to be agnostic, arguing that only pragmatic or empirical arguments can solve this issue. Even gender might be considered a categorical phenotype with underlying dimensionality at the behavioral and also at the hormonal level. Unless convincing evidence for one of the two positions is available, classifications might be taken as handy markers for a set of closely related data-points in a multivariate space defined by continuous dimensions, or considered real categories to be found in vivo, while for some purposes approximated most adequately with a set of intersecting continua. The developers of the AAI seemed to have had the latter option in mind, and to consider dimensional scales as practical steps toward the ultimate goal of categorical classification of discourse strategies (Hesse, 2008; Main et al., 2003–2008).

The approach of Roisman, Booth-LaForce et al.'s monograph to this thorny issue brings to mind the so-called Münchhausen paradox, in particular the circularity variant of it. Baron Von Münchhausen allegedly pulled himself and the horse on which he was sitting out of a swamp by his own hair, or in other versions of this narrative, by the straps of his own boots, from which statistical bootstrapping has been derived. In the taxometric analyses of the NICHD data set the state-of-mind rating scales of the AAI coding system are used to test the "categorical assumption." Through sophisticated statistical exercises it is demonstrated that the indicators of dismissing versus secure attachment representations provide evidence in favor of a continuous instead of categorical "nature" of the phenotype. In contrast, as the authors admit (Fraley & Roisman, Chapter 3), similar analyses do not falsify the categorical nature of preoccupied attachments.

Baron Von Münchhausen's paradox emerges in the use of the same source of coded data for categorical classifications and continuous scales of the AAI scoring procedure. In our experience, AAI coders score state-of-mind scales and classify overall discourse strategies in an iterative process that makes scales and classifications inherently connected and intertwined, and in some basic way circular or rather spiraling. Coding AAIs is a process of creating hypotheses about the kind of discourse a specific interview presents and a continuous critical search for supporting and falsifying evidence for these hypotheses. It is not a neat linear process starting with scoring inferred experiences and state-of-mind ratings without any thought of final classification, resulting in an "independent" overall categorical impression of the discourse. Instead, it is pattern recognition going back and forth between various levels of the discourse in an attempt to gradually approximate the "true nature" of the transcript.

For statistical analyses of AAI scales and classifications this is a serious limitation. Only independent coding of classifications and rating scales would create the statistical independence needed for the taxometric analyses. But even in the ideal case of independently coded scales and classifications we would still need a validity criterion outside of the AAI to calibrate the statistical parameters. In the real world, Baron Von Münchhausen needed a tree or a rock to pull himself out of the swamp. Such an external criterion is lacking, and as the authors acknowledge no statistical procedure in and of itself is able to "carve nature at its joints." Nature will not make the decision between categories or dimensions for us, whatever sophisticated statistical means we use to torture the data.

The ultimate criterion might be the heuristic value of a categorical or continuous interpretation of attachment representations. As the authors note, the value of attachment theory does not hinge on the categorical status of measures of security (p. 50). If continuous attachment dimensions serve us better in understanding individual differences in development compared to attachment categories there may be sufficient reasons to opt for a dimensional interpretation. This may be the case in the long-run because individual idiosyncrasies can be better represented in a complex multidimensional space than in four fixed categories. In the meantime, however, the pragmatic use of both categorical and continuous measures as heuristics of adult attachment might work best.

## TWO DIMENSIONS INSTEAD OF ONE?

The authors of the monograph submit that the kind of dimensionality of the AAI is more important than the discussion about its categorical or continuous nature. They argue that the AAI "captures two modestly correlated state-of-mind dimensions—one that reflects the degree to which individuals either freely evaluate or defensively discuss their early experiences (i.e., dismissing states of mind) and the other reflecting attachment-related

162

preoccupation (i.e., preoccupied states of mind)" (Roisman & Booth-LaForce, Chapter 8, p. 129).

In adult attachment research traditionally the most important dimension is considered to be the dimension represented by the central coherence scale, with high scores on coherence inevitably leading to a secure classification and a low coherence score implying dismissing, preoccupied or (in some cases) unresolved classifications. But it takes $k-1$ dimensions to fully differentiate $k$ categories. The difference between the insecure classifications is determined by the pattern of scores on other state-of-mind scales. In samples with roughly equal numbers of dismissing and preoccupied subjects one might expect a second dimension beyond security-insecurity to emerge, namely a dismissing versus preoccupied dimension.

Whereas low scores on the Booth-LaForce et al. dismissing dimension would imply a secure attachment representation, in the traditional view low scores on scales indexing dismissing attachments such as idealization still leave room for an insecure preoccupied classification, for example, when scores on the anger scale would be sufficiently high. Indeed, in the Main et al. (2003–2008) coding system preoccupied and dismissing states of mind are incompatible in the sense that insecure adults are assigned either to the dismissing or the preoccupied group for analysis, but not to both (as Roisman & Booth-LaForce, Chapter 8, p. 128, correctly argue). Thus, in that system secure states of mind reflect the combination of low levels of dismissiveness *and* low levels of preoccupation. In fact, if the AAI discourse shows strong indications of a dismissing as well as a preoccupied state-of-mind the implication is a Cannot Classify (CC) decision (Main et al., 2003–2008).

Hesse (1996) suggested that CC subjects show a global breakdown of coherent discourse about attachment experiences, for example, high anger in the first part of the interview and strong idealization in the second part, whereas the dismissing and preoccupied subjects display an incoherent but systematic strategy to discuss attachment issues throughout the interview. In normative-risk samples CC interviews are infrequent, but in clinical samples their numbers can be substantial. We found a substantial number of CC cases in our study of personality-disordered criminal offenders in maximum-security forensic psychiatric hospitals, some of whom had been raised in institutional care settings (Van IJzendoorn et al., 1997). For the purpose of statistical analyses these CC subjects are usually added to the unresolved category as they seem to have similar traumatic backgrounds but more research is needed to establish the precise nature of this sub-group (Hesse, 1996, 2008).

At this juncture, we note the impact of truncated distributions in the low-risk, late-adolescence NICHD SECCYD sample with nonrandom nonre-sponse. The study does not report any CC cases, and a very small percentage of preoccupied and unresolved cases. Those classifications that are critical for the assessment of attachment in clinical samples (Bakermans-Kranenburg & Van IJzendoorn, 2009) are lacking or severely underrepresented. The logical implication is that the findings of the current NICHD SECCYD can be generalized to a small section of the population. For example, in the NICHD SECCYD sample a large part of the variance in the rating scales associated with attachment preoccupation must be ascribed to variation in the range of the secure discourses, from securely classified subjects with mildly elevated anger scores (Main et al., 2003–2008). It comes as no surprise that in this truncated case factorial solutions are dominated by the two largest groups, dismissing and secure participants, representing 94% of the sample, and that therefore a low score on the dismissing dimension is identical to a high score on security. Thus, the reason that scores on the dismissing dimension can be related to scores on the preoccupied dimension is simply due to participants with low scores on both dimensions, the absence of CC interviews, and the very low rate of preoccupation in this low-risk, late-adolescence NICHD SECCYD sample.

## THE UNRESOLVED ISSUE OF UNRESOLVED LOSS

The truncated AAI distribution also causes the merging of unresolved features of the interview into one dimension that consists of anger, passivity, and unresolved trauma. Although the authors used an oblique rotation instead of a Procrustes rotation, their factor-analytic approach runs the risk of creating a Procrustean bed for the AAI. Procrustes, son of Poseidon, was a criminal blacksmith who forced his guests to fit into an small iron bed by cutting their limbs. The authors suggest that there may be no empirical distinction between preoccupation and unresolved discourse, and that the unresolved features of the AAI would be sufficiently covered by the preoccupied dimension. It should be noted that the unresolved state-of-mind category was originally conceived as orthogonal to the other categories, and indeed is linked to a separate coding system and set of interview questions (Main et al., 2003–2008). Thus, the authors' claim seriously undermines a major component of the AAI coding system, and their surgery indeed costs an arm and a leg.

Of course, quite a few unresolved classified individuals (but by no means all of them, see Bakermans-Kranenburg & Van IJzendoorn, 2009) come from the preoccupied category but this is not sufficient reason to conclude that one may abandon the idea of an independent status as a classification or dimension on its own. In a low-risk, late-adolescence sample with relatively few losses or other traumas unresolved indicators are rare, and thus a separate unresolved dimension might only be identifiable in adult or clinical samples. In a study on Dutch veterans half of whom were suffering from deployment-related posttraumatic stress symptoms (PTSS), we found almost half of the

164

veterans to be classified as unresolved; at the same time, half of these unresolved veterans were classified into the secure category as their secondary classification (Harari et al., 2009). Unresolved loss or trauma is an essential component of the AAI, and crucial for clinical applications and understanding of individuals' socio-emotional functioning after experiences of loss of attachment figures, abuse, or other traumatic events. Whether unresolved loss or trauma shows sufficient incremental validity beyond established measures for posttraumatic stress symptomatology is however not beyond discussion, given the overlap between PTSS measures and the coding guidelines for unresolved loss or trauma (Harari et al., 2009), and this may be considered an unresolved issue.

## PROOF OF THE PUDDING IS IN INCREMENTAL VALIDITY

Throughout the monograph Booth-LaForce, Roisman, and colleagues break a lance for the use of continuous AAI dimensions, and they are right in doing so if no ontological strings are attached to this claim. Indeed, they correctly state that "the statistical power advantages associated with assessing AAI-related variation as continua argue in favor of routinely doing so" (Roisman & Booth-LaForce, Chapter 8, p. 127). Of course, there are sufficient pragmatic reasons to work with categorical as well as dimensional measures in empirical studies—even though the taxometric tests of the authors remain surprisingly ambiguous as to the nature of the categorical versus dimensional structure of the AAI (Chapter 2) and even though the proposed two-dimensional structure can only be accepted for late-adolescence samples with high rates of dismissing classifications and low rates of the other insecure categories.

Nevertheless, the field started with classificatory systems for the Strange Situation Procedure (Ainsworth, Blehar, Waters, & Wall, 1978) as well as for the AAI (Main et al., 2003–2008), so any alternative approach should prove to be better than this original system—which necessitates incremental validity as a way out of the Münchhausen paradox. Incremental validity is essential to prove the empirical superiority of the dimensional system over the categorical approach, and it is crucial for demonstrating the superiority of a specific two-dimensional structure over a more conventional set of dimensions. The authors are in an excellent position to test incremental validity of the dimensions for use with low-risk adolescents as they have at their disposal the incredibly rich NICHD SECCYD dataset. For example, it would be possible to test whether early experiences with parental sensitivity predict the dismissing and preoccupied dimensions of the AAI significantly better after controlling for the conventional AAI classifications or the coherence dimension.

The authors stipulate, however, that incremental validity might be difficult to demonstrate for two reasons. First, simulation evidence supports the use of AAI dimensions over categories only when sample sizes are moderate (rather than either small or large, but see Fraley & Spieker, 2003, who suggest that differences would most clearly emerge in the case of medium effect sizes). Because the NICHD SECCYD is a large sample it might be worthwhile to test incremental validity in a random part of the sample. As the call for replication has become increasingly louder in recent years (Pashler & Wagenmakers, 2012) the added advantage of this approach is the opportunity to replicate any outcome in the second part of the sample. Second, the various approaches to measure variations in AAI discourse converge strongly. That is why the authors did not expect nor find more evidence for continuity of security from infancy to adulthood using dimensional versus categorical assessments (Chapter 4). According to Roisman and colleagues, categorical or continuous AAI measures do not make much of a difference in empirical practice. But then one wonders: why all the fuss?

Adding the AAI to the NICHD SECCYD study Booth-LaForce, Roisman, and colleagues created a real gold mine. We have not yet seen its bottom.

## ACKNOWLEDGMENTS

M. van IJzendoorn and M. Bakermans-Kranenburg were supported by the Dutch Ministry of Education, Culture, and Science, and the Netherlands Organization for Scientific Research (Gravitation program number 024.001.003, SPINOZA, and VICI).

## REFERENCES

Ainsworth, M. D. S., Blehar, M. C., Waters, E., & Wall, S. (1978). *Patterns of attachment: A psychological study of the strange situation.* New York, NY: Lawrence Erlbaum.

Bakermans-Kranenburg, M. J., & Van IJzendoorn, M. H. (2009). The first 10,000 adult attachment interviews: Distributions of adult attachment representations in clinical and non-clinical groups. *Attachment & Human Development,* 11, 223–263.

Fraley, R. C., & Spieker, S. J. (2003). Are infant attachment patterns continuously or categorically distributed? A taxometric analysis of strange situation behavior. *Developmental Psychology,* 39, 387–404.

Harari, D., Bakermans-Kranenburg, M. J., De Kloet, C. S., Geuze, E., Vermetten, E., Westenberg, H. G. M., et al. (2009). Attachment representations in Dutch veterans with and without deployment-related PTSD. *Attachment and Human Development,* 11, 515–536.

Hesse, E. (1996). Discourse, memory and the adult attachment interview: A brief note with emphasis on the emerging cannot classify category. *Infant Mental Health Journal,* 17, 4–11.

Hesse, E. (2008). The adult attachment interview: Protocol, method of analysis, and empirical studies. In J. Cassidy & P. R. Shaver (Eds.), *Handbook of attachment: Theory, research, and clinical applications* (2nd ed., pp. 552–598). New York, NY: Guilford Press.

Main, M., Goldwyn, R., & Hesse, E. (2003–2008). *Adult attachment scoring and classification system.* Unpublished manuscript, University of California at Berkeley, Berkeley.

Main, M., Kaplan, N., & Cassidy, J. (1985). Security in infancy, childhood, and adulthood: A move to the level of representation. In I. Bretherton & E. Waters (Eds.), Growing points in attachment theory and research. *Monographs of the Society for Research in Child Development*, **50**, 66–106.

Parker, G., Tupling, H., & Brown, L. B. (1979). A parental bonding instrument. *British Journal of Medical Psychology*, **52**, 1–10.

Pashler, H., & Wagenmakers, E.-J. (2012). Editors' introduction to the special section on replicability in psychological science: A crisis of confidence? *Perspectives on Psychological Science*, **7**, 528.

Pearson, J. L., Cohn, D. A., Cowan, P. A., & Cowan, C. P. (1994). Earned and continuous-security in adult attachment: Relation to depressive symptomatology and parenting style. *Development and Psychopathology*, **6**, 359–373.

Roisman, G. I., Fortuna, K., & Holland, A. S. (2006). An experimental manipulation of retrospectively defined earned and continuous attachment security. *Child Development*, **77**, 59–71.

Roisman, G. I., Padrón, E., Sroufe, L. A., & Egeland, B. (2002). Earned-secure attachment status in retrospect and prospect. *Child Development*, **73**, 1204–1219.

Sroufe, L. A., Egeland, B., Carlson, E. A., & Collins, W. A. (2005). *The development of the person: The Minnesota Study of Risk and Adaptation from birth to adulthood.* New York, NY: Guilford Press.

Van IJzendoorn, M. H., Feldbrugge, J. T. T. M., Derks, F. C. H., De Ruiter, C., Verhagen, M. F. M., Philipse, M. W. G., et al. (1997). Attachment representations of personality disordered criminal offenders. *American Journal of Orthopsychiatry*, **67**, 449–459.

# INVITED REJOINDER

PULLING OURSELVES UP BY OUR BOOTSTRAPS: A REJOINDER TO
VAN IJZENDOORN AND BAKERMANS-KRANENBURG (2014)

*Glenn I. Roisman, R. Chris Fraley, and Cathryn Booth-LaForce*

**ABSTRACT** This rejoinder addresses two interrelated concerns raised by Van IJzendoorn and Bakermans-Kranenburg (this volume): (1) the degree to which it is reasonable to expect some of the results reported here to replicate given the low rates of preoccupied and unresolved classifications in the SECCYD sample and (2) whether the results from the taxometric and factor analyses we report should be used to guide scholarly thinking about the latent structure of individual differences in AAI narratives.

## IS THE SECCYD SAMPLE AND ITS AAI DATA UNUSUAL?

Van IJzendoorn and Bakermans-Kranenburg (this volume) characterize the age 18 year SECCYD sample as "low risk" based on evidence that the attrited sub-group differed significantly on various risk indicators from those who were administered the AAI. They also claim that the SECCYD AAI assessment underrepresents preoccupied and unresolved states of mind in light of a lower proportion of preoccupied and unresolved classifications observed in the dataset than might be expected based on the meta-analytic "norms" reported in Bakermans-Kranenburg and Van IJzendoorn (2009).

Although space limitations preclude a detailed assessment of these issues, we make three relevant observations here. First, the AAI sample of the SECCYD is accurately described as *normative*-risk. Second, the meta-analytic data Van IJzendoorn and Bakermans-Kranenburg (this volume) refer to are not necessarily informative about whether the SECCYD under-represents unresolved and preoccupied cases. Neither the AAI sample of the SECCYD nor the data sets meta-analyzed in Bakermans-Kranenburg and Van IJzendoorn (2009) were designed to be representative of the populations of interest. Moreover, Bakermans-Kranenburg and Van IJzendoorn's (2009) estimates of the rates of preoccupied and unresolved AAI classifications in the

168

non-clinical adolescent population are based on an aggregate sample size ($N = 617$) that is considerably smaller than the SECCYD ($N = 857$). Third, although it is true that the number of categorically preoccupied and unresolved cases is low in the SECCYD in an absolute sense, the taxometric and factor analytic results presented in this Monograph are *already well replicated findings*, in a number of cases based on datasets in which the rates of preoccupation and unresolved discourse are demonstrably higher than in the SECCYD.

## TAXOMETRICS AND THE AAI

Van IJzendoorn and Bakermans-Kranenburg (this volume) also take issue with our use of taxometric techniques to investigate the latent structure of individual differences in the AAI. Specifically, they claim that there is an inherent circularity involved in using data based on fallible indicators to draw inferences about the latent distribution of the constructs they purportedly indicate.[1] They reference one of the tall tales associated with Baron von Münchhausen, who allegedly pulled himself and his horse out of a swamp, not with external assistance, but (in some versions of the story) by the straps of his own boots.

Van IJzendoorn and Bakermans-Kranenburg (this volume) argue that, to resolve the latent structure of the AAI, one must evaluate the ratings against an external criterion. But the problem is that there is no gold standard. The absence of a gold standard in the measurement of psychological entities is one of the challenges that led Cronbach and Meehl (1955) to conceptualize construct validity as a dynamic process in which we, as researchers, lift "ourselves by our bootstraps" (Cronbach & Meehl, 1955, p. 286). Specifically, in the absence of a gold standard, one has to rely upon the pattern of statistical relations among fallible indicators to uncover the latent structure that organizes them. And through the process of evaluating the data in light of theoretical assumptions and, importantly, evaluating those assumptions in light of the data, one comes to a better understanding of what the measures are measuring and the meaning of the constructs in that theoretical space. The power of Cronbach and Meehl's (1955) approach is that it explains how knowledge can advance in incremental steps in the absence of a gold standard.

What have we learned through this process to date? For one, we are relatively confident via taxometric analyses that individual differences with respect to the free-to-evaluate versus dismissing distinction in AAI research reflect continuous and not categorical variation. We are open to evidence that suggests otherwise, but after examining data from two distinct and large samples, it strikes us as untenable to advocate for a categorical interpretation of those individual differences. Second, we have learned that the evidence regarding preoccupation is not conclusive. We have suggested that, in the absence of strong evidence that preoccupation is categorical, researchers treat the variation as if it were continuous. But we should be clear that we are not suggesting that researchers call off the search for latent structure and treat the matter as a settled issue. If anything, the lack of compelling evidence regarding preoccupation should be taken as a call to further investigate this matter in samples that contain a higher rate of purportedly preoccupied individuals.

## FACTOR ANALYSIS AND THE AAI

### Two Weakly Correlated Dimensions?

Van IJzendoorn and Bakermans-Kranenburg (this volume) caution researchers on the dangers of using factor analysis in a Procrustian fashion to impose latent structure where it does not exist. However, the oblique rotations we use allow, but do not force, factors to be uncorrelated. If indicators of dismissing and preoccupied states of mind were "naturally" correlated with one another, the exploratory factor analyses presented in Chapter 2 of this volume would have been capable of revealing this. In other words, the use of oblique rotation did not *force* the indicators of dismissing and preoccupied states of mind (or indeed indicators of preoccupied and unresolved states of mind) to be independent of, or to correlate with one another in an unnatural manner. All factor analyses of the AAI of which we are aware (see Chapter 2 for a review) demonstrate that preoccupation and dismissing states of mind reflect largely empirically distinct observations about AAI discourse—this despite the fact that the AAI classification system implies that dismissing and preoccupied stances are mutually exclusive.

### Unresolved Versus Preoccupied Discourse

Van IJzendoorn and Bakermans-Kranenburg (this volume) next observe that it might be premature to conclude that indicators of unresolved and preoccupied states of mind load on a common factor in light of the limitations of the SECCYD dataset. We would note that the first and second authors of this rejoinder were surprised to discover when conducting analyses related to Roisman, Fraley, and Belsky (2007) that indicators of unresolved and preoccupied discourse loaded on a common factor. Nonetheless, we have at present no reason to doubt the replicability of those results for two reasons. First, the Roisman et al. (2007) report was based on a large sample with more representation of preoccupied and unresolved cases than was the SECCYD sample (9% and 10%, respectively). Second, evidence that indicators of preoccupation and unresolved discourse "travel together" has been replicated in a number of studies (see General Discussion Section).

We are sympathetic to the possibility that, in higher risk and/or clinical populations, unresolved and preoccupied discourse might well represent distinct psychological phenomena. However, the scientific literature currently demonstrates no such distinction in normative risk samples and no one has yet published any factor analytic evidence that supports the assumption that preoccupied and unresolved discourse are distinctive phenomena in clinical samples.

## INCREMENTAL VALIDITY

Van IJzendoorn and Bakermans-Kranenburg's (this volume) final claim is that the only real test of the value of the dimensional approach is to engage in "head to head" comparisons of the performance of the state-of-mind dimensions with the original AAI classifications. Although it is tempting to suggest that the true value in a "new" measurement system lies in its ability to predict various outcomes, we caution against this temptation for two reasons. First, we are not proposing an alternative coding system. The latent structure we identify reflects what trained raters using both current coding systems for the AAI (Main, Goldwyn, & Hesse and the Kobak Q-set) *already* appear to be coding, at least through the prism of factor and taxometric analysis. Second, and more importantly, the dismissing and preoccupied dimensions we highlight—in contrast to the AAI categories—differ in at least two distinct ways, which makes simple "head to head" comparisons ambiguous. If the AAI dimensions outperform the categories, is it because of the use of dimensions per se or due to the use of a factor structure better suited to study the associations of interest?

Van IJzendoorn and Bakermans-Kranenburg (this volume) recognize this, and make two suggestions for furthering tests of what they refer to as incremental validity. One of their ideas is to use the results of simulation studies—which delineate the conditions under which true dimensions scored dimensionally are expected to outperform their categorically scored counterparts—as a basis for attempting to recover the latent structure of the AAI individual differences. The focus here is to examine whether, say, a categorically coded "preoccupied versus not" variable better predicts a theory-predicted outcome than does the corresponding preoccupied dimension, over various levels of statistical power (i.e., by varying sample size across analyses). This is an intriguing idea, but, without further elaboration, it raises more questions about implementation than it might hope to answer in execution. In particular, there is at present no simulation evidence of which we are aware that demonstrates that such patterns of predictive validity can be used to bootstrap one's way to knowledge about the dimensional versus categorical character of individual differences.

The other suggestion Van IJzendoorn and Bakermans-Kranenburg (this volume) make can be construed in relation to the issue of factor structure. Let us back up a moment and note that incremental validity tests typically refer to the examination of whether some construct B (incrementally) predicts outcome Y statistically controlling for construct A. In the current case, however, we are not dealing with different constructs at all (i.e., secure-insecure versus dismissing and preoccupied dimensions), but different ways of partitioning the same individual differences (i.e., different rotations in the same construct space). Let us imagine such a test. Will an AAI security-insecurity (i.e., coherence) dimension predict observed sensitive-responsiveness after controlling for dismissing and preoccupied dimensions? It will not. Why? Dismissing and preoccupied states of mind are $45°$ rotations of a secure-insecure dimension (see Figure 2.1, this volume). And, indeed, when one regresses the secure/autonomous dimension simultaneously on the dismissing and preoccupied state of mind dimensions using the SECCYD AAI data, the resultant $R^2 = .99$. That is, dismissing and preoccupied discourse are collinear with security-insecurity. This is why we state in the General Discussion of this volume that, under conditions of adequate statistical power, the value of using the dimensions that fall out of factor analysis of the two coding systems for the AAI is entirely dependent on one's research questions.

To return to our broader point, the questions we are asking are largely questions of construct validity. What is the latent structure of individual differences in adult attachment? The answer to this question cannot be articulated in the language of incremental validity coefficients. The answer to this question emerges gradually from attempts to compare the predictions of alternative models against the data through an iterative process. It could very well turn out to be the case that dimensional models predict the same pattern of outcomes as does a categorical model. But that fact in and of itself would not speak to the latent structure of individual differences. Understanding that structure is a worthy goal on its own, and a necessary one for those who are interested in understanding individual differences in adult attachment organization.

## REFERENCES

Bakermans-Kranenburg, M. J., & Van IJzendoorn, M. H. (2009). The first 10,000 Adult Attachment Interviews: Distributions of adult attachment representations in clinical and non-clinical groups. *Attachment & Human Development*, 11, 223–263.

Beauchaine, T., & Waters, E. (2003). Pseudotaxonicity in MAMBAC and MAXCOV analyses of rating scale data: Turning continua into classes by manipulating observers' expectations. *Psychological Methods, 8*, 3–15.

Cronbach, L. J., & Meehl, P. E. (1955). Construct validity in psychological tests. *Psychological Bulletin, 52*, 281–302.

Main, M., Goldwyn, R., & Hesse, E. (2003–2008). *Adult attachment scoring and classification system.* Unpublished manuscript, University of California at Berkeley, Berkeley, CA.

Roisman, G. I., Fraley, R. C., & Belsky, J. (2007). A taxometric study of the adult attachment interview. *Developmental Psychology, 43*, 675–686.

## NOTE

1. To clarify, none of the taxometric procedures we used involved the rater-scored classification data from the Main, Goldwyn, and Hesse (2003–2008) AAI coding system, as the reader might infer from Van IJzendoorn and Bakermans-Kranenburg's comment. Van IJzendoorn and Bakermans-Kranenburg (this volume) correctly note that the AAI state-of-mind scales (i.e., the indicators used in the taxometric procedures) are not independent of the classifications in that coders are free to adjust their state of mind coding in light of "top down" considerations (e.g., fit with a classification) in addition to using the state-of-mind scales inductively to identify a best fitting category. Interestingly, however, there is experimental evidence that when raters are informed that they are using rating scales to identify categories, taxometric procedures like MAXCOV are at risk of revealing pseudo-taxa (Beauchaine & Waters, 2003). What this means is that, if anything, our taxometric analyses may have been biased toward a *categorical* rather than a dimensional account of the AAI data.

# ACKNOWLEDGMENTS

Cathryn Booth-LaForce, Family & Child Nursing Department, University of Washington; Glenn I. Roisman, Institute of Child Development, University of Minnesota. Glenn I. Roisman completed much of the work associated with this monograph while an Associate Professor of Psychology at the University of Illinois at Urbana-Champaign.

This research was supported by Grant HD054822, awarded to C. Booth-LaForce, from the *Eunice Kennedy Shriver* National Institute of Child Health & Human Development. Additionally, genotyping for the Online Supplement to this monograph was supported by a Research Board grant from the University of Illinois at Urbana-Champaign to Philip C. Rodkin and Glenn I. Roisman. Co-editors Booth-LaForce and Roisman contributed equally to the production of this monograph.

We thank Sumi Hayashi, Project Coordinator; the AAI interviewers; the AAI transcribers; the primary AAI coders (Keren Fortuna, Ashley M. Groh, John D. Haltigan, Katherine C. Haydon, and Ashley Holland); and the data analysts for the Chapters 1 and 5 (Hsiao-Chuan Tien, John Sideris, and Pan Yi). We are grateful to the parents and their now-adult children who have continued their study participation since the birth of these children.

Correspondence concerning this monograph should be addressed to Cathryn Booth-LaForce, University of Washington, CHDD 106 South Building, Box 357920, Seattle, WA 98195-7920, email: ibcb@uw.edu.

174

# CONTRIBUTORS

**Marian J. Bakermans-Kranenburg** is a Professor of Child and Family Studies at Leiden University, the Netherlands. Her research is on attachment and emotion regulation in parents and their children, with special emphasis on neurobiological processes in parenting and development.

**Cathryn Booth-LaForce** is a developmental psychologist and the Charles and Gerda Spence Professor of Nursing in the Family & Child Nursing Department at the University of Washington. Her research focuses on individual differences and contextual influences on social-emotional development and relationships, within an attachment framework.

**Margaret R. Burchinal** is a Senior Scientist at the FPG Child Development Institute, Research Professor in the Psychology Department at the University of North Carolina at Chapel Hill and Adjunct Professor of Education at the University of California-Irvine. Her research focuses on improving the quality of child care and school readiness skills for low-income and other at-risk young children.

**Martha J. Cox** is a Professor of Psychology at the University of North Carolina at Chapel Hill. Her research focuses on family relationships as a context for children's social and emotional development, with a particular focus on parent-child interactions and attachment relationships.

**R. Chris Fraley** is a social-personality psychologist in the Department of Psychology at the University of Illinois at Urbana-Champaign. His research involves the study of attachment processes in close relationships, personality dynamics and development, and research methods.

**Ashley M. Groh** is a postdoctoral fellow with the Center for Developmental Science at the University of North Carolina at Chapel Hill. Her contributions to the monograph were supported, in part, by a postdoctoral fellowship (T32-HD07376) through the Center. Her research focuses on the significance of children's early relationships with primary caregivers for social and emotional development across the lifespan and the mechanisms by which such experiences contribute to developmental adaptation.

**Katherine C. Haydon** is an Assistant Professor of Psychology and Education at Mount Holyoke College. Her research examines the developmental organization of the adult attachment system, including its antecedent and concurrent correlates, in relation to interpersonal functioning across the lifespan.

**John D. Haltigan** is a postdoctoral fellow in the Faculty of Education at the University of Ottawa. His research focuses on the dispositional, environmental, and contextual determinants of maladaptation and competence in early human development.

**Margaret T. Owen** is the Robinson Family Professor of Psychological Sciences at the University of Texas at Dallas and Director of the Center for Children and Families. Her research focuses on mother-child and father-child relationships and connections between contexts of children's development.

**Glenn I. Roisman** is a Professor at the Institute of Child Development at the University of Minnesota. His program of research concerns the legacy of early interpersonal experience as an organizing force in social, cognitive, and biological development across the lifespan.

**John Ruscio** is a Professor of Psychology at The College of New Jersey. His scholarly interests include taxometric methodology and its application, the science and policy implications of behavioral economics, citation-based indices of scholarly impact, and modern and robust statistical methods.

**Marinus H. van IJzendoorn** is a Professor of Child and Family Studies at Leiden University, the Netherlands and a Research Professor of Human Development at Erasmus University Rotterdam, the Netherlands. His work concerns attachment and emotion regulation across the life span from a multidisciplinary perspective.

# STATEMENT OF EDITORIAL POLICY

The SRCD *Monographs* series aims to publish major reports of developmental research that generates authoritative new findings and that foster a fresh perspective and/or integration of data/research on conceptually significant issues. Submissions may consist of individually or group-authored reports of findings from some single large-scale investigation or from a series of experiments centering on a particular question. Multiauthored sets of independent studies concerning the same underlying question also may be appropriate. A critical requirement in such instances is that the individual authors address common issues and that the contribution arising from the set as a whole be unique, substantial, and well integrated. Manuscripts reporting interdisciplinary or multidisciplinary research on significant developmental questions and those including evidence from diverse cultural, racial, and ethnic groups are of particular interest. Also of special interest are manuscripts that bridge basic and applied developmental science, and that reflect the international perspective of the Society. Because the aim of the *Monographs* series is to enhance cross-fertilization among disciplines or subfields as well as advance knowledge on specialized topics, the links between the specific issues under study and larger questions relating to developmental processes should emerge clearly and be apparent for both general readers and specialists on the topic. In short, irrespective of how it may be framed, work that contributes significant data and/or extends a developmental perspective will be considered.

Potential authors who may be unsure whether the manuscript they are planning wouldmake an appropriate submission to the SRCD *Monographs* are invited to draft an outline or prospectus of what they propose and send it to the incoming editor for review and comment.

Potential authors are not required to be members of the Society for Research in Child Development nor affiliated with the academic discipline of psychology to submit a manuscript for consideration by the *Monographs*. The significance of the work in extending developmental theory and in contributing new empirical information is the crucial consideration.

Submissions should contain a minimum of 80 manuscript pages (including tables and references). The upper boundary of 150–175 pages is more flexible, but authors should try to keep within this limit. Manuscripts must be double-spaced, 12pt Times New Roman font, with 1-inch margins. If color artwork is submitted, and the authors believe color art is necessary to the presentation of their work, the submissions letter should indicate that one or more authors or their institutions are prepared to pay the substantial costs associated with color art reproduction. Please submit manuscripts electronically to the SRCD *Monographs* Online Submissions and Review Site (Scholar One) at http://mc.manuscriptcentral.com/mono. Please contact the *Monographs* office with any questions at monographs@srcd.org.

The corresponding author for any manuscript must, in the submission letter, warrant that all coauthors are in agreement with the content of the manuscript. The corresponding author also is responsible for informing all coauthors, in a timely manner, of manuscript submission, editorial decisions, reviews received, and any revisions recommended. Before publication, the corresponding author must warrant in the submissions letter that the study has been conducted according to the ethical guidelines of the Society for Research in Child Development.

A more detailed description of all editorial policies, evaluation processes, and format requirements can be found under the "Submission Guidelines" link at http://srcd.org/publications/monographs.

Monographs Editorial Office
e-mail: monographs@srcd.org

Editor, Patricia J. Bauer
Department of Psychology, Emory University
36 Eagle Row
Atlanta, GA 30322
e-mail: pjbauer@emory.edu

## Note to NIH Grantees

Pursuant to NIH mandate, Society through Wiley-Blackwell will post the accepted version of Contributions authored by NIH grantholders to PubMed Central upon acceptance. This accepted version will be made publicly available 12 months after publication. For further information, see http://www.wiley.com/go/nihmandate.

# SUBJECT INDEX

Page numbers in *italics* refer to tables and figures.

# CURRENT